Jetsun Pema, a sister of the Dalai Lama, was educated in India, Switzerland and England and, since the invasion of her country, has played a major part in the education of refugee Tibetan children. She was also the first woman minister of the Tibetan government in exile and was awarded the title Mother of Tibet by its National Assembly.

TIBET

My Story
AN AUTOBIOGRAPHY

Jetsun Pema

with Gilles Van Grasdorff

[signature: Jetsun Pema]

ELEMENT

Shaftesbury, Dorset • Rockport, Massachusetts
Melbourne, Victoria

First published as *Tibet, mon histoire* by Éditions Ramsay in 1996

This revised edition © Element Books Limited 1997
Text © Éditions Ramsay, Paris 1996

Published in Great Britain in 1997 by
Element Books Limited
Shaftesbury, Dorset SP7 8BP

Published in the USA in 1997 by
Element Books, Inc.
PO Box 830, Rockport, MA 01966

Published in Australia in 1997 by
Element Books and distributed
by Penguin Books Australia Limited
487 Maroondah Highway, Ringwood,
Victoria 3134

Translated by Geraldine Le Roy and James Mayor
Commissioned for Element Books by Ian Fenton
Cover design by Mark Slader
Design by Roger Lightfoot
Typeset by Bournemouth Colour Press
Printed and bound in Great Britain by
Creative Print and Design, Wales
and in the USA by Courier Westford Inc, Westford

British Library Cataloguing in Publication
data available

Library of Congress Cataloging in Publication
Jetsun Pema, 1940–
    Tibet: my story, an autobiography / Pema Jetsun
    p. cm.
Includes bibliographical references and indexes.
ISBN 1 – 86204 – 124 – 5 (alk. paper)
    1. Jetsun Pema, 1940 – . 2. Cabinet Officers—China—Tibet—
Biography. 3. Tibet (China)—Biography. I. Title.
DS786. J47 1997   97–18273
                                                     CIP

ISBN 1 86204 124 5

Contents

APPENDICES

To the children of Tibet,
and to all those who support them
and help them to find meaning in their lives.

Acknowledgements

The author would like to thank: Dawa Thondup, the former representative of His Holiness in France, the Benelux countries and the Iberian Peninsula, for all his help and advice; Gilles Van Grasdorff, for his help, patience and understanding; Gilbert Leroy, for his assistance; to Matthew Cory, for his editorial assistance in preparing this English edition, Hélène Morel, my friend and publisher; Daniel Radfort, for his support and his interest in this book; Tashi Lhamo, Kesang Lhamo, Sonam Yangzom and Lhamo Youdon, for their hard work checking and typing my notes; Wangpo Bashi and Rachel Brévière, for their assistance; Vincent Dupont, for his help; Ngawang Dakpa, for his contributions as translator, critic and guide – and also his family, who warmly welcomed me in their Parisian home; to Tenchon Yangzom and Choedak, my children, for their enthusiasm, interest and understanding; Tempa Tsering, my husband, for his constant encouragement and his suggestions; and, especially, His Holiness the Dalai Lama, who is my guiding source of inspiration and strength.

Preface

The tragedy of the Tibetan people cannot and should not leave us indifferent. The suffering resulting from their oppression by China should give rise to reactions other than silence or acceptance. As with all other civilizations in the world, Tibet has a right to religious freedom as well as to its own ideas of happiness and fate. This is the message of Jetsun Pema, which overwhelms us with its deep human truth as much as with its determination never to yield to force or to the rule of the conqueror.

I do not know the author, but I know her famous brother. Jetsun Pema is the sister of a man who honours me with his friendship: the Dalai Lama. His spirituality is admired in religious and cultural circles everywhere where there is faith in human dignity.

We have known for a long time that Tibet was going through a heavy and unfair ordeal. The Dalai Lama has shown us that there is a non-violent way of dealing with this situation, which is not the same as resignation.

The people of Tibet consider divinity to be more important than politics, so why does a great power like China stubbornly persist in stifling their need to live in peace. Does not China understand that it has much to gain from recognizing the spiritual sovereignty of Tibet?

The first time I met the Dalai Lama, he questioned me about

the survival of the Jews, my kin. He found a striking similarity between the history of our two peoples. To his mind, Tibetans are now undergoing the exile that Jews have experienced for 2,000 years, and he asks them a simple question: could you teach us how you survived without being annihilated by our oppressors? With such an approach this great spiritual leader has inspired believers all over the world to come together.

In a sense, although told in more personal terms, Jetsun Pema's autobiography will have a similar effect on its readers. She describes her education in India, Switzerland and England before the Dalai Lama put her in charge of the education of exiled Tibetan children. It is for her a vital mission to care physically and mentally for children who have been deprived not only of their childhood but also, to some extent, of their future. To devote herself wholeheartedly to her task, Jetsun Pema has given up her other activities to work for the women of Tibet and for organizations run by the Dalai Lama. In reading this book about her life and her struggle, let us listen to her message of hope: it breathes optimism.

Elie Wiesel

New York 1997

Introduction

In June 1995, I received a letter from Gilles Van Grasdorff saying that he wanted to tell my story. At the time I wondered who would read such a book because it seemed to me that there was not all that much to talk about. However, he insisted. He said that in it I could talk about the work to which I have devoted so much effort: the education of children in the Tibetan Children's Village (TCV). The book would also provide an opportunity to describe the life of Tibetan refugees, both adults and children, during the first years of exile.

We need the support of other peoples of the world. With the aim of a better understanding of the tragedy which has been plaguing my country, I felt that I could use my own 56-year-long life to tell the story of the suffering of an entire generation of Tibetans. In this way, my account would not be limited to the life of a single Tibetan citizen but would be the story of a whole nation.

For these reasons I agreed to write the book: to present the history of Tibet between 1940 and 1995 as clearly as possible, and to relate the traumatic events that characterized this period. I ask the reader to forgive me for any lapses of memory.

His Holiness the Dalai Lama sent me to Tibet in 1980 as head of a mission to verify what was really happening in the country. The 105 days of my journey still remain an unforgettable experience and I thought this evidence might be of interest to our friends.

Nowadays strength is often considered to be the only legitimate value. But I know that many men and women still believe in truth and justice, and still stand up for these principles. I am sure that my people's voice – today smothered, even though we are blameless – will always be heard somewhere. It is for those that hear it that I have decided to tell our story.

Jetsun Pema

Jetsun Pema

PART I

1939–1964

1

The First Years in Lhasa

As Buddhists, we Tibetans believe in reincarnation. So, when I reflect on my life, I believe that I had good *karma*. I was born a sister of the man who became the present Dalai Lama and I grew up in a family in which two more reincarnations were recognized – Takseter Rinpoche, our eldest brother Thubten Jigme Norbu and Ngari Rinpoche, our youngest brother Tenzin Choegyal. (According to the concept of reincarnation and karma, the whole of life is a learning process. Each personal act – be it mental, physical, spiritual – shapes our being, leaving us imprints of who we are due to our past deeds. Karma, in this sense, is conditioning and not fate. Buddhism suggests that we rid ourselves of this conditioning through the achievement of awareness and sensitivity, thereby behaving with full consciousness.)

I was born in Lhasa in 1940, on the seventh day in the seventh month of the Tibetan calendar. The Tibetan year begins with the new moon, a month or two before the Western spring. It consists of twelve lunar months with fluctuating days and months. According to Tibetan astrological calculations, some days in a month could be missed out or repeated and sometimes in a year a whole month could be missed out or repeated.

Amala (I prefer to use this Tibetan word for mother as it is an honorary term showing love and respect) gave birth to sixteen children, nine of whom died in infancy. Our family comes from

Taktser, a small village in the province of Amdo in the North-East of Tibet.

When I was old enough to understand, Amala explained to me that in 1933, *Pala* (father) had gone to the monastery of Kumbum where he had learnt of the death of the thirteenth Dalai Lama, Thupten Gyatso. He had returned to the village bearing this tragic news.

Immediately following the news the search for the new reincarnation began. Each Dalai Lama is considered both to emanate from Chenrezi, the *Bodhisattva* of Compassion, and to be the reincarnation of his immediate predecessor. About the time when the family's thirteenth child, then named Lhamo Thondup, was just over two years old, some officials arrived in the Amdo area. They soon discovered a house in Taktser with turquoise tiles, which the Regent had seen in a vision in 1935 (the year of the Wooden Pig in the Tibetan calendar) when he had visited the sacred lake of Lhamoe Lhatso, in Chokhorgyal, about 100 miles from Lhasa. The house belonged to my parents.

Two men, a *lama* and his companion, appeared at the house. Kewtsang Rinpoche, the abbot of the monastery of Sera, then asked to see my brother. He spent the entire day there observing his every gesture. Amala said that she could sense the lama's growing interest although she was not aware of the real purpose of his visit. As the sun set, the two men asked if they could spend the night in my parents' house.

The following morning, my brother woke as they were getting ready to leave and said that he wanted to go with them, but he was not allowed to do so. Then, a few days later, the family had another visit, this time from the lamas and other Tibetan dignitaries. I think that even then my parents did not know that the important visitors were looking for the reincarnation of the Dalai Lama of Tibet.

Finally, my brother had to go through various tests. These eventually proved conclusive and the dignitaries and lamas were satisfied that they were indeed in the presence of the fourteenth Dalai Lama.

In the sixth month of the year of the Earth Hare (1939), part of my family left Taktser for Lhasa with His Holiness, who had just reached the age of four. The journey lasted three months and thirteen days. It must have been such a wrench for my parents to leave house, farm, village and friends without knowing what the future would have in store. There was nobody to reassure them, but the overriding compensation was that they had a son who was the Dalai Lama. This was an exceptional event in the life of any Tibetan family, and of historical significance for the whole of Tibet. Yet, while they no doubt experienced a legitimate feeling of pride, my parents remained truly humble.

On their arrival in the capital, my parents were given by the Tibetan government everything they could possibly need – and had probably never even dreamt of. Servants were assigned to look after them and they were told that a house was to be built for them half-way between the Potala and the town. In the meantime they were to live in a house near Norbulingka, His Holiness's summer palace. *Achala*, her husband Phuntsok Tashi, and my two brothers, Gyalo Thondup and Lobsang Samten, also left Taktser to join my parents in Lhasa.

At the time of my birth, my parents had not yet moved, but by the time I was five they were in the huge new house in Lhasa, with the name that sounds so beautiful in Tibetan – Changtse-shar. Tsering Dolma, my elder sister by 20 years, often told me about their previous home where they had to work in the fields, and I will never forget the day when she told me that I was born with a silver spoon in my mouth. So it is perhaps natural that I remember a very happy childhood, while she remembers more about life in Taktser.

Before 1940, Taktser was a village of about 30 houses on the caravan trail between Siling and Labrang Tashi Khyil (an important monastery in the province of Amdo), crossed by a stream and surrounded by rich pastures. The slopes of the nearby mountains were covered by conifers which made the air fragrant with their scent, and delicious berries grew in the woods. During the rainy season the stream was full of brownish earth. In the fifth and sixth months of the year, after a few days of rain, it was almost impossible to go out of the house, as the boggy ground gave way beneath your feet.

The village dates back to a nomadic settlement. Originally, black tents made from yak hair had been pitched on the surrounding heights. The nomads had quickly realized that barley, oats, potatoes and all kinds of vegetables such as radishes, parsnips, cabbage and garlic, could easily be grown in this fertile soil. They had then built solid houses and the village had gradually expanded.

My parents' house overlooked the village and was built around a large inner courtyard between two other houses. At sunset, the gate and small windows were shut and the family felt as secure as if they were in a fortress. The roof had two chimneys and three ventilation holes set in it. The water from the melted snow or rain ran through drainpipes made from juniper, often of extraordinary shapes, into the courtyard.

In Lhasa, I often thought of my parents and their village life, imagining the strange sound made by the prayer flags flapping in the wind at the approach of a violent storm. My curiosity was particularly aroused by my sister's account of the building of a new house. Foundations were built with clay bricks which had been dried in wooden moulds. The roof was covered with logs and finished off with a layer of brushwood treated with a mixture of trodden-down earth and oil that made an excellent form of insulation. The house was then white-washed and the prayer flags raised. (The flagpole that stood in our courtyard was 30 feet high.) The door lintels were decorated with tridents and dragons.

My sister's descriptions of the inside of the house also caught my imagination. Although my family was not rich, they were self-sufficient. A magnificent carpet hung over the front door that swung on wooden hinges. My father had lined the door with sheepskin so that it could be opened and shut without making any noise. On the northern side of the house was my parent's room and the altar room, on the western side the cow shed, guest room and storeroom, and on the southern side the stables, kennels and sheepfold. The courtyard and the corridor connecting all the rooms were tiled with flat stones and Pala had put down a wooden floor in all the rooms.

The family spent most of their time in the kitchen, which had been divided into two unequal areas separated by the stove and a wooden partition. You entered the larger of the two areas from the courtyard. The beamed ceiling supported a terracotta watertank, covered with a beautiful green glaze. On the brick stove sat the pot that was used for tea, which was refilled several times a day. The kitchen utensils were made of copper or brass, and there were also jars and containers in terracotta. Amala liked to keep the milk in a wooden container, though. Behind the stove, three steps led up to a platform where the whole family ate and slept in the winter because it was just above the chimney pipes. The other part of the kitchen had an earthen floor. In one corner my parents stored materials used for fuel such as wood, yak or *dri* dung, and twigs and dry hay for roasting the barley.

I often asked my sister to tell me about the time when Amala took my brother, the future Dalai Lama, to the cowshed. We had eight cows and seven *dzomos* that Amala liked to milk herself. My brother was allowed to drink a bowl of warm milk before running to the henhouse to collect the eggs. I always collapsed with laughter when she used to tell me how he had once been found perched on a cage, clucking like a hen.

My first childhood memory of Lhasa is of our house there, an imposing building of some 60 rooms, that opened onto a magnificent garden and huge park. I was always surrounded by small children of my own age. Apart from Tenzin Choegyal, the little brother who was born when I was five, there was my sister's first child (my nephew Tenzin Ngawang, born when I was only nine months old), followed shortly afterwards by my niece, Khando Tsering. There were also the children of the servants who lived with us. We all had tremendous fun together. The house with its garden and surrounding property was separated from the outside world by a wall that was too high for us to climb over, and behind which we lived a life of considerable freedom, playing hide-and-seek for hours. The basic unit in Tibetan society is the family, which often comprises not only parents and children but also numerous uncles and aunts with their children too. Amala and my sister looked after the younger children with the help of my aunt (my father's sister).

I cannot really remember the brother who was born when I was two, and who sadly only lived a couple of years. My sister told me that when he died, my parents consulted oracles and astrologers. It is a Tibetan tradition that astrologers (who are often lamas) determine the correct funeral procedure according to the time of birth and death. The most common forms of funeral are those involving air or fire (cremation, mainly used for religious dignitaries), earth (burial) or water (immersion in a river). If these procedures are not followed, then all sorts of misfortunes such as illnesses or poverty may strike the dead person's family. Astrologers also prescribe the rituals to be performed throughout the period of mourning: fasting, the reading of sacred texts and the offering up of butter lamps to purify the deceased's soul and guide it towards a better reincarnation. The astrologer consulted by my parents said that the body should not be buried, but embalmed in salt in the cellar so that the dead boy could be reborn in the same house. The procedure also required that the body be marked with butter, an instruction that my family followed. When the next child (a boy and the last of the 16 brothers and sisters) came into the world, he bore a mark exactly where the butter had been rubbed on to his elder brother's body.

Amala used to visit His Holiness the Dalai Lama, then aged about ten, two or three times a month either at the Potala or at Norbulingka. My mother was very busy on these days preparing dishes for him, especially *Amdo* bread. Sometimes I was allowed to accompany her with my nephew and niece. We loved these occasions when we had special permission to leave the property and I shall never forget our visits. However, my mother's visits to His Holiness were to become less frequent because his teachers said that the time had now come for him to stop playing and devote himself completely to his studies.

Sometimes we rode on horseback to the Potala, leaving our mounts behind the palace. But usually we went on foot, which meant climbing the many hundreds of steps up to what was undoubtedly one of the largest buildings in the world. The Potala had been built up by the Tibetan king, Longsten Gampo and enlarged by the fifth Dalai Lama in the seventeenth century. The central part of the edifice was 13 floors high with large ceremonial rooms, chapels, cells for meditation and the mausoleums where the Dalai Lamas were embalmed. The west wing housed a community of monks, and in the east wing were the administrative offices, with meeting rooms and a school for the monks to be employed by the government.

On the days that Pala accompanied us, I used to hold his hand tightly to climb the stairs. When I complained of being tired, he encouraged me with a tender smile. Later on, Amala told me that the Potala, besides being the home of His Holiness the Dalai Lama, contained armouries, ammunition stores, and cellars where the government's archives were kept. Libraries with thousands of volumes testifying to the life and development of Tibetan culture. These libraries held ancient parchments, books written on the bark of palm trees and imported from India several centuries before, as well as volumes of sacred texts written in a special ink made from a blend of gold or silver, and iron or copper powder, or sometimes from the powder of ground stones or shells.

His Holiness's residence was at the top of the stairs, 400 feet above the town. To reach it we had to pass the monastery of Namgyal and cross a courtyard, then climb more stairs, which led up to the mausoleums of the previous Dalai Lamas. Covered in gold and precious stones, some of these were 30 feet high. Then we walked through a temple where my mother placed a *khata* in front of the altar. There was another dark corridor, with more very steep stairs which I found difficult to climb with my little legs. At last we emerged on to a terrace where the dazzling sunlight compelled me to shut my eyes tight. His Holiness would be waiting impatiently for my mother in a room that seemed very dark to us after the brightness of the terrace.

I shall always remember these audiences when His Holiness gave us his blessing, even though they involved a lot of waiting for us children. My mother went towards her son, greeted him and showed him what she had brought with her. I realized much later on how much these moments meant for my mother. As for me, I had to show my elder brother a great deal of respect because he was the Dalai Lama.

I must admit that I preferred Norbulingka to the Potala. It had been built in the eighteenth century by the seventh Dalai Lama, and its name means 'jewel park'. The residence consisted of a series of small palaces and temples with marvellous gardens surrounded by a huge wall. At the first signs of spring His Holiness used to go there with a long procession made up of dignitaries from Lhasa.

His Holiness would receive my mother on the veranda of the house. From there it was only a short walk down a few steps to the gardens, where there were poplars, willows, junipers and fruit trees, some of which were very beautiful, particularly the walnut and cherry trees. Cherry trees in Tibet are different from the European variety as they are very tall and have an extremely acid fruit. We particularly enjoyed windy days at Norbulingka because we were able to gather up walnuts, although we occasionally received bumps on the head as they fell off the tall trees.

Sometimes we would go to a part of the garden where the

peacocks used to play, a place of dreamlike beauty. When we had been out for too long, His Holiness would become worried and ask my mother to call us back. We came immediately because we knew that we should not displease him. We knew very well that there were certain limits we should not overstep, but we could go on playing so long as no one worried about our absence.

Pala died in 1947, just after my seventh birthday. My childhood then became much more dependent on my mother, but my father's image remains engraved in my memory. Tibetans usually get up very early and every morning at sunrise, Pala, who had a passion for horses, went to the stables. He owned about 20 horses and was among the first to buy thoroughbreds from Amdo when they were sold in Lhasa. Often, when a servant heard me calling, I was wrapped in a blanket and carried to the stables where I stayed with my father until it was time for us to return to the house together. Pala was so fond of horses that he had a special staircase built that led down to the stables.

Another memory of my father concerns an event which was of great interest to me at the time. The high-ranking Tibetan civil servants started work at eight in the morning. At ten, they would gather around the Dalai Lama to discuss current affairs and plan the day. My father attended these meetings, in the course of which the civil servants, who had all brought a wooden bowl with them, were served salty Tibetan tea with rice soup, occasionally rice mixed with raisins. Every day, around eleven o'clock, I would watch for my father's return as he always brought me back some little delicacy in his wooden bowl. I was very angry with him when he did not bring me anything.

One apparently normal day, when I wanted to go to his room to wish him good morning, I was prevented from doing so. Unable to understand why, I cried for ages. I was then told that children cannot go into a room where an adult is unwell. However, Amala said that I could see my father later in the day. But a visit became impossible as his strength waned. The other children kept on asking me to go and play with them, but I refused, explained that my father was ill and might need me.

Pala had begun to complain of acute stomach pains. Shortly before the beginning of the New Year celebrations, the symptoms became more severe and his health began to deteriorate. Members of the family and servants took turns at his bedside day and night. Doctors came regularly to the house and prescribed remedies, but nothing seemed to make him feel any better. Everybody busied themselves around him, the servants ran to and fro, and nobody answered my questions about my father.

My father's condition began to worsen fast. Amala immediately sent a messenger to His Holiness to ask him to excuse the family from attending the New Year celebrations.

After a bad night, during which my mother feared that the worst might happen, my father suddenly felt much better and insisted on making the traditional New Year offerings in front of the altar. He even asked to have tea with the family and servants.

As my father did not appear to be suffering any more, my elder brother decided to return a New Year visit to some friends. Shortly after he left, a messenger was sent after him to tell him that my father had had a serious relapse and that my brother should return home as soon as possible. When he arrived, my father was already dead.

The winter days were cold and gloomy and I remember that I cried continuously. The more my nephew and niece implored me to stop, the more tears I shed. I remember my mother's face being marked with pain, and my youngest brother sitting on her lap with Lobsang Samten squatting at her side. When my elder brother arrived, Amala explained that Pala had died without too much suffering.

Gonsar Rinpoche, a lama friend of ours, recited prayers for the dead and monks came and prayed at my father's bedside. Once more, astrologers were called on and, following their recommendations, my father's body was dressed in new clothes and placed in an upright position. Before sunrise on the third day, the body was taken to the mountains and ceremonially cremated. According to tradition, the period of mourning lasted for 49 days.

My father's death was a terrible loss for our family of seven children, and particularly for my mother. I was still very young at the time, but I could feel an infinite sadness hanging over the house. The period that followed was a very difficult one. Seven years had gone by since our arrival in Lhasa and then, overnight, not only did Amala have to run our everyday life, but she also had to look after the family interests in various parts of Tibet from which we derived our income. Fortunately, the government appreciated the difficulties she now had to face and rapidly appointed a special adviser for her, as a result of which she was able to rest for a few days in our property near Gyantse.

At the time of Pala's death, Amala had just given birth to her sixteenth child, Tenzin Choegyal. When he reached the age of two, he was recognized as the reincarnation of Ngari Rinpoche, a close friend of the thirteenth Dalai Lama. When they used to meet during their lifetime, the thirteenth Dalai Lama had often said to his companion that they would be much closer in their next lives. In fact, through reincarnation, they had now become brothers! It was extraordinary to have this third reincarnation in an ordinary peasant family (first of all, that of my eldest brother, as head of the monastery of Kumbum, and then that of the Dalai Lama), and it was certainly a great honour for my mother during this sad period of mourning. Normally my little brother would have been educated in a monastery, but Amala was firmly opposed to this, believing that he was far too young to be separated from her. So, instead, monks came to live with us and devoted themselves to the task of his education.

All the attention given to the youngest member of the family might possibly have caused a little jealousy amongst the other children, as it was obvious that Tenzin Choegyal was given special treatment and that everyone – servants, monks, friends and visitors – waited on him hand and foot. In Tibet, the influence of Buddhism is present from an early age, completely permeating the life of the household with its notions of tolerance and respect. It is only natural for Tibetans to show a monk total respect. This respect is even more marked in the case of a rinpoche, a reincarnated monk like my little brother. So when we played with him, we always had to take his every wish into consideration and be nice to him all the time.

In every family, whether they be rich or poor, a room is always reserved for an altar. Sometimes, as was the case in our house, a room is is also kept as a prayer room. I remember that there were always monks praying all day long, and sometimes at night too. Their prayers were for the peace and prosperity of the household as well as for His Holiness the Dalai Lama. There was also a part of the house that we were forbidden to enter, reserved, as in many Tibetan households, for the hermits who my parents took in. The hermits stayed for anything from one to three years and when they left were always replaced by others. The servants brought them food and Amala sometimes visited them.

In this kind of atmosphere, children grew up to consider religion as something inseparable from the rest of their lives. When they see their parents making *puja* for instance, they will spontaneously imitate them. However, this observation calls for some comment. Even though Tibetans experience an inner awareness of Buddhism, as a result of growing up with it, this does not necessarily mean that they understand the fundamentals of their religion. Most Tibetans would probably be unable to explain the reasons for their daily behaviour. Buddhist teaching in Tibet is not institutionalized and it is up to each individual to decide how much he would like to know about his religion.

Religion permeates the life of a Tibetan. There are various ways of receiving religious teachings. Tibetans go to see a reincarnated lama or learned geshe for teachings. They ask monks to their house to recite prayers, attend religious ceremonies or follow the public teachings of the great lamas. In Tibetan Buddhism, there are four schools of thought – Sakyapa, Gelugpa, Kagyupa and Nyingmapa. More often than not, each lama gives teachings according to his lineage. The approach to Buddhism, therefore, varies from lama to lama and the teachings received depend a lot on individual choice.

The practice of Buddhism pervades the life of a Tibetan and Tibetans are in general pious. But it has to be understood that their religion is in no way imposed on them. Only those who wish to become monks and nuns have to go to a monastery to study the sacred texts and adhere to a life of discipline and strict education for many years.

Since he was destined to become a monk, my younger brother's education was different to ours. At home, he regularly received visits from teachers to instruct him in prayers and sacred writings. I am sure that we must have disturbed these lessons on a great many occasions. When I was playing with my nephew and niece, my eyes sometimes met those of my brother and I saw an expression of envy in his face.

Amala gradually realized that we would not be able to live on fresh air, games and childish squabbling for ever. We would now have to receive the education that she, as the daughter of a Taktser peasant family, had not. In the past, my parents had of course owned property in the village and this had produced enough income to feed the family. The property had been given to them when my elder brother was recognized as a reincarnation and became the head of the monastery of Kumbum. But once His Holiness was recognized as the reincarnation of the Dalai Lama, this simple farm life changed for good.

2

Memories of Childhood

I recently read an extract from a speech given by His Holiness to the Tibetan Women's Association: 'Mother is the first Lama/Guru of compassion. Our spiritual lamas come later in life. The foundation of love and compassion built by our first lama or mother determines our propensity and ability to internalize these values when they are taught to us later in life by our spiritual lamas.

'Take the case of we Tibetans, our Mahayana lamas may teach us the values of compassion. But that comes later in life, when we are at least about 15 years old. On the other hand, our mother teaches us the power and value of compassion right from our birth, and that too through its sheer practice and application.'

Lama means 'master' in Tibetan. His Holiness was right to say that the mother is the first lama; she is also probably the best (this can be regarded as a universal truth; it is after all the mother who sets an example to her child).

When I was a child, there was no powdered milk in Tibet. A mother breast-fed her child until the next baby was born. In some aristocratic families the children had wet nurses, but this was not the case in families like ours. It was therefore a common sight to see a two or three-year-old child sucking at its mother's breast. This long period of breast-feeding created a very close bond between mother and child. Modern psychology now acknowledges the benefits of this relationship, and doctors stress the nutritional value of mother's milk.

Women were the real heads of the family. Within the traditional structure of society the family existed as an economic unit, with women responsible for material matters. When an important decision had to be taken, the entire family gathered around the mother. If no general agreement was reached, the mother had to arrange a compromise that would please parents, children and any other members of the family circle who lived under the same roof.

Although polyandry and polygamy existed in Tibet, monogamy was the most widespread form of married life. Divorces were unusual, but could be obtained easily, at the request of either the husband or the wife. Marriage was in fact considered a contract between two families. Therefore, when the bride went to live with her new family, everything she brought with her was written down and, in the event of separation, she was able to have her possessions back.

In spite of all they had to do, Tibetan women devoted a lot of time to their children's education, and this was so in my mother's case. When she lived in Taktser, Amala used to work in the fields, carrying a baby on her back. She always used to place him in a corner of the field, protected from sun and wind by an umbrella tied to a post stuck into the ground. That baby was His Holiness.

Until the age of five a child spends all his time with his mother. He grows up following her example. I was in fact to learn a great deal from three exceptional women: Amala, my elder sister and my aunt (my father's sister).

I now realize how essential it is that a mother always be available. Nowadays, most children do not receive all the attention they need. When they get home from school, they are often left to their own devices, because their parents work. Some people would say that children are more independent now, but is this really a good thing in the end? I personally believe that a child who is given a lot of attention will grow up happier and acquire more confidence and, later on, will in turn be able to pass on the attention and love he received.

Some readers may find my analysis a bit old-fashioned. But anyway, Tibetans allow their children to grow up gradually, remaining carefree and happy, as all children should be.

There was always someone to listen to us and take care of us in our large house. Nevertheless, when I was nearly seven, Amala thought that it was time for us to be taught outside the home.

In Tibetan society, teaching was traditionally dispensed by several different kinds of establishment. Monks taught in the monasteries and there was also a very well-organized university system. The Tse School, founded by the seventh Dalai Lama, trained monks who formed government cadres. Graduates from this school who wanted to work in the civil service then underwent higher training at the religious school. Lay civil servants were mainly trained at the Tse School. The acquisition of practical skills held an important place in this system of education. The medical centre at Chakpori was one of the oldest in Tibet and was reserved strictly for monks. Other medical students studied at the Mentsikhang Medical College, which was also the best place for astrological studies.

Lhasa also had a number of private schools started by civil servants, frequented mainly by their children and those from a similar background.

Amala, who wanted me to receive the best possible education, did not want me to be taught with too many other pupils. My two elder brothers had been taught by a brilliant tutor, but once his task was over the government had assigned him to another region of Tibet. Amala therefore asked his assistant, a monk who had remained in Lhasa, to take charge of our education.

Up until then, my nephew and niece, our servants' three children and I had been close playmates, so my mother thought it would be best if we all received the same education. From then on we also became classmates. Our small group was joined by the son of a civil servant.

Classes started very early in the morning and, as our tutor's house was 20 minutes on horseback from our own, we had to rise before daybreak. We did not like doing this and the servants often found it hard to drag us from our beds. My nephew and niece were sometimes in such a bad mood (they were only six and four) that the servants suggested that they follow my better example. This was a way of giving me a sense of responsibility as the elder child, and today I can admit that I rather enjoyed it.

In spite of getting up so early, we were always very excited, not at the prospect of going to school, but at the thought of our daily ride. At an altitude of 10,500 feet, the mornings were pretty cold, so we would set off wrapped in blankets, after swallowing hot tea and *tsampa*. I can also recall an Amdo tradition. In winter, when it is extremely cold, the wind is often very strong. Amala and my sister would prepare a mixture of milk and honey that the servants would rub onto our faces and hands. They would also cover our lips with beeswax to prevent them getting chapped; this was extremely agreeable and I loved to lick my sweet lips as I rode along.

We often arrived before our tutor, who would be kept away all morning by his important duties in the Tibetan civil service. We were welcomed by his assistant who would begin the lessons. Prayer is the first thing taught to Tibetan schoolchildren, and the first prayer they learn is dedicated to Jampal Yang, the Bodhisattva of Wisdom. As we did not yet know how to read, the monk taught it to us line by line until we were all able to recite it by heart. Then he taught us the mantra.

The lessons seemed to me to be endless. Once the recitation was over, our teacher would give us a small wooden board about one foot wide, dusted with chalk powder. He would stand behind each of us and trace horizontal lines in the chalk. Then he carefully drew the shapes of the letters of the Tibetan alphabet using a bamboo stick-pen. Placing the boards on our knees, we would then write with ink on these letters, carefully following the forms that he had made, because the slightest mistake would make us go over into the powder. This is how we learnt to write.

In fact his method became rather tedious. When the board had been completely filled, we had to wash and dry it carefully before once again dusting it with chalk powder. The assistant then drew new lines with new letters and we would copy from him over and over again. It was such painstaking work that I got blisters on my hands, and I can assure you that when you have to keep on writing the pain becomes almost unbearable. However, writing and calligraphy were so important in Tibetan schools that I managed to put up with my discomfort.

The best time of the day was at around half past ten, when a servant brought us our lunch. This servant loved opera and, every day, as soon as our little tummies began to cry out for food, we would listen out for his voice. When we heard him singing loudly in the distance, we knew that lunch was on the way.

Lunchtime was our daily break. I shared my meal, lovingly cooked by Amala, with my nephew and niece as well as with our servants' three children and the civil servant's son, who had food brought to him by another servant. My mother always said that you should share food. However, sometimes when our little companion's meal did not tempt us, we would refuse to swap dishes: something which Amala would certainly not have appreciated. The boy would look at us sadly, obviously not understanding the reason for our strange behaviour.

The afternoon was devoted entirely to reading. Unlike my nephew and niece, who managed very well, I showed little aptitude for this subject. Once our tutor arrived, he would greet us and then go off to have his lunch. As I was a bad reader, he would call me into his room and ask me to read to him throughout his meal. This was a terrible experience! As we did not have many books, he gave me religious texts to read, or else petitions addressed to the government, written on long scrolls.

Seating me opposite him, he first of all made me start with texts that were very easy. Then the texts would gradually become harder. The smell of his meal tickled my nose while I read and sometimes I even felt hungry, although I had just finished my own lunch. In vain I hoped for the moment when my tutor might offer me a mouthful of his delicious meal. Sometimes he was pleased and cut short my suffering. But as he was very strict, he often asked me to repeat sentences endlessly. The time then seemed to go by terribly slowly.

Lessons ended around three o'clock and the horses were then brought round so that we could return home, where we would gobble up the delicious meal Amala had cooked for us.

Throughout their schooling, Tibetan children are given very little homework so, once our meal was over, we were once again free to play.

The huge family house was marvellous for playing hide-and-seek, one of our favourite games. We thought that we knew every recess of this house but, even so, many corners must have remained unexplored. Our large group of children was often joined by the older servants.

The girls also liked to skip with a rope or to play on the swing hanging from the huge tree next to the stables. This game was the cause of many quarrels. As soon as the meal was over, we rushed into the garden, because the first to reach the swing had to be pushed by the others.

We also used to get bags full of sheep knucklebones from the servant in charge of the food stores. We would dry them and then polish them by rubbing them against a large stone to transform them into pieces that would stand up by themselves which we would colour in green yellow or red. Tibetan children have few toys and therefore have to be very inventive. There were various games which could be played with these knucklebones. One of them involved digging small holes in the ground. Each child would then choose a coloured knucklebone and place it in a hole. Taking turns, we then threw a flat stone in the air. If the stone fell into the hole with your knucklebone, you won and were allowed to gather up all the other knucklebones. But if the stone landed in someone else's hole, you lost. I was very good at this game and, being sure of myself, I sometimes bet on two or three knucklebones at a time.

Tibetans love kites and, from the first fine spring days onwards, the sky is dotted with these multi-coloured objects, decorated with the motifs of their owners. Grand aerial battles were organized. Of course, it was really an adult game, but we little ones were fascinated by the magic of the gracious movements against the blue sky. Sometimes a kite fell into the garden, making a shrill whistling sound. We would all rush to pick it up.

My brother, Lobsang Samten, nearly 18 at the time, shared this Tibetan enthusiasm with the other inhabitants of Lhasa. One of his friends often used to come to our house with his kite and we spent hours helping them prepare it for combat. We broke bottles and mixed the pieces of glass with glue before dipping the string of the kite into the mixture. This first operation was rather tedious, but we performed it with great care, hoping that my brother would win.

Once the kite was ready, our excitement soared. We climbed up onto the roof of the house and Lobsang Samten let the kite flutter in the wind, searching for its adversary. The two kites did not engage immediately, every kind of ploy being first used to intimidate the enemy, such as dives, encirclements, sidesteps and fake assaults. Suddenly, Lobsang Samten would start to attack, cheered on by our shouts. The object of the game was to get up close to the enemy kite and cut its string. Losing its balance, the kite would then crash to the ground. But the handler of the enemy kite was also experienced and the battle would rage for some time. Our shrill cries encouraged my brother to surpass himself. Tradition had it that the loser arranged a celebration for the winner or invited him to lunch and, in this way, my brother managed to win quite a number of meals.

Even at school, our tutor sometimes climbed up on to the terrace to practise flying his kite while we were busy with our writing. We would then have to go up there in order to show him our boards. Needless to say, we hurried to wash and dry them before doing more letters so as to be able to return and see him as soon as possible. Sometimes, he was so absorbed by his kite's magnificent flight that he paid no attention to our work. We would then sit silently in a corner and watch him handling the string, feeling a certain amount of admiration.

The boys, including my nephew, often followed more destructive pursuits. In the spring, they loved to roam the property in search of birds' nests. When they found one, they would throw stones at it. My niece and I, and the other small girls did not like this kind of behaviour at all, so we would walk behind the boys and pick up the young featherless birds, or the eggs if they were unbroken. We discovered that a mother would unfortunately not feed her little ones or sit on the eggs after we had touched them. So we regularly brought the poor little birds to my aunt, who then had to feed them. We seemed to think this was the only thing she had to do.

The ground in our property was relatively uneven. When it rained, small pools formed. We used to take off our shoes and splash about happily in the water which had been pleasantly warmed by the sun.

I think that this is now the right moment to describe my first encounter with the Western world. It took place in 1947, when I was just over seven. Two Austrian prisoners had escaped from an Indian prison and taken refuge in Tibet. Lhasa was in a state of great excitement, with everybody wanting to see them.

My brother, Lobsang Samten, became friends with them, especially with the one called Heinrich Harrer. Heinrich was the first European I ever saw. On his visits, which became more and more regular, he would lift me up on to his shoulders and carry me round the property. He loved nature and even planted poplars and fruit trees in our garden. Perched high up on his shoulders, I found it hard to hide my amazement. I had never seen a man like this, so tall and thin, dressed in canvas trousers and a shirt. I was particularly puzzled by his blue eyes and fair hair. Clinging to him, I was fascinated by his silky hair, which I was allowed to touch as much as I wanted. The other thing I remember even now is that he had a strange smell.

The Austrian had made numerous friends in Lhasa. He often went up into the mountains with Lobsang Samten and his other companions. Heinrich had taught them how to ice-skate, an activity unknown in Tibet and one which they enjoyed hugely. We children loved to listen to the stories of their adventures and falls, which they recounted with much laughter. We used to say that they were setting off to 'walk on ice'.

Heinrich often ate with us. One day, he surprised us with a Western recipe. I remember vividly the moment when he entered the room where we used to eat, bearing a steaming dish which he laid on the stove exclaiming: 'Try it. Tell me what it's like.' After a long moment of hesitation, my mother and sister tasted this strange delicacy. Visibly appreciating it, they gave a piece to each of the children present who, up until then, had been awaiting Amala's opinion with curiosity. I remember the food being delicious and from that day on I have loved roast chicken.

When I left Lhasa with my eldest sister, Heinrich was still in Tibet. I saw him again in Kalimpong and later, on his way back to Europe, he stopped in India to visit my mother.

One evening, Amala told us about the official reception given for His Holiness the Dalai Lama in Lhasa on 7 October 1939. His enthronement took place shortly after the New Year celebrations for the year of the Iron Dragon, in 1940. At the time, I had not yet been born and His Holiness was only four. At this ceremony his new names were proclaimed: Jetsun Jamphel Ngawang Lobsang Yeshi Tenzin Gyatso.

Before the arrival of the fourteenth Dalai Lama in the Tibetan capital, the government had repainted the palaces and prepared a temporary abode for our family. The monasteries made banners for the procession and the whole population awaited this exceptional event with growing impatience. Foreign envoys crowded into the town, some bringing magnificent presents for His Holiness. The Chogyal of Sikkim offered him two beautiful white horses.

The yellow satin Peacock Tent, which is only put up to welcome a new Dalai Lama to Lhasa, had been repaired and cleaned as it had not been used for a long time. About 13 feet high, it covered an area of some 90 square feet.

According to custom, a camp was pitched at Rigya, two miles from Lhasa. All the civil servants, whether monks or lay officials, had to place their tents within the encampment around the area reserved for His Holiness. Some officials had new tents made for themselves, others had to make do and make repairs, but all the families were kept busy. The tailors worked non-stop, overwhelmed by requests for new fabrics, banners and clothes.

When His Holiness the fourteenth Dalai Lama finally arrived, practically the entire population of Lhasa was in Rigya to greet him. He then gave his first audience to the Kashag, the prime minister, and then ministers and the abbots of the monasteries of Drepung, Sera and Ganden, important centres of Tibetan Buddhism. Traditional dances followed songs and prayers. Cakes and dried fruit were handed round and everyone was able to help themselves to as much smoked yak meat as they could eat, a sign of prosperity.

Our family stayed in Rigya for two nights. Then, in accordance with the government astrologer's instructions, the procession set out for Lhasa. His Holiness's palanquin, born by 16 young officials dressed in green satin and wearing red hats, was in the middle of this impressive and continually growing procession. The Lonchens (ministers) rode in front of the palanquin on a beautiful horse, dressed in Mongol costume with silk headgear decorated with gold braid. The Regent followed next, in his finest clothes, riding a horse clad in brocade with golden trappings.

The procession was led by the astrologer, dressed entirely in white and carrying the banner of Sipakhorlo. Important figures such as the *shap-pes* and the *tsi-pons* walked next to His Holiness. The order of the procession had been decided on before setting out from the encampment and an impressive escort of monks and police took care that everyone remained in their place.

Pala, on whom the title of *gyalyap* (father to the Dalai Lama) had been conferred, was dressed as a shap-pe. Amala, now the *gyalyum* (mother to the Dalai Lama) looked splendid in a magnificent Amdo dress, a costume the inhabitants of Lhasa were not used to seeing and which aroused their curiosity.

As the procession set off, you could hear the beating of the *Dhama*, a drum from Ladakh, used only on great occasions, as well as the *suna*, a flute whose sound that morning seemed particularly pleasing to the population's ears. Tibetans consider that when these two instruments are used together they express great dignity and intense happiness.

The dhama and suna were accompanied by the ringing of numerous bells and, behind the musicians, 20 small boys danced to the rhythm of folk songs. Two dhama with different tonalities had been fastened to the flanks of a pony covered in silk and satin that was being led by a man wearing a black shirt, brocade jacket and white turban. The drummers and flautists also wore brocade costumes, with white shirts and flat-topped hats and long golden earrings.

As His Holiness entered Lhasa, multi-coloured flags and silk banners floated in the wind, their bright colours shining in the sun. Lines had been drawn in yellow and white chalk at the edge of the road to be followed by the Dalai Lama and the ever-lengthening procession accompanying him. Every 100 feet, incense burners gave off dense smoke. Rows of monks and the regiments of the Tibetan army followed His Holiness in an impressive guard of honour. Openings had been made on each side of the palanquin so that the young Dalai Lama could see the crowd which had come to welcome him, a crowd crying with happiness and showing signs of deep devotion.

As the procession entered Lhasa, it was approached by the Nechung oracle. The man was in a state of trance, and Amala told us that his face looked even more ferocious than one of the masks from the temple. He offered His Holiness a khata, placing his head against the Dalai Lama's forehead. His Holiness surprised everyone when, entirely naturally, he placed the khata around the oracle's neck, as if they had both known each other a long time. The oracle then accompanied the palanquin until His Holiness, with our entire family and a large number of officials, entered the Jokhang.

The Dalai Lama was placed on a raised throne, just in front of an image of the Buddha. The lamas and monks prayed, the festive crowd offered khatas to the various temples, and the private altars, heaped with offerings, glittered with a multitude of lights as a symbol of their gratitude and happiness. His Holiness was then led to the temple of Ramoche Tsuklakhang, and finally to

Norbulingka. In the hall of the Dalai Lama's summer palace, the Regent, the Lonchens, and a great many officials, lamas, monks and foreign envoys attended a performance of folk and sacred dances. Attendants brought round cakes and Tibetan tea (salted tea mixed with milk and butter).

Amala ended her story by explaining that His Holiness remained for a while at Norbulingka, awaiting the day chosen by the government astrologer for his move to the Potala.

One day, in front of some of our friends, my mother told the story of my birth and explained the origin of my name. I was very surprised and amused by this story.

Shortly after His Holiness's arrival with our family in Lhasa, the capital was once again in the state of ferment brought on by the performances of the Shotoen opera. For several days these operas were performed by various troupes at Norbulingka. This was the first time that His Holiness had attended.

The house that our family occupied temporarily was right next to His Holiness's summer residence, indeed so close that we could see the stage from it. Although Amala was expecting me at the time and nearly at the end of her pregnancy, she was very busy during the festivities. Needless to say, I did not choose a very convenient moment for my arrival.

On the fifth day of the Shotoen, the servants were all going about their tasks and the officials, our friends and all the other guests were attending the opera performances. As she was by now used to giving birth (I was her 14th child), my mother was equipped with a pair of scissors and pieces of cloth and towels, which she hid in her *ambag*, a kind of breast pocket formed by the two overlapping sides of her *chuba*, and in which Tibetan women put their important personal items. I was born in the pantry of our family house inside Norbulingka compound, this being the only part of the building that was out of sight, with my sister as witness to the event. I was the first and only child born in the Norbulingka compound.

A few days after my birth, Amala went to see His Holiness and asked him to give me a name. Without a moment's hesitation the Dalai Lama replied: 'Jetsun Pema' (virtuous lotus). It was the first time that the fourteenth Dalai Lama, then only five years old, had given a name to a child. In fact, Jetsun is the first part of His Holiness's own very long name.

3

Traditional Celebrations

The Tibetan New Year is officially known as Losar. At the end of each year, an astrologer would draw up a new calendar for the coming year. Celebrations began on the twenty-ninth day of the last month of the old year with the Torgya at the Potala.

Tibetan months do not have names but are designated by numbers. The seven days of the week are represented by the sun, moon and the five visible planets. In ancient Tibet, the calendar followed a 12-year cycle. Each year was associated with an animal: horse, sheep, monkey, bird, dog, pig, mouse, ox, tiger, hare, dragon and snake. In the eleventh century, a 60-year cycle was introduced, combining the animal names with the five elements: wood, fire, earth, iron and water. In this system, each element was combined twice with the same animal. In order to differentiate the two years bearing the same name, the first was called 'male' and the second 'female'. In this way, a Wood Female Ox year can be distinguished from a Wood Male Ox year. This cycle, known as Rabjung, began in 1027. A year is called a Lokhor. Day and night are divided into two-hour periods, designated by the 12 animals as follows: daybreak/hare; sunrise/ dragon; morning/snake; noon/horse; afternoon/ sheep; evening/monkey; sunset/bird; dusk/dog; early night/ pig; midnight/mouse; late night/ox; dawn/tiger.

The entire population prepared for Losar with great care. The temples and houses were specially cleaned and repainted, and the white lace that surrounded the outside of the windows and doors was changed. Families used the occasion to change the brocade or satin sheets which surrounded the icons of the deities. Two weeks before the New Year, we planted shoots of wheat or barley (*lo-phud*) in a jar. Tsampa mixed with butter (*chemar*) and offerings of wheat were put in special wooden boxes decorated with golden and silver paper banners and coloured butter. The offering was accompanied by a bowl of *chang* and *khabse*.

But let us go back to the festivities known as Torgya, which closed the year at the Potala. A colourful performance was put on by the monks at the monastery of Namgyal. The yellow silk curtains of His Holiness's apartments flapped in the wind. This delighted the people, as a strong wind is considered to be a good omen for the new year. Dancers mimed various legendary scenes from Tibetan history. At intervals, soldiers clad in coats of armour several centuries old, fired guns into the air. The resulting smoke was so thick it became extremely difficult to distinguish what was going on on stage.

The public burst into laughter when monks wearing animal masks appeared. Their dances, known as *cham*, lasted for hours. When the skeleton dancers appeared, a heavy silence fell on the crowd and a wave of emotion swept through it for everyone knew that these characters represented demons. The dancers wore chains made from human bones (*rugyen*) over their black costumes; these made sinister, almost supernatural, noises at the slightest movement.

The performance ended with a pantomime. A huge sheet of rice paper picturing a man was spread in the courtyard. All the dancers gyrated round the sheet, to the sound of drums, horns and cymbals. This symbolic act released all the harmful influences of the old year onto the paper. The frenetic dancing became more and more intense. Suddenly, the great wizard seized hold of the sheet and, screwing it up into a huge ball, threw it into boiling oil. Then he drew some alcohol from a human skull and poured a large glassful onto the oil. Fatty, smoky flames rose high into the sky, carrying the bad influences of the old year with them.

That evening, each Tibetan family ate *guthul*, a thick soup with small pieces of vegetables, cheese, meat and dough in it. Some of the dough pieces would be made bigger than the rest and filled with small objects such as wool, paper, salt, chilli, stones or peas. Everyone in the household would receive one of these bigger pieces in his or her bowl. There would be great excitement to see what each one got and there would be much laughter when the interpretation for the objects was made. Funnily enough, what was received did speak about the person's character: wool would be someone who is kind and gentle; paper – whimsical; salt – lazy; chilli – sharp-tongued; stone – conscientious; pea – tight-fisted or miserly.

After the third day of New Year, the exchange of food and presents began between friends, as well as the offering of gifts to the poor. The flags and banners of the houses were changed. Each family made special Losar biscuits (deep fried savouries) known as khabse. I remember that a couple of old, grey-haired Tibetans would come to our house to make them. They worked in a room specially set aside for this purpose, with a large chimney. As happened in all families, the couple made an enormous quantity of khabse so that a room was completely filled from floor to ceiling. There was of course a reason for producing such a vast number: besides being placed on the altars in the houses, khabse were also distributed to members of the family, servants, hermits, visitors and friends – and to monks and the poor. Huge trays full of khabe with khatas were sent to friends. According to the custom, these khatas were then returned with their thanks. The cakes were cooked in oil or butter and the smell of khabse frying enveloped Lhasa and probably all the other towns of Tibet too. Families were very proud to be known as the best khabse makers in town.

At New Year when guests visited a home they would be offered chemar which is placed in a beautifully painted wooden box with two compartments, one holds barley and the other a mixture of tsampa, butter and sugar. One would take a pinch of chemar and throw a bit of it into the air as an offering to the gods and a bit would be eaten. Chang was also offered in a bowl and one would dip the ring finger in the bowl and flick it in the air and then a drop of chang would be put on the tongue. Sheep's heads decorated with coloured butter always adorned the altars to welcome in the New Year. We cooked sweetened rice, called *dresil*, mixed with potentillas (*dro-ma*) and raisins.

In the morning, we would always get up as early as possible

to welcome in the New Year. After the Tashi Delek ceremony, sweet boiled chang (a mixture of cheese, tsampa and potentilla) was served. Then the family withdrew to pray in the altar room and to bow down before the deities. The younger members of the family gave khatas to their elders, and the servants gave them to their masters. On the third and final day of Losar, the khatas were returned to the servants. They were also given chang and spent the entire night dancing and having a good time. On the early morning of the first day of the New Year the sky was filled with the sound of a myriad firecrackers and the bursting of multi-coloured fireworks.

After celebrating at home, the inhabitants of Lhasa all went to the Jokhang and queued to visit the temples. The weather was still extremely cold and, on the first day, there were official ceremonies at the Potala.

On New Year's Day, the children were dressed in new clothes and the adults put on their best costumes and jewellery. It is a custom that one must wear something new on this day. The houses were repainted and katas are tied on the water jugs and other jars to bring about good luck. It was also customary to draw lines of white sand between the gate and door of the house and mark symbols in the middle of the path, for instance a conch symbolizing the splendour of dharma.

I did not like putting on new clothes, and I made a great nuisance of myself to the servants who were meant to dress me, screaming and crying and demanding that they return my old and, in my opinion, far more comfortable, clothes. Amala found my behaviour very peculiar, repeating several times: 'What a funny little girl, not caring about her appearance!' Perhaps I should search among my earlier lives to find an explanation for this behaviour.

Clothes worn by the rich Tibetans are mostly made from brocade and covered with embroidery. The fabrics usually came from China, and later on from India, and were rather coarse, which partly explained my reluctance to wear new clothes. Better woollen garments were imported from Britain. Women's fashion had developed slowly in Tibet, and many women wore brocade clothes with warm linings. My elder sister was more interested than most in clothes and fashion, but then she was 25! We children loved hiding and observing the women of the nobility and well-to-do who came to visit Amala. Tibetan women adored making themselves up and covering themselves with cosmetics from India and Europe, especially from Paris and London. There was one product that I longed for with all my heart and soul whenever a servant washed my frequently dirty face: Pears soap from London. As Pears soap is translucent, I spent long moments looking through it at all the objects in the room, which suddenly seemed very strange.

All the same, apart from the torture of pulling on the new clothes, I was delighted, and so were my nephew and niece, for celebrations such as Losar or Monlam (which I shall soon describe) provided us with our only opportunities to leave the property and mix with the crowd, both religious and lay. In the evening, I fell asleep exhausted in our bedroom, on a large mattress which I shared with my niece and nephew. My aunt told us stories before we went to sleep and then watched over us.

My father's sister had become our ally. She kept our little secrets and did not tell anyone about the food we stole from the storeroom, something that we used to do at least once a week. Normally, we were not allowed to go down to the cellar except for when, at the approach of winter, the servants took all the plants and flowers down there to protect them from the cold, and we would help them. But, once or twice a week, someone went down to the storeroom to fetch rice, flour and barley to make tsampa. Hidden in the darkness, we listened out for footsteps and, above all, for the creaking sound of the large old lock. We would then crawl into the storeroom on our stomachs after the servant. It was a perfect opportunity to stuff ourselves with dried meat, popcorn, and butter that was kept in a lump in a yak skin. We brought some of the food up to my aunt, who promised not to say anything to Amala.

According to Buddhist scriptures, the Great Prayer Festival of Monlam on the evening of the full moon in the first month commemorates the Buddha's victory over the heretics at Sravasti. The great Tsongkhapa introduced these festivities, which had been celebrated since the Earth Female Ox year of the seventh 60-year cycle (1409).

The first two days of the New Year in Lhasa were celebrated only by the government and lay inhabitants, with the Monlam Chenmo beginning on the morning of the third day. Monks and pilgrims then arrived from every direction. The capital's population suddenly grew from 25,000 to 100,000 people. The main hall and corridor of the temple of Jokhang were full of monks from the three great monastic universities of Sera, Ganden and Drepung, who each year were in charge of the festivities. The celebrations lasted for three weeks under government patronage.

The monks' day began at four o'clock, with a short break at sunrise. The monks served tea and a rice dish with meat, butter, and dried fruit is also served which the monks mixed into the tea in small wooden bowls. The people of Lhasa made offerings and donations to the monks.

Then it was time to go to the Sungchorawa. The monks who had finished their studies to attain the supreme title of Lharampa by taking part in philosophical debates. These events, which always attracted large crowds, were attended by the abbots of the monasteries and a jury decided what rank to accord each participant.

His Holiness sometimes visited the Tsuklakhang, carried there in a solemn procession of senior monks, members of the Kashag and rinpoches. From a seat which had been prepared for him in the temple, the Dalai Lama would bless the crowd that gathered round in ever increasing numbers.

After the three weeks of celebrations for the New Year and Monlam, Lhasa emptied again very rapidly. The town's renewed calm lasted only 12 days, though, before the Tsogcho Monlam, known as the 'small New Year celebration', began. Once again, the streets of Lhasa were invaded by crowds. This second celebration was customarily the occasion for further philosophical debates in which the monks tried to obtain the title of Tsokrampa. This title was undoubtedly less important than Lharampa, but it gave the monk who held it the distinction of *geshe*.

During Monlam, anyone could make a written request for prayers to be said. The pilgrims wrote their requests on pieces of paper that they tossed among the monks. They in turn threw the papers up into the air towards the Superiors of the monasteries who caught them as they fell. One of the Superiors then read the paper and recited the prayer that had been requested.

During the Monlam riding was forbidden in the Barkhor, and even the shap-pes had to walk. Women only went out in their finest clothes with their hair well arranged. On the night of the fifteenth day of the first month, the great butter festival took place. The butter was coloured with powdered dyes and then sculpted, with some of the sculptures reaching as high as 36 feet. They represented Tsongkhapa and his disciples, the Buddha's five disciples, the eight good luck signs, dragons, lions, birds and so on. I loved going to see the beautiful butter sculptures. Sometimes the monks also had a small puppet show and this was the climax of the evening for all Lhasa children.

The New Year festivities culminated in the exhibiting of the banner known as the *goeku*. A procession of monks crossed the turquoise bridge in the direction of the Potala. Many wore papier mâché masks of demons and extraordinary animals. The monks displayed the flags and banners of the monasteries, as well as silk and brocade umbrellas and other symbols of good fortune. An enormous crowd danced in front of the Potala. Cries of admiration at the sight of the precious embroidery and the magnificently coloured banners rose up to His Holiness's residence. After a few hours, the goeku was put back into its cover, and this act marked the end of the New Year celebrations.

Before leaving Lhasa to rejoin his monastery, each monk threw a stone into the river, to strengthen the dikes. This custom dates back to the year 1562, when there had been a great flood in the Tibetan capital. At the close of Monlam, the monks took part in rites that lasted for several days and were meant to drive away evil. An entire day was devoted to burning and throwing *tormas* to keep away all the malevolent spirits who might harm the country and its religion.

After Monlam, the two Lhasa magistrates, whose authority had been turned over to the monks during the festivities, were once again placed in charge of maintaining the law, and life in the city returned to normal.

The celebration that I particularly enjoyed was His Holiness the Dalai Lama's birthday, on the fifth day of the fifth month of the Tibetan calendar (he was born on 6 July 1935). The event was celebrated throughout Tibet and was one of the most important days in the life of the country.

The day began with offerings of juniper incense, with the prayer flags floating over the Potala and Norbulingka. Our family went to His Holiness's residence to offer him our best wishes. Members of the Kashag, the palace administrative staff and other officials gathered in the audience room. The tutors gave His Holiness longevity pills, wished him long life on earth and prayed for his health. In turn, the Kashag, administrative staff, and government officials presented their best wishes. Then they set out for Trung-lha Yarsoel, a mile outside Lhasa, where they took part in different rituals in the Dalai Lama's honour. More prayer flags were raised and juniper incense was once more offered up.

The Tsechag Lekhung, the Treasury department of the Potala, gave a party for our family lasting for two days. In return, we organized two days of festivities for the officials. It was very important for these officials to appear on the list of those invited to His Holiness's birthday celebration, and they went there dressed in their finest clothes. We exchanged khatas, and dancing and singing went on for several days at the top of the hill.

Trung-lha Yarsoel was a magnificent place, with a garden crossed by a stream. In the summer, extremely beautiful flowers grew in and around Lhasa, especially long-stalked irises with very delicate leaves, entirely different from the Western varieties. The children had been waiting for just such an opportunity to run off. We did not, however, go very far as the servants followed us. In fact, we only wanted to go to the banks of irises. We were able to pick as many of these beautiful flowers, which were taller than we were, as we wanted to. The servants would then plait our short hair with them. Sometimes, if our 'transformation' had not been completed, we would not reply to the servants that Amala sent to look for us, and just snuggled up against one another. Our servants became our allies. Then, once the danger was over, they hurriedly completed their work. Only then would we suddenly reappear – and we did look stunning.

Still accompanied by the servants, we would sit down by the banks of the river. The water was icy and flowed fast. The servants immediately spread a carpet on the ground and made a small bed from our clothes which we had taken off. We then slipped into the water for a marvellous dip; sometimes both the men and women servants joined us. On getting out, shivering with cold, we quickly dried ourselves and hid under the clothes for a well-earned nap. Later on, in the shade of the willow trees, we sometimes managed to catch tadpoles that we then put into bottles.

Tibetans, including our family, loved to picnic along the irrigation canals fed by the Kyi Chu river. These canals went through fields of oats and peas, and one of our favourite games was to go in small groups of seven or eight children and steal the peas. When the peasants saw us, we got chased and the servants had to distract their attention when we were threatened with slingshots.

I also loved the wonderful moments when our entire family was seated around the table, except of course for His Holiness and my elder brother, now installed at the monastery of Drepung. My sister busied herself amongst us and my mother devoted herself to her passion, cooking. We ate Amdo food at home which is very different from the food of other Tibetan regions. Lobsang Samten often asked the servants to bring him sweetened tea (with condensed milk imported from India), which was then the fashion in Lhasa, instead of the usual Tibetan tea with salt and butter.

As there was not yet any piped water in Tibet there was a tank in a corner of the kitchen, from which we helped ourselves with large copper ladles. Often my sister or Amala would bake potatoes in the ashes of the wood stove. We ate them with butter and salt and they were delicious. Sometimes Amala put dough in a tray and baked this in the ashes too, making crusty golden bread. By mixing molasses into the dough it became soft and sweet inside. Amala also liked to add sesame seeds. When I asked her to, my sister would prepare a kind of fudge with molasses and butter. When we had eaten too much, my mother would say, 'It's not good for your teeth!'

As far back as I can remember, His Holiness was aware of his exceptional position. When I was four or five and accompanied my mother to the Potala or Norbulingka, there were always advisers present. At the time His Holiness was ten years old but he was already unlike other children. Boys of that age usually go to school and are only interested in playing. His Holiness, though, showed a precocious sense of responsibility and gave an impression of great dignity. Whenever I was in his presence, I felt great respect for him, even at such a young age.

His attitude would, however, change according to which counsellors were present, as there were probably some he felt more at ease with than others. I instinctively knew that my visits with my mother to the Potala in winter, and to Norbulingka from the spring onwards, were privileged moments. When my nephew and niece came with us, we were all aware of the changed atmosphere.

At the same time, another reincarnation was living in our house: my youngest brother, Tenzin Choegal, a rinpoche or spiritual master to whom we also paid great respect. He, however, shared our everyday life and was also sometimes very mischievous. At meal times, he did not think twice about getting down from his chair and joining us to be naughty, much to his tutor's distress. He too was unlike other children, although this did not prevent him from getting up to every possible kind of adventure. Everyone let him do exactly what he wanted, because of his position as a rinpoche. I was particularly struck by an event which occurred when he was five. He loved riding, and at this time my sister had a beautiful black mare which had just given birth to a gorgeous foal. As the foal grew up, my brother asked to ride it, but not just anywhere ... on the roof terrace of our house! The servants, completely obedient, went to fetch the foal who was then made to climb the stairs. Some of the servants pulled the reins while others pushed from behind. My young brother waited in a dignified manner, commenting on the animal's reluctance. Once it was up on the terrace, the foal made an extremely impressive sight. No one could remember ever having seen a horse on a roof. On the way down, once my brother's whim had been satisfied, the servants had to hold the foal by the tail to prevent it from falling and breaking its legs.

I experienced two very different kinds of feeling for the reincarnations in my family. His Holiness the Dalai Lama, although my brother, lived in his palaces, the Potala and Norbulingka, whereas my younger rinpoche brother lived with us at home. I should also say that I was still growing up in my own little world of school, games, and companions – my nephew and niece, the servants' children and my aunt, whom I easily confided in. At this time I adapted to our particular circumstances with a young child's spontaneity.

When we visited him, His Holiness addressed our mother as 'Amala' and spoke about 'Pala' whenever he talked about our father. He called us by our first names. In the spring he liked to walk in the gardens at Norbulingka with Amala. With a great shout of laughter, he would show her his tame parrots and the fish which appeared at the surface of the lake as soon as they heard his voice or footsteps. We followed silently at a distance, waiting for the moment when His Holiness would turn round and say: 'You can go and play now.' Amala talked at length to His Holiness, telling him about everything that had happened at home. I am certain that these moments were very important for her, especially after my father's death. His Holiness also talked about his studies and the need for me to study too. It was probably on one of these occasions that Amala asked for his advice on my future.

When just my mother and I visited, I stayed by her side with His Holiness, listening to their conversation. I remember his keen interest in watches, which he used to take to pieces to study their workings before putting them together again, though sometimes failing entirely. He was also fascinated by the electric generator at Norbulingka, and old cars. The thirteenth Dalai Lama had had two 1927 Baby Austins delivered, as well as a 1931 Dodge, but it had been a long time since these cars had been driven. However, one day, His Holiness showed us the Dodge, which he had succeeded in repairing with the help of a young mechanic. The electric generator often broke down. His Holiness explained to Amala that he had repeatedly repaired this obstinate machine and that, thanks to his tinkering, he had managed to understand how a combustion engine worked and how a dynamo could create a magnetic field.

4

Boarding School in India

Up until now, our lives had been spent in and around Lhasa. I vaguely remember a trip to Gyantse with my sister, but I was still too young at the time to have retained any detailed memory of it. My family owned ten properties in different parts of Tibet, one of which was run by a cousin of mine, my aunt's son Chen Chen La.

When they arrived in Lhasa, my parents had been given everything they owned, including their house, by the government at the time of the Dalai Lama's enthronement. It was customary that these possessions should then be passed on through the family.

The government also provided agricultural land for the peasants, who were therefore able to farm, knowing that they would be able to feed the following generations. It was like leasing from the state. Monasteries as well as lay members of society owned land and, in this way, all kinds of Tibetans took part in improving it.

The peasants paid rent in exchange for the land they received. Some of them had to give over a part of their harvest to their landlords, as well as to the state, who then redistributed some of this rent to the army, or to lay officials and those monasteries unable to support themselves. Others paid for their lease with their labour. This system, similar to sharecropping, was perhaps not an ideal one and there may have been abuses on both sides.

Sometimes, though only in exceptional cases, the government reclaimed the land when a peasant could not make his contribution. On the other hand, the state gave support grants when there were bad harvests and families were in difficulty.

It would seem that this means of managing natural resources worked reasonably well, in spite of its imperfections. Indeed, Tibet never knew famine until the Chinese invasion and, even though the land technically belonged to a small number of people, each family had enough to eat.

However, some Tibetans were discontented and no longer had respect for our country's traditional essential values, based on reflection and honesty; their belief in non-violence and the karmic doctrine of reward had seriously declined. Some members of the ecclesiastical orders no longer respected their moral codes and preferred trade and profits and all kinds of other things that had nothing to do with spiritual matters. Those who remained religious often found themselves relegated to the lowest ranks of the social ladder. A particular kind of man seemed to be becoming more common, the kind who took no account of morality or of the spirit of our culture. The fourteenth Dalai Lama therefore decided to undertake important reforms, particularly concerning the management of aristocratic properties. Having enjoyed these properties for many generations, some owners abused their rights and exploited the peasants. This kind of behaviour was contrary to His Holiness's wishes for his people.

Buddhism, generosity and kindness form part of a Tibetan education from early childhood on. According to our religion, we have to behave with merit in order to influence our next life. This includes knowing how to give and to receive. Tibetans are inclined to accept the inequalities that may result from these Buddhist principles.

In 1949, my life suddenly changed. My sister fell seriously ill and my mother decided to have her treated in India, and to send me with her. At this time, many Tibetan families used to send their children to Indian mission schools. Amala's decision for me was thus very different from her earlier treatment of my brother, Gyalo Thondup. He had been invited by Chiang Kai-shek and his wife to visit Shanghai to finish his studies there.

We carefully went about preparing the details of our

departure, including luggage, horses and escort – the roads to India often being bad and dangerous. All the secretaries and stewards were very busy and the usually quiet life of our household became one of great upheaval. Amala had a great deal of work to do, for my sister and brother-in-law were unable to help her. We had to get a very considerable sum of money together to cover the expenses of our stay in India, as well as the medical costs. This no doubt explained the tremendous comings and goings which upset the normal routines of the house. Tibetan, Nepalese and Indian merchants came to the house very often, and it was through them that Amala could change our Tibetan money. I was amazed by the huge pile of Tibetan notes that we gave them for their currency. I think that at this period there were 15 Tibetan *sang* to an Indian rupee. Today I realize the significance of this transaction. We were in fact able to exchange our currency because Tibet was an independent free state.

As the time of our departure neared, the tension in the house increased. For my part, I felt a mixture of excitement and sadness at the idea of the journey: excitement because I had never travelled before, my life having being restricted to Lhasa, the Potala and Norbulingka; sadness, because my sister was so ill. For her sake, I so wanted to speed up our departure, but at the same time I was appalled by the thought that something awful might occur on the journey.

Our good-byes were very sad. In 1949, for the first time I was going to leave Amala, my grandmother (*mola*) and my little brother, Tenzin Choegal; I would also be away from His Holiness. When would I see them again? Although I was desperate for an answer, I knew that my mother was unable to reply to this question. I would have to say goodbye to my family, friends, the officials, the servants and their children – all the people I had grown up with. We exchanged khatas ... everyone cried. My feelings were a confused mixture of joy and anxiety. But when I thought of His Holiness, who had given us his blessing, I felt encouraged.

Round crafts lined with yak skins awaited us on the river Kyi Chu. An advance convoy had already left Lhasa with our luggage and it preceded us throughout the journey. The first stage of our journey was as far as our property in Gyantse. We descended the river without the slightest difficulty and then continued our journey on horseback.

Besides the first convoy of about a dozen people, who were to unpack our luggage at each halt, prepare meals and find us rooms in an inn or private house, we took two additional servants with us. There were a lot of travellers on the road from Lhasa to Sikkim. For the first time I saw nomads and convoys of mules, horses or yaks. They mostly carried wool, which was Tibet's main export, particularly to the United States via India. In the evening, I enjoyed visiting the different encampments. The merchants always smiled at me and had a kind word to say.

Without the worry of my sister's health, the journey would have been rather enjoyable. As she was not allowed to travel on horseback, the servants had made a palanquin borne by two mules, one in front, one behind. My niece, nephew and I each had a horse. Amala had made a kind of basket, rather like a cot, and one of these was attached to each saddle by four very strong rods and a cord. The road was going to be very long, so if we were to fall asleep, we would not fall off. A servant led the horses. In Tibet it was customary to dismount when climbing a rise but, as we were only children, we were allowed to remain seated.

Amala had also prepared provisions for us. We each had a box of English biscuits, sweets and nuts. In fact, the journey was rather like a big picnic. We advanced by short stages, which were arranged in the following way: departure early in the morning, a pause to have our meal and, finally, the halt at our stopping place in the early afternoon.

One day, while crossing an immense green plain that stretched in every direction, we arrived at a lake which glimmered in the sunlight. I was fascinated by this landscape surrounded by mountains whose summits disappeared in the mist. How could I ever forget this fairytale spectacle which made me want to touch everything around me?

Children are, of course, attracted by anything new. I discovered yellow and blue wild flowers unknown in Lhasa, spread like a marvellous many-coloured carpet beneath our feet. On the other hand, the streams of clear water reminded me of those in the capital. We could see fish in the middle of the streams and admire the magnificent pebbles. Everywhere nature revealed its treasures to us.

Once, when we were at the edge of the lake, my niece wanted to take a box of biscuits that I fiercely guarded in a bag attached to my saddle. An argument followed and the servants had to intervene: 'Your niece is younger than you are, give her the box. She won't eat them all ...' I finally gave in and held out the box to her. As she seized it, the box banged heavily against one of the rods of her basket frame, making a loud noise. Horrified, the horse set off at a frantic gallop with my niece, who was then seven, jolting about in her saddle like a puppet. There was general consternation amongst the convoy and my uncle left in hot pursuit, while the servants rushed shouting in every direction. My nephew and I began to cry.

As soon as the horse began to tire, my uncle, who was an excellent rider, managed to catch it. My niece, though livid and in a state of shock, owed the saving of her life to her children's saddle basket.

Naturally, we had other adventures, but nothing else quite as serious – our journey had undoubtedly been very carefully prepared. At the frontier between Tibet and Sikkim, we passed through the valley of Chumbi, which is known as the valley of flowers. Even in those days, the British used to come in large numbers to visit this magical spot where we were able to count thousands of flowers and wild strawberries.

Once we had crossed the frontier, the servants returned to Lhasa with the family horses that had shown such endurance.

With its huge mixture of cultures, Sikkim was very different from Tibet and I felt that I was in another world. For the first time in my life I rode in a motor car arranged by the Chogyal of Sikkim. Cars were to be seen everywhere. Although I remembered the old Dodge that His Holiness had repaired, I had never seen a modern car at close hand. I was very frightened, to the extent of being ill when we dismounted at the frontier and climbed into a jeep; the winding road that followed the edge of precipices was too much for my bravery.

Many of the Tibetan merchants left their mules in stables and continued by car to make their purchases in Kalimpong or Darjeeling. On their return, they loaded their animals for the journey back to Tibet. The Tibetans did business with the Indian, Nepalese and Bhutanese traders. For the first time I saw many people dressed in the Western manner.

After several days in Gangtok, the capital of Sikkim, we set off in the direction of Kalimpong where my sister had friends.

Thanks to them, we were able to get admission to the convent school in Kalimpong, run by Catholic nuns from Ireland, in the middle of the school year.

My niece, my nephew and I were suddenly torn from our childhood routines. We had to replace our Tibetan clothes with school uniform: a brutal change. Sometimes we felt we were living in a bad dream and that we would soon wake up again in Lhasa. But the nightmare was real. And so began our tough apprenticeship at boarding school, where only one language was spoken, English. Luckily, there were about 20 other young Tibetans from Lhasa who shared our fate. I can remember some of their names (the others must forgive me): the four children of Ngapo Ngawang Jigme: (Peme La, Norin La, and two boys); Tsering La and Angyi; Tapel La Yuthok, Thochu La Yuthok, Norla and Norzin La, Surkhang Yangchen La, Ongmo La Pondatsang, Soden La and Chimi Phungkhang, Pema La and Tse Dolma La Lanthon. Some of the Sikkimese children spoke Tibetan as well, so there was always someone to act as interpreter. Even so, we had to learn English pretty quickly.

The nuns also proved to be sympathetic. Our class of 25 included pupils of several different nationalities: there were children from Tibet, Nepal, Western Bengal and Burma, as well as Anglo-Indians and children from various regions of India. At night we slept in an immense dormitory of at least 50 beds. I adapted to this change quite easily, though my niece, who was used to sleeping with her mother, had problems. The sisters decided to put her next to me for our first night. Suddenly I was woken from a deep sleep by moaning and stifled sobs. My niece had fallen out of bed. I took her into my bed and she fell asleep in my arms.

My sister's health improved. After being treated in Calcutta she decided to rent a house with her husband in Kalimpong. We were therefore able to spend the weekends and holidays together as a family. We frequently went to Sikkim, the only place from where we could establish radio contact with Lhasa. The news from Tibet was very alarming. Chinese troops had invaded part of the country and were occupying Chamdo. Extraordinary rumours were circulating and even a march by the Communist forces on the capital was talked about.

Then came the winter of 1950/51. At a family meal during the holiday period, my sister announced that His Holiness had assumed state responsibility for the Tibetan nation. According to tradition, the Dalai Lamas were not entrusted with leadership of the state until the age of 18. But, because of the national crisis, the Tibetan government, the monastries, the people and the Regent emplored His Holiness to take charge of the leadership of the country. Thus it was that at the age of 16, His Holiness became the spiritual and temporal leader of Tibet.

The government wanted His Holiness to leave Lhasa so as to preserve the country's independence, and also for his own safety, in the event of the Chinese seizing the capital. His Holiness went to Yatung with a heavy escort, taking gold dust and ingots with him. His Holiness would then be able to take refuge in India should it be necessary. This small treasure was hidden in an underground store in Sikkim and used several years later, notably for the first refugees.

In spite of the increasingly worrying news from Kalimpong, I was extraordinarily happy. My sister had told us that we were going to see His Holiness again, with Amala, my brothers Lobsang Samten and Tenzin Choegal, in the valley of Chumbi, near the Sikkim frontier. It must be said that we children (at the time I was only ten) did not really know the exact reasons for His Holiness's presence there, nor did we understand the political problems that now confronted him. Nevertheless, I was aware that serious events were taking place in Tibet. It was at about this time that Lobsang Samten, who was just over 20 years old, became an important official in the Tibetan government.

We would go for long walks along the water's edge, leaving our elders to their meetings which sometimes lasted for the entire day and often continued late into the night. Heinrich Harrer, who had accompanied Lobsang Samten, loved these walks. Several servants would also join us on our escapades. We built dikes with enormous pebbles and caught huge fish. Heinrich would have liked to transform them into delicious delicacies, but we threw them back into the water. It was only a game for us, and there was no question of letting our Austrian friend do what he wanted, especially as we considered his manners to be rather strange. Imagine eating a fresh trout!

One day a servant accidentally killed one of the fish by throwing a pebble into the torrent. I vaguely remember that that evening Heinrich cooked an excellent feast.

One afternoon we learnt that the United Nations, who for the Tibetans represented the last chance to prevent total Chinese invasion, had decided not to raise the Tibetan problem at the General Assembly in New York, and that the British were behind this decision. I saw an expression of deep distress and great sadness on His Holiness's face. With the passage of time, it became easier to understand the reasons behind this terrible abandonment (though as I child, I was of course incapable of analyzing the situation).

The isolation of the Tibetan people in some way explained the inertia of the UN member countries towards us. Was not the Tibetan capital, Lhasa, described as a 'forbidden city'? The country's particular geographical conditions, considered by the Tibetan government to be a protection against conflicts and invasions, were partly responsible for this attitude. The traditional view that Tibet was protected was borne out by the fact that the thirteenth Dalai Lama did not sign any treaties with China, nor did he consider it worthwhile appointing ambassadors to the world's capitals or joining the League of Nations between the two World Wars. He and his countrymen thought there would never be any doubt or quarrel over the country's independence. The thirteenth Dalai Lama had re-established Tibet's independence in 1913 and had carried out a series of very important reforms. He printed stamps and created a postal system that served all the large towns. The telegraph was connected to the Indian system and the central bank issued bank notes. As additional proof of our independence, he had created a Tibetan passport that was internationally recognized.

A delegation of five Tibetan officials had been sent to Beijing at the invitation of the Chinese government to negotiate. On 23 May 1951, a 'Seventeen Point Agreement' had been signed under duress, which Beijing still uses today to convince the international community of China's right to occupy Tibet. Because I was too young, I had to wait several years before I could understand the immense political significance of this act. This 'agreement' had simply delivered Tibet into the hands of China. To obtain it, the Chinese authorities had even forged the Tibetan state seal in Beijing and then, by making threats, had forced the delegation to sign. As I have said, this document has been the basis of Chinese strategy to this day. Later it was the

Chinese Government which violated all the articles of the 'agreement' which they forced on the Tibetan delegation.

While the Tibetan delegation was in Beijing, the holidays came to an end and we had to return to the convent at Kalimpong. His Holiness, who was still living in the monastery near Yatung, met a Chinese emissary there in order to decide whether he should return to Lhasa or take refuge in India. In the end he chose the first alternative. Before returning to Tibet, my mother and my little brother accompanied us to Kalimpong, where we stayed in a house that my sister rented. The Dalai Lama was now the only person who could appeal to the invader and this is probably the reason why he later accepted the Chinese invitation to visit Beijing. The entire population of Lhasa trembled at the thought of this journey for they did not believe that His Holiness would return.

During my mother's stay in Kalimpong, we were surprised to see my brother Gyalo Thondup arrive with his wife and, shortly after, my eldest brother Thubten Jigme Norbu. He had managed to escape from the monastery of Kumbum, which had fallen into the hands of Chinese troops. Before coming to Kalimpong, he had gone to Lhasa, hoping to warn the government and His Holiness of the atrocities committed by the aggressor. My two brothers told us how they had first of all met in Shanghai, before going on to Formosa where they spent several months. Thubten Jigme Norbu then decided to leave for the United States. He was not to see Kumbum again until 1980, 30 years later on.

1951 was a terrible year and my family finally had to split up. My nephew went to North Point St Joseph school and my niece and I were going to board at the convent of Loreto in Darjeeling in the spring of the following year. My mother, my sister and her husband chose to return to Tibet to help His Holiness face his new responsibilities. I was to remain separated from them until 1956. My brother Gyalo Thondup settled in Darjeeling with his young Chinese wife, Chu-tang (who now bore the Tibetan name of Diki Dolkar that His Holiness had given her). During this period China completely occupied Tibet.

At our boarding school, which we very rarely left, we knew very little of events in Tibet. Sometimes we received a letter from Lhasa, but Amala was always extremely careful. She had hidden our photographs in the house in Lhasa and took every precaution when writing to us. Indeed, a large number of young Tibetans studying in India were suddenly required to return to Tibet, apparently at their parents' request, but actually under pressure from the occupying authorities. It is possible that if the Chinese had seen pictures of us, they would have immediately asked where we were and demanded our return. We would then have had to attend the Chinese schools which had been set up in Lhasa for the children of the Tibetan aristocracy.

Naturally the children did not understand the reasons for these sudden departures in the middle of the school year. My niece Khando Tsering, my nephew Tenzin Ngawang and I also asked ourselves why it was no longer possible to go and see our parents during the holidays, while all our non-Tibetan companions left Darjeeling and Kalimpong.

We were lucky that Gyalo Thondup and his wife had remained in Darjeeling. The couple fulfilled the roles of father and mother to us and we spent the holidays with them. As time went by, however, we asked ourselves many questions about Tibet. When we talked to my brother he described a situation that was becoming more and more critical.

I made many friends at the Loreto convent, most of them foreigners like myself. I was in this way sometimes able to talk about the events overwhelming my country, especially when in the company of two Nepalese princesses, Shanti and Sharada Shah. I can also remember Tin Tin Oo from Burma, whom we all called Tiny; Duengkeo Kosin from Thailand; Puchin, a Chinese girl whose parents lived in Calcutta; Nima and Pem Pem Norgay, the daughters of Tenzin Norgay, the first man to have climbed Everest; Legjin Tsering; Grace Hughes, an American; and Heidrun Bartch, a German whose parents lived in Jamshedpur (her father worked for Mercedes).

Shanti, elder sister to the present King of Nepal, was my best friend at school. Even today, I visit her when I am in her country and we correspond regularly.

The nuns who ran the Catholic schools at Kalimpong and Darjeeling were very strict. Every day we went to mass and in the evening we said our prayers. As Buddhists, we were let off the catechism, although we studied both the Old and New Testaments of the Bible, subjects which figured in the school curriculum.

I began to think about the content of this teaching and all that it implied. Some of the nuns showed a highly developed sense of missionary zeal and some of the things they said bothered and irritated us; for example, that only Catholics would go to heaven, with everyone else being burnt in hell. If we had still been too young to react in Kalimpong, this was no longer so in Darjeeling. Besides, 80 per cent of the pupils were Buddhists or Hindus.

One evening, fed up with the attitude of the nuns, we organized a revolt and decided to go on strike. Most of us were then nearly 14. When everyone was gathered in the church for evening prayers, we threw our books onto the floor and began to kick up a terrible racket. The nuns were horrified. The mother superior summoned us and listened attentively to our remarks and demands. From that day onwards, things changed. But I have to say that only some of the nuns were guilty of this abusive behaviour. For a Buddhist, all faiths share the same essential belief: you must be good, and not lie, steal or kill. I was very interested to read the stories in the Bible about Moses, Isaac, Mary and, of course, Jesus. But our religious education remained very rigid. We learnt to recite prayers such as 'Our Father' and 'Hail Mary', as well as psalms and songs.

While the nuns explained the catechism to the Catholic girls, the others had a class known as 'moral sciences'. I must say that the work we did in these classes had an enormous influence on all of us. The teacher always told us an anecdote to illustrate her remarks. Her lessons were marvellously prepared and I think that she was responsible for giving us a good grounding in our education. We also learnt to read and write in English, besides having singing and piano lessons, and lessons in history, geography and mathematics. The Catholic nuns developed our ability to analyze and we no longer just had to learn our lessons by heart.

Except for a very few rare exceptions, the nuns were women of great devotion. Most of them had left their family and friends in Ireland to work with a mission in India. They understood that their efforts should be concentrated entirely on education and they did not use the school as an opportunity to preach. They respected our cultural and religious differences because, as we grew up, those of us who were Buddhists could not accept the Catholic dogma without raising essential questions. The values of our religion had been instilled in us through strong family influences and no one could ever take them away.

Tenzin Ngawang, Khando Tsering and I spent all our holidays with my brother Gyalo Thondup and his wife Diki Dolkar. They devoted an enormous amount of energy to the Tibetan cause, maintaining permanent contact with the Indian government and the Americans. At night they often printed pamphlets in Tibetan and we helped to roll them up. Encouraged by my sense of curiosity, I sometimes dared to ask an indiscreet question: 'What are these sheets going to be used for?' The reply seemed like a joke: 'Oh, we are going to throw them over Tibet!'

We had to wait a few more months before we understood that these pamphlets left Darjeeling early in the morning for an American air base. An aircraft then dropped them over Lhasa and the region of Kham, whose inhabitants still opposed the Chinese troops. The texts encouraged the population to resist. However, we did not really understand the role that my brother played in all this.

5

The Train of Hope

The education I received in India prepared me to take up the challenge of my future responsibilities and to carry these out more effectively, and I considered that the knowledge provided by the nuns was adequate for this purpose. I never felt the slightest inward conflict between my Catholic education and my Buddhist convictions. I knew where I came from and who I was.

A spirit of tremendous tolerance prevailed among the girls at the school. As we were aware of our different origins, on the whole our life together worked out very well. In any case, the nuns believed in the same teaching for everyone, and they were probably right. However, when an official or some important person came to the school, the two princesses, Shanti and Sharada, in their position as the daughters of the King of Nepal, my niece, and myself as the Dalai Lama's sister, were always presented to the visitor. This was not really preferential treatment, but it enabled us to become aware of the role that awaited us in society.

Under these conditions, it was impossible not to feel a little different. The nuns gradually gave us special responsibilities. When they were busy, they often asked Shanti or me to watch over the class. Later, the mother superior asked us to distribute the other pupils' pocket money. Shanti and I rapidly made friends among the older pupils of the school, and the youngest often came to ask our advice on some difficult problems. The girls gave each of us a nickname. I became 'Grandmother 1' and Shanti 'Grandmother 2'. But our advice cannot have been too bad, because the nuns approved of our behaviour.

One day in 1954, I learnt of His Holiness's departure for Beijing at the invitation of the Chinese. I heard that the entire population of Lhasa was opposed to it, but His Holiness was determined to negotiate with the Chinese authorities in the hope of reaching a non-violent solution. 'Tibet's autonomous position', as set out in the 'Seventeen Point Agreement', was formally adopted by the Chinese People's Congress. I believe a 'resolution for the establishment of the Preparatory Committee for the Autonomous Region of Tibet' (PCART) was passed by the Congress. This was aimed at the absorption of the Tibetan government by the People's Republic of China. This Committee was to function in place of the legitimate Tibetan government. The Dalai Lama had been designated as the Chairman of the Committee but in actual fact he did not hold any real authority over it. It was simply a facade, the actual policy decision being in fact made by the Chinese Communist Party.

A strange atmosphere reigned in Darjeeling. We were very worried about His Holiness; he was to be accompanied by Amala, Achala, my brother-in-law, my younger brother Tenzin Choegal and a large group of Tibetan government officials, and we feared that the Chinese would prevent them from returning to Lhasa. They were in China for just over a year. In spite of the dearth of news, there was a man who seemed to know everything that was going on in Tibet. This was my brother Gyalo Thondup who regularly explained the political situation of our country to us and gave us news of all the family.

When His Holiness returned to Lhasa, Gyalo Thondup took my niece and nephew and me to Sikkim where we were able to exchange a few words by radio with Amala and Tsering Dolma, my sister. We remained very careful, however, because the Chinese authorities were increasing their pressure on the three of us to return to Lhasa to take up studies in Tibet. Amala and my sister visited us and spent a few days in Kalimpong. When they left, Gyalo Thondup went with them. The Chinese had insisted that he return to Lhasa. Indeed, as my brother spoke Chinese fluently, he could serve as an interpreter for His

Holiness. Gyalo Thondup quickly understood how rapidly the situation was deteriorating and that Tibet could no longer expect to gain anything from China. He asked to be allowed to go to our property near the Indian frontier. The Chinese gave him authorization to do so after he had promised to follow the Communist party line. Gyalo Thondup had already told Amala and Tsering Dolma of his intention to return to Darjeeling. His Holiness was not informed of his intention of going back to India. Gyalo Thondup's wife, Diki Dolkar, who was in Darjeeling was unable to hide her anxiety. She was pregnant at the time and already had two children: Yangzom Dolma, born in 1950, and Tenzin Khedrup, born in 1952.

One morning at dawn, Gyalo Thondup gave us a terrible fright by arriving at the house in an awful state. He had caught malaria and lost a lot of weight and had to be supported by two servants. I was 14 at the time and so did not really appreciate that the couple had financial difficulties. All the same, they left for Calcutta for medical treatment for Gyalo Thondup and for Diki Dolkar to give birth to her baby, Ngawang Tempa.

My niece, my nephew and I remained in Darjeeling. During the winter holidays, Lhamo Tsering, Gyalo Thondup's secretary, took care that we were not cut off from our roots. He taught us Tibetan as well as our country's history. Now, I suspect that he knew much more than he appeared to about Gyalo Thondup's activities. Lhamo Tsering became a minister of the Tibetan government in exile (1994–6), elected by the National Assembly of Tibetan People.

My brother recruited young Tibetans who were sent to Arizona to be trained by the CIA. They then returned and were parachuted in small groups over certain regions of Tibet. Very few people knew about this at the time, and no one talked about it. Some of the people were captured and tortured, others had a cyanide pill to prevent them from falling alive into the hands of the Chinese.

I was still too young to understand everything that was going on at home. Sometimes the telephone would ring during dinner and Gyalo Thondup would disappear in the car towards an unknown destination.

It was now 1956. The Chinese had begun democratic reforms in Kham and Amdo, destined for the whole country, and this provoked acts of increasing violence. The monasteries and their monks were attacked. The Seventeen Point Agreement had said that no reform should be imposed without the consent of the Tibetans, but the Chinese authorities took no notice of this. Armed conflicts broke out and repression became more and more brutal in these two regions. The troubles then spread to other areas of Tibet and the summer of 1956 saw the emergence of all-out guerrilla warfare. A large number of refugees from the north-eastern part of the country made their way towards Lhasa. Within a year the resistance had spread to central Tibet.

Gyalo Thondup contacted the Mahabodhi Society of India, an old institution whose aim was to spread the teachings of the Buddha. An invitation was sent to His Holiness asking him to take part in the Buddha Jayanti, the 2,500th anniversary of the birth of the Buddha. In Lhasa the negotiations got under way and, in Darjeeling, we asked ourselves whether the Chinese would allow him to leave.

The event was an important one. Besides the spiritual dimension, there were obvious political considerations. Since 1950, His Holiness had tried to negotiate with the Chinese authorities; according to what was said in Darjeeling at the house of Gyalo Thondup, the discussions were interminable, discouraging and pointless. The Chinese communists had set themselves the objective of both controlling the country and destroying our culture.

Tibet's isolation should again be emphasized. Gyalo Thondup wanted the Dalai Lama to use the Buddha Jayanti to make contact with the leaders of the neighbouring democratic countries, particularly Prime Minister Nehru. But since Buddhist wisdom was far removed from international politics, the designs of Communist China unfortunately benefited from our inexperience. His Holiness hoped that Mahatma Gandhi's disciples would come to his aid.

The Buddha Jayanti is above all a religious celebration. When the announcement of the arrival of the Tibetan delegation, consisting of over 200 officials, reached Gangtok, we were overwhelmed with joy and set off to meet them in Delhi. His Holiness took the route through the valley of Chumbi, which Tibetan merchants had used before the Chinese invasion, and from Bagdora he took the flight to Delhi.

My niece and nephew and I met up with Amala, my younger

brother Tendin Choegal, Lobsang Samten, my sister and my brother-in-law. Thubten Jigme Norbu had returned from the United States to meet His Holiness, but he did not take part in the journey across India.

The delegations of the Dalai Lama and the Panchen Lama were composed of Tibetan dignitaries, lamas and Chinese officials. I noticed that His Holiness and the Panchen Lama were always accompanied by one of these Chinese officials, and most of the time it was difficult to speak freely. The Indian welcome was magnificent, however. The Indian President, Dr Rajendra Prasad, received His Holiness at an official state luncheon given in his residence, the Rashtrapati Bhavan. All the Tibetan guests, the Vice-President Dr Rada Krishna and Prime Minister Pandit Nehru, as well as the important government officials were also invited. His Holiness was received as an important head of state. We then went to Rajghat, where Mahatma Gandhi had been cremated, and His Holiness prayed there for a long while.

For the first time I heard His Holiness the fourteenth Dalai Lama give a speech. A thrill went through my body when I heard him speak about mankind's salvation through the faith present in every single being, and when he developed his thoughts on the pacifist nature of Buddhism.

After the festivities, His Holiness had a meeting with Chou En Lai, the Chinese Prime Minister. They talked together about the situation in Tibet, which deteriorated daily. His Holiness expressed his anxiety. A few days later Chou En Lai gave a dinner at the Chinese embassy, to which Thubten Jigme Norbu and Gyalo Thondup were invited. However, no positive result came from this meeting.

The Indian government had arranged a special train for the Tibetan delegation that was to travel all over India. In this way we visited the principal religious sites: Sanchi, Ajanta, Benares, Bodh Gaya. These places shone with a rare beauty. Everywhere, the Dalai Lama and the Panchen Lama were welcomed as official guests. Unfortunately the continual surveillance by the Chinese authorities spoilt these moments of intense joy.

My niece and nephew and I had requested permission to accompany our family during this three-month journey. In the train, Indian cooks prepared meals for us and, as Amala immediately made friends with them, she was also able to prepare a few Tibetan dishes that were very much appreciated by His Holiness and the rest of the family.

The Chinese officials who accompanied us on the journey had mostly held positions in Lhasa and understood Tibetan perfectly. I was not very happy with their constant presence and I made this obvious. One day they said to Amala: 'We can see that your daughter doesn't like us!' The resentment that I felt towards them went back a long way. When I was younger, I had not been able to understand clearly what was happening in Tibet, but I had instinctively rejected the Chinese because they prevented my niece and nephew and me from going to Lhasa during the school holidays. We knew that they were to blame and we did not forgive them the long months spent without seeing our parents. We also knew that if we were to return to Tibet, they would not hesitate to send us to China to undergo Communist education and indoctrination there. Moreover, I had learnt that many of my friends had been sent in this way to Beijing.

It was during this journey across India that I really got to know His Holiness. I was then 16 and he was 21. We visited the aircraft factory in Bangalore and the site of the hydroelectric plant in Nangal. He was fascinated and did not miss any opportunity to compare his journey to China in 1954 with his impressions of India. He talked a lot about the differences between Communism and a young democracy in which liberty soared.

His Holiness often sat down next to Amala, Lobsang Samten and Tsering Dolma and they would speak in low voices. At about this time the problem arose of whether His Holiness should seek refuge in exile. At the close of a meeting with Chou En Lai, Nehru had insisted that His Holiness return to Lhasa. Chou En Lai had reassured the Indian Prime Minister, promising him that he would not undertake any more reforms in Tibet and to give the Tibetan people real autonomy. Unfortunately, this was not to be the case.

I went from compartment to compartment with the other children, but sometimes I also had long talks with His Holiness. He urged me to continue my studies, and took an interest in my experiences in India with the nuns. He approved of the teaching that I had received. Nevertheless, I asked Amala if I could return to Tibet. She explained that it was preferable to remain in Darjeeling for security reasons. We always had to be careful what we talked about, because an official would often stroll through our carriage. The Chinese always pretended to be very kind to the children and tried to get them to talk by offering them sweets or playing with them. Amala and my sister told me that they were used to being very cautious because this was how they now had to live in Tibet. You had to be careful of everyone, because there were some Tibetan informers. Much later, returning to my country for the first time in 1980, I was able to observe my countrymen's strange behaviour. You could see the fear in their eyes and, when I spoke, they did not dare to express themselves openly and cast anxious looks about them.

When we stopped for several days in the same town, guest houses was placed at our disposal by the Indian government. We took our meals all together. For the first time, I saw His Holiness as an ordinary human being. Even if I retained an enormous amount of respect for the Dalai Lama, I realized at this point in my life that he was also a marvellous man. There no longer existed between us the distance that there was when I used to have to climb the steps to the Potala.

His Holiness proved to possess an astonishingly eclectic mind. Admiring the landscape, he made comparisons with Tibet. He was very interested in technical matters and asked all sorts of questions. I spent a great deal of time observing him. In the cockpit of an aircraft, he would question the pilot in detail and the latter would be fascinated by the interest that the Dalai Lama showed in the plane's complex workings. I discovered a young man of 21 who was continually alert, and I understood the importance of Buddhist teaching, which is not a fixed doctrine, because nothing is ever acquired. I also understood why I was always advised to ask questions and to try and reach a conclusion, with all doubts dispelled. His Holiness had followed these principles from a very early age and for him our journey in India was a stimulating application of these ideas.

Everywhere, the Dalai Lama roused the passion of the crowds. His speeches were listened to in deep silence, followed by an explosion of joy. He excited the curiosity of the Indians who, of course, knew of the existence of the Dalai Lama and the Panchen Lama, but had never had the opportunity to approach them. Their enthusiasm knew no bounds, especially when they saw about 200 Tibetans in brocade costumes, getting off the train to escort their spiritual and temporal leader, who was dressed in a simple monk's tunic, smiling at the crowds and always in total harmony with them. At these very special moments, I experienced two sensations: I acknowledged His Holiness as the reincarnation of the Dalai Lama, and at the same time I felt very proud of this elder brother who remained so humble in front of the crowds who admired and acclaimed him.

I can assure you that my thoughts did not dwell on the past; this trait is another part of the Tibetan character. However, my childhood years in Lhasa always remained engraved on my heart. But one thing was certain: this journey had brought me much closer to his Holiness and strengthened my decision to serve both him and the Tibetan cause as soon as my studies were over.

During the journey, I met the Panchen Lama for the first time. Although the Dalai Lama expressed his thoughts easily, the Panchen Lama seemed rather an introvert. He did not often smile and I found him very intimidating.

The Panchen Lama's mother was also of peasant origin. She came to our compartment whenever she could and spoke at length with Amala and Tsering Dolma, touching on everyday subjects such as embroidery, knitting or cooking. They were relatively unaffected by this strange atmosphere of mistrust, with its absence of free expression.

Amala was always calm and managed these complex situations with an enormous amount of good sense. At this time, her main worry was my education and, to an even greater extent, that of Tenzin Choegal; in 1956, my younger brother was ten and a bundle of energy. He ran up and down the corridors of the train and amused himself enormously with the Indian servants. Amala treated him with more affection than ever before, now that the rest of the family was dispersed. I believe that it upset her to have one son, Thubten Jigme Norbu, in the United States; another, Gyalo Thondup, in India; and two sons, the Dalai Lama and Tenzin Choegal, in Tibet. Lobsang Samten had also left to go and live in India but had been taken seriously ill and had had to undergo surgery mid-way through the journey. In these circumstances, was it wise for the young Tenzin Choegal to continue his studies in this foreign land? She eventually asked my elder brothers for their advice: they replied that a reincarnated lama's place was in Tibet, for as long as this was possible.

I also spent a lot of time with Amala. We talked about school as well as our country. She taught me to embroider and to knit. My mother loved the circus and the cinema, so whenever we stayed several days in a large Indian town, we spent the evening at a circus or visited a zoo, such as those in Madras or Calcutta. In the evenings we went to performances of traditional dancing or concerts of Indian music given in honour of His Holiness the Dalai Lama and the other guests of the Indian government. During the day, we visited temples. In New Delhi we were able to go to performances of the great Moscow Circus and watch a show on ice.

This journey through India with the family was a marvellous experience and separating at the end of it was therefore very difficult. I saw His Holiness wearing an expression of great weariness, and I also heard him confiding in my mother and sister how disturbed he was by all the negotiations that had resulted in nothing useful for our country. If the survival of the Tibetan people had not been involved, he would have willingly retired from politics to devote himself to meditation and the study of sacred teachings.

6

The Road to Exile

At the end of our train journey, the Dalai Lama returned to Lhasa. As the situation in Tibet was worsening, Gyalo Thondup strongly advised Amala to spend a further month in Calcutta with my sister Tsering Dolma, my niece Khando Tsering, my nephew Tenzin Ngawang, and myself.

We devoted the month in Calcutta to rest and relaxation. In fact it was a real holiday. Amala was able to indulge her passion for the cinema, taking a member of the family with her to translate the dialogue into Tibetan. We also went to the zoo and the botanical gardens, as my mother loved animals and flowers.

We stayed in a small hotel that Gyalo Thondup knew well in the centre of the town. Every time that he and his wife visited the city, they would stay at this hotel which was run by a charming Armenian couple, the Martins. It was not a large tourist establishment, but a kind of small family boarding house. I loved the garden which surrounded it and I often used to linger there at nightfall.

Mrs Martin took great care of us. She always asked Amala if there was anything in particular that she wanted to eat for dinner and she would take a great deal of trouble in preparing it for us. She considered Amala to be a very fine cook, and I would not be surprised if they exchanged a few recipes during their long conversations. In fact it is often said that the Tibetans took the roots of their religion from India, their culinary knowledge from China, and their costume from Mongolia. It seems to me that we knew how to choose the best from our neighbours' traditions.

I used to go out a lot with my friends. When I got back, my mother and sister would ask me to tell them about my escapades. We enjoyed ourselves very much, all the time knowing that this situation would not last for ever as Amala would soon have to return to Lhasa. One day, two friends, with whom I had been at the convent in Darjeeling, dragged me into a hairdresser run by a Chinese woman, and they persuaded me to have a permanent wave. Tibetans, of course, usually have straight thick hair, as I have, and the permanent wave quickly became the prologue to an amusing catastrophe. Above all, I remember the smell of the liquid with which the hairdresser liberally covered my head, then the placing of the curlers which pulled my hair horribly. My friends made fun of my misfortune. The more time went on, the worse I felt, and I ended up regretting that I had let myself be led into this. When I returned to the hotel, my sister and mother uttered cries of horror: 'What have you done to your hair?' I rushed to the bathroom and put my head under water for a long time, hoping to make the curls disappear. I washed my hair again and again, but the permanent wave remained and I had to put up with my strange appearance for several days. In fact, my hair took a long time to regain its original straightness. I realized that one should not always listen to friends.

Amala and my sister returned to Lhasa, and our parting was very sad. As for me, I had to finish my studies. After his stay in hospital, Lobsang Samten was to remain in India to convalesce and then go back to the United States, where my elder brother Thubten Jigme Norbu who was a research worker at the Natural History Museum in New York had begun writing *Tibet is My Country*. We wrote to one another frequently. Chola did not yet know much English and, as for myself, I had forgotten the Tibetan alphabet. He therefore wrote to me in Tibetan, using the letters of the Roman alphabet. It was an unusual but effective way of writing. Wherever he went, he never forgot to send me a postcard or a few scribbled words. We got on very well and I enjoyed reading about life in America.

I returned to boarding school routine with some difficulty. Up at six, wash, prayers, breakfast. Then back up to the dormitory to make our beds, about which the nuns were very strict, insisting that we turn the mattresses every morning. Then we had half-an-hour's recreation, most often spent talking in small groups, following morning classes.

We had lunch in a large hall at tables of six. I always sat next to my niece and Princess Shanti. Before beginning the meal, we had to say grace. The nuns watched our behaviour: we had to sit up straight, eat correctly and hold our cutlery properly. After a short silence, we impatiently awaited the tinkling of the bell indicating that we could talk. A further tinkling signalled that we had to finish our meal in silence and a final tinkling announced that the meal was at an end. There was then half-an-hour's recreation, followed by afternoon classes.

The nuns were particularly keen that we should play various sports: hockey, badminton, table tennis or roller-skating. It was very important for the pupils of the higher classes to be selected for basketball or hockey teams. The different missionary schools organized contests around Darjeeling and, since the founding of the convent in 1860, the sisters of Loreto prided themselves on several resounding victories.

These contests generally took place at the boys' school, where my nephew was. The school of North Point St Joseph was run by Jesuits and was twinned with Loreto. The competition was not only sporting as we also played against the teams of the Protestant schools and, in this case, victory became very important to us. The nuns took training extremely seriously and did not hesitate to give privileges to those preparing for the matches: richer food, larger helpings and other signs of extra consideration.

Before an important competition we would get up very early to catch the bus to the boys' school to practise on the hockey or basketball pitches. Being a little older than the others, I was part of both the basketball and hockey teams for the seventh year onwards. I think I often preferred sport to lessons. However, the nuns tested us on our knowledge very rigorously.

A first exam was held during the school year and a second one took place at the end of the year. We were not all always very proud of our marks, especially as, for the last 20 years, the nuns had recorded the results of all the boarders, with comments, in a big book. If we were not among the top of the class, this could make our situation even more difficult.

I always found myself in the bottom half of the class. I made excuses for myself, such as my having begun my schooling in India very late. However, when the nuns awarded prizes to the best pupils at the end of the year, they always gave me one for trying hard and good behaviour. In this way I received a recompense, even though some considered it a consolation prize.

When it was fine, the nuns organized picnics in the botanical gardens. After lunch, they left us free to amuse ourselves on the grass for the rest of the day. We looked at the trees and flowers and played hide-and-seek. In this way, the nuns tried to break the routine and monotony of boarding school life with weekly distractions.

Another point in the school year also proved to be of great importance. From the seventh form onwards we went on a three-day retreat. The nuns did not take any part in these retreats, which were with Jesuit priests. There were no lessons, but every morning and evening we took part in sessions in which we examined our thoughts and feelings. We analyzed the past and discussed life's meaning. We asked ourselves what our aspirations were and how we could be of use to others.

In addition to this work on ourselves, we read in groups. The choice of texts was very important. Novels were out of the question, and the works had to be written by authors who had done good for others. I must admit that these texts made a great impression on me. I particularly remember the story of Father Damien, whose life as a priest was completely devoted to the lepers of Africa. I was, of course, very struck by the life of Albert Schweitzer, and I can also remember an American doctor who looked after Vietnamese refugees from Communism. This story made me think of Tibet and the situation which existed there after the invasion of the Chinese Communists.

Between the ages of 15 and 19, I particularly appreciated these periods of contemplation. The Jesuits replied to our numerous questions, and sometimes a priest talked to me about the situation in Tibet. He asked me how, as the Dalai Lama's sister and being educated in a Catholic school, I regarded the events in my country. Today, I am convinced that these retreats and long conversations made me and my niece more mature and aware of our origins. We did not have to be embarrassed by our Buddhist culture and way of thought.

My last year of school at Loreto was in 1960. These months were particularly difficult to live through as I received very bad news from Tibet. Without the support of the nuns and my friends, my courage would probably have failed. My brother Gyalo Thondup and his wife Diki Dolkar encouraged me to continue my studies and prepare for my exams, believing that later I would be able to help the Tibetan cause. To this tragic situation was added the feeling that I had reached a turning point in my life. I was soon going to be 20 and I had just spent half of my existence with a group of girls whom I must now leave. We all felt very sad at the prospect of this inevitable separation; we promised to write often to each other and never to break our ties of friendship, whatever might happen to us.

We were in the ninth form and the subjects for the final exam arrived from Britain. In the seventh year, I had done well in the intermediate exam, the Cambridge Junior. Gyalo Thondup then asked that we be taught Tibetan. And so, for our last two years, a teacher taught us our history and culture in our own language. For the Cambridge Senior, London even agreed to include Tibetan as a second language. The subjects seemed easy to me. There were translations from and into Tibetan and some grammar and spelling questions.

17 March was particularly important at Loreto. The nuns were mostly from Ireland, and so each year they celebrated St Patrick's Day. The occasion was marked by a basketball match. However, that year I did not feel much enthusiasm for practising for my final competition: Gyalo Thondup and Lobsang Samten had joined us in Darjeeling, bringing very alarming news with them.

The Indian and British newspapers led with the events in Tibet on their front pages. We learnt that there had been an uprising on 10 March 1959 in Lhasa. The most worrying rumours were circulating. Some said that the Dalai Lama was a prisoner of the Chinese, others that there was no news of His Holiness and his family. The BBC also reported on the subject. When I went to see my brother Gyalo Thondup at the weekend, there was a tremendous coming and going at the house. Faces were marked by anxiety. In spite of the attempts to reassure us, my niece and I knew that something very serious was happening. I was frightened for Amala, my sister and her husband, and for Tendzin Choegyal and, of course, His

Holiness. I trembled at the idea that their lives might be in danger. I was also worried for the Tibetans that I knew personally, and for our people who were going through the most terrible times. However, anything I was imagining was a far cry from the reality of the tragedy being played out beyond the Himalayas.

In Loreto, the nuns collected the newspapers for us. Morning and evening, they asked everyone to pray for 'Pema's family'. Everyone at the school therefore knew about our tragedy. In spite of everything, I could not hold back my tears when I heard the announcement of the firing of guns and cannons by Communist troops – tears of revolt and despair.

Three long weeks went by. Suddenly the news spread like wildfire. The Dalai Lama and his entourage had succeeded in crossing the Indian frontier and had reached Tezpur. Gyalo Thondup had left a few days earlier to meet his brother. In Tezpur hundreds of journalists and photographers welcomed the spiritual and temporal leader of the Tibetans.

My sister-in-law, who had remained in Darjeeling, came to Loreto to tell us the happy news. My niece, nephew and I were allowed to listen to the BBC, which had interrupted its programmes to broadcast newsflashes from Tezpur. My relief was complete when at last I heard the journalist announce that the Dalai Lama and all his family were out of danger. They were going to Mussoorie, Northern India, a resort in the Himalayan foothills, by special train. The radio then announced a message from the Indian prime minister to His Holiness the Dalai Lama: 'Upon your safe and sound arrival on Indian territory, my colleagues and I welcome you. We are happy to offer you, your family and your entourage, the facilities necessary to reside in India. Our people, who hold you in profound veneration, will without doubt show the traditional respect due to your person.'

The mother superior of Loreto gave us a day off. My niece, nephew and I were able to accompany Diki Dolkar to Siliguri where the train carrying His Holiness was due to arrive. On the way we passed the Tibetans living in the region of Darjeeling and Kalimpong, eager to welcome the Dalai Lama.

When the coach entered the station an enormous crowd surged on to the platform. Everyone showed deep veneration on this exceptional day. The Indian people also expressed their rejection of the expansionist politics the Chinese Communists had been practising for the last ten years.

We had great difficulty in making our way to the platform. Suddenly a shout of joy went up. The door of the carriage opened, revealing bodyguards and then, finally, His Holiness, who seemed to have been terribly affected by events and had lost a lot of weight. His Holiness seemed exhausted and anxious. The few paces that separated us seemed to take an eternity to cover. I offered him a khata, received his blessing and was then literally thrown into the train by the bodyguards. At last I was able to embrace Amala whom I had missed so much during these difficult times, and then my sister and brothers. We were all together again at last, for the first time since 1956, three years earlier.

Of course, my niece, nephew and I did not want to go back to Loreto, and it took some strong persuasion on Amala's part to make us accept that we must return to boarding school. We therefore left for Darjeeling two hours later, with the assurance that we would see all the family during the holidays. Two hours … two hours of intense emotion, of tears and questionings. What fate awaited our families? What was going to happen to His Holiness, and to the Tibetans who had remained behind in our country? The questions came from all sides, but no one had the time to give us replies, still less to explain the situation to us. In fact, we were simply living the happy conclusion to a long month of fears and anxieties.

I was, however, able to imagine how terrible it must have been to leave Lhasa. My family was exhausted and completely dejected. They had fled without luggage and had worn the same clothes for several weeks. Diki Dolkar had brought a few clothes and a little food. Indeed, we no longer owned anything, but I was so pleased to find them alive that nothing else seemed very important. Nevertheless, at that precise moment, I realized that we were starting a new life: a life of exile as political refugees.

That evening and all the following ones, I had great difficulty in getting to sleep. Images continuously rose up into my mind: the house in Lhasa, our games in the gardens with the servants and their children, school, the kites. I was very worried about His Holiness and my mother. However, Amala remained confident in the future and an imminent return to Tibet. As for His Holiness, he also showed enormous courage. He believed, and still does, that a solution exists for all difficulties. He also, with his strong belief in justice and faith, placed his hope in the support of the Indian government and other nations.

A little later we had four days holiday and my brother Gyalo Thondup came to collect my niece, nephew and myself. Darjeeling–New Delhi was to be our first journey in an airplane, a flight during which we experienced wonderful sensations. However, when we arrived in the capital, it was so hot that we had only one thing in mind: to leave that furnace as fast as possible. The journey to Mussoorie was made by car.

My family had fairly good lodgings. His Holiness occupied two rooms in a fine house that belonged to Birla, a rich Indian industrialist. Amala and my youngest brother shared a bedroom, and so did my sister and her husband. His Holiness's secretaries and advisers lived in two further rooms. Amala and my sister looked after the cooking, helped by one of our servants who, in spite of her great age, had managed to follow my family into exile. The Indian government had also placed several servants at our disposal, and they were responsible for the smooth running of the house.

Gyalo Thondup rushed around the house. Concerned for His Holiness's comfort as well as for that of the rest of the family, he continually asked them if they needed anything. In fact, they needed everything. At meal times, Amala complained that she did not have enough cups or saucers and that she needed spoons. My brother would go out for several hours and return laden like a mule. If my sister said that she no longer had a dress or shirt, Gyalo Thondup would go out once again. I could imagine Tsering Dolma's unhappiness as she was very attached to her clothes and now had nothing. Sometimes she discreetly wiped away a tear.

Mussoorie was at this time a holiday resort for Indians fleeing the suffocating heat of the capital. When my brother was unable to find everything he needed in the town, he prepared a long list and went to New Delhi for his purchases.

I spent only four days with my family. Even though sadness was visible on their faces, they all reacted in a positive manner. They refused to become demoralized by the situation but, on the contrary, gave much thought to the future of the Tibetan people, such as whether the United Nations should be contacted, or whether help should be solicited from elsewhere in the world.

As soon as he arrived in Mussoorie, His Holiness decided to open a school to teach English to 50 young Tibetans. Mr and Mrs Taring gave the lessons. This was the beginning of the first Tibetan school in exile. This wonderful couple continued working for the Tibetan children for almost three decades, and came to be considered as Pala and Amala to hundreds of students who passed through this school. Many of their students later held important positions in the Tibetan government and in the Tibetan settlements scattered around India.

One evening my mother and sister asked my niece and nephew and me to join them in the drawing room. I learnt that my long-time companions were to continue their studies in Mussoorie and that I was to return alone to Loreto. They insisted on the usefulness of this training. The Dalai Lama was also convinced that a modern education could help serve the Tibetan cause. Confronted with the sight of my family so penniless, I regretted that I was still only a simple schoolgirl. I felt that I was both powerless and at the sme time invested with an important mission: to finish my studies as fast and as well as I could.

That evening, listening to Amala and my sister, I felt how much I had grown up. They talked slowly, without omitting the slightest detail, though sometimes needing to restrain a sob. I listened attentively to the story of their escape from Lhasa on 17 March 1959, and their account of the following awful days.

Several days before this fateful date, the Chinese invited His Holiness the Dalai Lama to go without escort to attend a performance of a play at an army encampment about two miles from Norbulingka. The invitation seemed suspicious to say the least, for His Holiness's personal guard and advisers had been 'forgotten'. In addition, the Chinese wanted this visit to be kept secret, whereas usually when His Holiness went out he was accompanied by a sizeable number of Tibetan officials and bodyguards who took up their position along the processional path.

On 9 March, wild rumours circulated in the capital: the Communists wanted to kidnap the Dalai Lama; the army intended to capture him and take him by force to Beijing. Tension rose dangerously amongst the population. For their safety, Amala and my sister were taken to Norbulingka.

On 10 March, the Dalai Lama rose at dawn, as he did every day. After prayers, he liked to walk in the gardens. It was from here that he heard the first rumblings of the uprising. The people were marching towards Norbulingka to protect my brother. The tumult grew throughout the morning as the Tibetans let their hatred of the invader explode. They were no longer prepared to accept this foreign occupation and appeared ready to resort to force.

The tension mounted over the following days. The Khampas armed themselves with old rifles and were joined by the soldiers. Monks, men with daggers and shouting women massed around Norbulingka.

On 16 March terrible news reached the palace: Chinese troops were preparing to bombard the Dalai Lama's residence and, indeed, at about four in the afternoon, two shells devastated the garden. The crowd was agitated. There were meetings in the palace and the decision was eventually taken that His Holiness the Dalai Lama must flee to protect his life and that of his followers – and to preserve the existence of the country and the future of its people. I believe today that if His Holiness had been captured Tibet would probably have been wiped from the map of Asia and the Chinese would have been able to complete their genocide without the knowledge of the international community.

Three groups were formed just before sunset. The first included Amala with my youngest brother and my sister, dressed in Khampa clothing. The second included the chamberlain, my brother-in-law, the commander of the guard, and His Holiness (who had put on a soldier's uniform and cap). The third group comprised the ministers of the Kashag, the tutors, and various other individuals who served the Dalai Lama.

Keeping the departure secret was no easy matter. At nightfall on 17 March, the three groups left one after another by the south door in the wall of Norbulingka. As the guards had been dispersed, everyone managed to leave the palace without difficulty. Norbulingka is on the northern bank of the Kyi Chu river. The Chinese encampment was on the same side of the river and there was a danger that the groups might meet an unexpected patrol, or that an army truck would catch one of them in the beam of its headlights.

They advanced slowly up river for several miles to a place where small boats made from yak skins awaited them. The three groups managed to cross without difficulty and meet up with Tibetan soldiers and national voluntary security forces on the other side. It was not possible to take the usual roads to India as the Chinese army had set up control posts everywhere. It was therefore necessary to reach the mountain range to the south of Lhasa as rapidly as possible. The crossing of the Che-la pass on the way was extremely difficult. Stony tracks, the increasingly thin air, and fear, all combined to increase the apprehension of the groups and to slow their progress. Amala told me that an old Tibetan suddenly appeared and offered His Holiness a magnificent white horse, then followed them for a while. In the circumstances, the present was considered a good omen.

The other side of the pass was less steep. Sandy paths allowed faster progress, and at last the Tsangpo river was reached and they followed it eastwards until they came to a ferry. On the opposite side of the river they stopped at the village of Kyeshong, and His Holiness and Amala were able to rest for a few moments. The soldiers and army volunteers who had joined them mounted guard.

The group now consisted of 100 or so people, protected by 400 soldiers and volunteers, but at this point it split up. A group of men and women stayed behind the Dalai Lama, determined to protect his flight even if it was to cost them their lives. The different groups found marching difficult in the moutain terrain.

After a night at the monastery of Ra-me, 100 men turned back to block the road in case Chinese troops came in pursuit. Rest was taken in monastries and houses placed at their disposal by the inhabitants. Rest was taken in monasteries and houses placed at their disposal by the inhabitants. Some of these people knew that the Dalai Lama was staying in their humble home, others will probably never know. During these halts, the groups were joined by the voluntary guerrilla leaders and His Holiness had what seemed interminable discussions with them about the future of Tibet.

The first objective was to rapidly reach Lhuntse Dzong, a fortress in the mountains that was virtually impregnable in case of attack. Two days earlier, His Holiness had learnt from messengers of the shelling of Lhasa on 20 March, as well as of the destruction of Norbulingka and a part of the Potala. The medical Institute of Chokpori and the monastery at Sera also suffered great damage. Thousands of Tibetans, men, women and children, had been massacred. The Chinese Communists' barbarous behaviour unhappily confirmed the appropriateness of the government's decision that flight was the only way to protect the lives of the Dalai Lama and his family.

The different groups crossed over various passes high above the snow line: the Che-la (Sandy Pass), the Yargo-tag-la and the Tag-la. They had even gone to E-Chhudhogyang (a small village) which is at an altitude of over 18,000 feet, and where nothing grows and the inhabitants live in extreme poverty. There is a Tibetan saying which says 'Better to be born an animal in a place where there is grass and water, than to be born in E-Chhudhogyang.'

From Lhuntse Dzong His Holiness sent several emissaries to the Indian government to ask for political asylum. At Jhora his group rejoined the one with Amala and my sister, who had been able to make better time after His Holiness had taken our youngest brother with him. They had even been able to rest in one of our properties.

Amala also told me how His Holiness, far too ill to ride during the last stage after Mangmang, crossed the border between Tibet and India on the back of a dzomo.

During the press conference held in Tezpur, His Holiness was for the first time able to express himself freely and rejected the 'Seventeen Point Agreement' which had been signed under duress in 1951, with a forged Tibetan seal made in Beijing.

When the Tibetans learnt that His Holiness had left his country, many of them decided to follow him. Refugees arrived in India via Bhutan, Ladakh and Nepal. On my return to Mussoorie, I found the Dalai Lama very occupied with the arrival of the first exiles who came to receive his blessing and recount their trials. They were now the living witnesses of their country's tragic history.

Amala soon decided to rejoin Gyalo Thondup, who had just rented a house in Delhi, and my sister and I went there too.

Both Amala and my sister visited an eye specialist in Delhi because their eyes had suffered as a result of their flight through the snow. My brother Gyalo Thondup tried to make their stay as agreeable as possible after all they had just been through. But the fact of living together was enough to make us happy and, little by little, family life was restored. Gyalo Thondup often went to Mussoorie, because the Tibetan Office, opened in New Delhi, now organized the official contacts between our government and the various Indian institutions.

Fortunately, the Indian government helped us considerably. It found residences for His Holiness, first of all in Mussoorie and then in Dharamsala, and also houses for our families; it also paid for food and for the first bungalows of the Tibetan schools.

At the end of the winter holidays I returned to Loreto to finish my last year of school. At the same time my family set out for Dharamsala.

7

The First Refugees in India

My last year at the convent of Loreto was 1960/61. The Senior Cambridge exams went well, and the papers were then sent to England to be corrected. We would not receive the results until March, but now winter was about to start.

My nephew, Tenzin Ngawang, was a brilliant pupil and often topped his class. He loved reading and I think he preferred it to eating. At meal times during the holidays we always had to look for him, and usually found him sitting on the stairs, book in hand. He was excellent in English composition and had even obtained a gold medal for one of his essays. Shortly before the exams, the teachers had advised me to read compositions, because I was not very good at this subject. At my request, my nephew gave me a bundle of his work. I discovered a marvellous text about the river Kyi Chu, which I practically learnt by heart. The subject of my English composition examination was … the river. I must confess that I made full use of Tenzin Ngawang's text and, indeed, gained excellent marks.

I began a regular correspondence with Amala and the rest of my family. Diki Dolkar still lived in Darjeeling, and Gyalo Thondup stayed more often in New Delhi, but I saw him when he came to visit his wife and three children.

Amala explained to me in a letter that, on his return to Mussoorie, His Holiness, at Nehru's invitation, was going to live in a town called Dharamsala in the foothills of Himachal

Pradesh, which at that time was part of the Punjab. His Holiness had sent an official to have a look at the place and the man had returned saying that it seemed very suitable. However, Dharamsala was not particularly easy to get to. Situated at an altitude of 6,000 feet, the small town is divided into two parts: Lower Dharamsala and Upper Dharamsala. The latter was also known as McLeod Ganj, a resort founded several decades earlier by the British.

When His Holiness arrived at this refuge, it was to discover a remote and isolated town a ghost village inhabited by a few Indians. The only shop was run by the Nowrojee family. This episode helps to explain the complexity of the political situation at the time. It was not easy for the Indian government to accept the Dalai Lama on Indian territory, especially as His Holiness had just appealed to the United Nations. It is possible that the New Delhi authorities preferred the Dalai Lama and his entourage to settle in a place not easily accessible.

And so I left for Dharamsala, first of all taking a train from Siliguri to New Delhi, then a night train as far as Pathankot, where a car had been sent by the Private Office to fetch me. The road was awful and it took more than three and a half hours to reach McLeod Ganj. We drove through numerous hamlets as we crossed the plain. I could see shops, but none of the usual Indian street life with its colourful stalls. As we climbed into the foothills, there was not a living soul in sight, although the countryside was magnificent. We drove through thick forests with luxuriant vegetation and, in the distance, saw high, snow-capped summits.

We seemed to be heading towards a place withdrawn from the world, far from civilization. I could not imagine what awaited me at the end of this potholed road that in places bore the marks of rock that had been recently cut, probably by Tibetans who had opened up the road for His Holiness.

In Lower Dharamsala, I noticed some small shops. The driver drove round the perimeter road of a military zone, towards McLeod Ganj. The scene here was one of complete chaos: three buildings, just one shop, and canvas tents everywhere. The Tibetans were in rags, children were crying and trembling with cold, and the women seemed stunned by the weight of their misfortune. What suffering must they have gone through before arriving at this town of misery?

My family occupied an old colonial-style bungalow called Swargashram. Amala had a bedroom and there was also a dining room and a kitchen. His Holiness used one of the other rooms as a prayer room. The veranda and the living room were used for receiving visitors. The officials and advisers were lodged nearby in other buildings that had been requisitioned by the Indian government.

Dispersed around the village were the offices and departments of the government in exile (comprising six ministers in charge of six departments: Education, Finance, Health, Home, Foreign Affairs, Religion, and Security). My sister had to walk nearly half an hour every day to reach the nursery, where she spent nearly all her time. I helped her in her various tasks, in particular making myself useful as an interpreter, as she did not speak much English.

Amala often talked about my future. My brothers, who still lived in the United States, had advised her that I should continue my studies there and, naturally, His Holiness raised the subject during one of our meetings. I had always known him to be very studious, and here too he worked very hard. He welcomed the refugees and often met with his government officials and ministers. However, in spite of all these responsibilities, he managed to find time for the study of sacred texts.

To find work for the refugees was no simple affair. The majority of them, having been nomads or farmers in Tibet, had no professional qualifications, so His Holiness had to turn to the Indian government for help. The temporary option that it proposed was road building in Jammu, Kulu and Manali, in the Himalayan region. Teams of 200 or even 300 refugees were formed for this task.

His Holiness was very preoccupied with the lot of the children who lived with their parents in these extremely difficult conditions. He attached a great deal of importance to education and liked to remind his officials of a meeting with Nehru when the latter had said that the provision of education was Tibet's hope for the future. It was with these words in mind that His Holiness set up the first school in Mussoorie.

His Holiness decided to send officials to the areas where the Tibetans were road building to persuade the families to entrust their children to the government and, if possible, to bring them back with them. The most important priority was to provide shelter for the children. Many children were dying of illness and some had been crushed by falling rocks, and this situation could not be allowed to continue. On 17 May 1960, 51 children arrived from Jammu in a deplorable condition. His Holiness immediately handed them over to our elder sister. They were then shared out between the families of officials, who, according to their circumstances, took charge of one or two children.

This policy was most successful, and within a few weeks, 100 children had arrived in Dharamsala. The Indian government helped us by providing a large bungalow called Conium House to put the children in. We assembled the children here but very soon it became overcrowded and proved too small. So once again the Indian authorities came to our rescue by putting another building at our disposal. This was Egerton Hall where the Children's Village stands today. When still more children kept arriving, we were given Kishore Nivas. The government of India started five boarding schools for Tibetan children – they were situated in Mussoorie, Darjeeling, Simla, Kalimpong and Dalhousie. After gathering the children in Dharamsala, my sister kept the youngest with her and sent those who were over eight, in groups of between 20 and 50, to the various boarding schools, according to where room was available. Soon these five schools were full and so we had to keep the children in the then 'Nursery for Tibetan Children'. More and more children would arrive from different parts of India, Nepal and Bhutan. We were faced with all sorts of problems.

In 1960, at the start of our exile, we did not have enough resources to look after all the refugees. His Holiness depended heavily on the Indian government for help and charity. It was not possible, though, to be too demanding, especially as Nehru and all his colleagues proved themselves to be understanding and generous towards our family and the other Tibetan refugees who were arriving in India in great numbers.

My family came to consider the choice of Dharamsala a good one. If Mussoorie, a much frequented resort, had been chosen, serious problems would soon have arisen when large numbers of Tibetans started to arrive. But, in Dharamsala, there were a few abandoned bungalows and, above all, lots of space.

We badly needed space. Before joining the road-building sites, refugees spent several days, sometimes several weeks, in Dharamsala. Tents were put up to lodge the numerous families. No sooner had 100 children been sent to the schools than twice as many more arrived. Dharamsala had certainly ceased to be a ghost village, but chaos was increasing.

A typical bungalow comprised three rooms. My sister, not having any training as a teacher, acted purely from maternal instinct. She gave a room to each couple or widow. The infants were put into the care of women who were used to babies, and slept in cardboard boxes. Sometimes the older children slept on the floor. There were not enough blankets, let alone cups, cutlery and plates. I can remember a young French woman of Jewish origins. She was called Marie and had joined the nursery on impulse, simply because she wanted to help the children. It was not easy for her to communicate with the Tibetans, but everyone got on very well.

In the meantime, the world was not insensitive to the fate of the Tibetan refugees. Clothing, blankets and tinned food reached us from Canada, Switzerland and Britain. Charities sent us provisions, including the Swiss Red Cross, the Save the Children Fund and Care United States. And, of course, the Indian government helped.

When I arrived in Dharamsala, I received a real shock. I had never before been faced with a similar situation. My sister had the greatest need of me. The children had to be washed, dressed and given their meals. Several elderly Tibetans volunteered to help. I served as an interpreter for the doctors and nurses of the Swiss Red Cross. The urgency of the task to be accomplished drove me to action rather than to despair. I also wrote to many friends. Legjin, a school friend whose Sherpa parents lived in Darjeeling, joined me shortly afterwards.

His Holiness was 25 at the time. For several years he had tried in vain to negotiate with the Chinese authorities. My main feeling towards him was one of admiration. He had apparently lost almost everything, but this did not prevent him from continuing to fight for his people. He was the voice of Tibet. In spite of his disappointments, the despondency of the refugees, and the illness and death that decimated our countrymen, he braved adversity and was for all of us like a beacon of hope. He explained that we were going through a crisis that was part of the collective karma of the Tibetan people and that we had to resolve it ourselves.

I was encouraged by the His Holiness's attitude. I was aware of his incessant efforts night and day. There was no longer any ceremonial pomp surrounding him and he lived like a simple monk. I sometimes asked myself whether the Tibetans respected him even more now. But he was certainly still the Dalai Lama, the officials were still there and the government in exile went about its business.

The main thing was for us to be free. In India, His Holiness was free to act as he wished; he was no longer under the pressure of having his every movement watched. And, above all, he could at last speak in his people's name without taking precautions.

A powerful feeling was born from this new reality. For the Tibetans, exile meant that they first of all had to learn to survive before they could attain a state of freedom. Everything needed to be rebuilt; in addition it was also necessary to think of the sufferings of those who had remained in Tibet. Our future depended on the preservation of our culture. The acts of the government in exile, the development of schools, the behaviour of the refugees and His Holiness's declarations, were all messages of hope and proof of an intense determination. This fundamental desire for freedom enabled us to resolve all difficulties and to overcome our sufferings.

Our people felt enormously relieved to learn that the Dalai Lama had arrived safe and sound in India. For the thousands of people who regarded him as their spiritual and temporal leader, Tibet without the Dalai Lama could have no meaning. In Dharamsala they were able to receive his blessing. The refugees who went straight to distant camps and who were unable to come to Dharamsala always asked for news of His Holiness from those who had had the good fortune to meet him. In fact, in Tibet, very few people had been able to approach the Dalai Lama, either at the Potala or Norbulingka. Here in India, there was more direct contact between the Dalai Lama and his people.

I saw people leave our bungalow in tears. They tried to hide their grief at having had to leave everything behind in Tibet, but they also cried with joy, because there was now direct contact between themselves and their leader and he was safe and free.

One morning we discovered that it had snowed all night and that it was impossible to open the doors of the house. His Holiness's guards and the Indian servants came to help us out of this ridiculous situation. Once the main door had been cleared, Tsering Dolma tried to go to the nursery but she was forced to turn back. Trees had fallen on the road, cutting the electricity cables, and there was more than 3 feet of snow.

A long wait then began. For nearly a week, in spite of several attempts, we were not able to go and see the children. I then realized to what extent we were dependent on ourselves. Supplies began to run out and food, which had to come from Pathankot, could not reach us. We were very worried to be separated like this from the children.

Luckily, some Tibetan women had stayed in the bungalows. These women, who were in their early 30's and 40's, had just been through terrible experiences. Their husbands were either dead or had been taken prisoner by the Chinese. They had marched for days before reaching the Indian frontier, had spent weeks living in tents in encampments, and had sometimes seen their children eaten on the road by wolves. In answer to my sister's plea, they had immediately devoted themselves to the nursery. These women who showed such extraordinary devotion to the children were known as *ayas* then, but today we call them foster mothers or home mothers. The younger women who help in the homes are called aunties.

However, when the children arrived, exhausted and suffering from malnutrition, the ayas' presence was unfortunately not sufficient to overcome all ills. Many children died during the first winter in Dharamsala, with only the toughest surviving. At Conium House and Egerton Hall there were not enough blankets, and food was terribly scarce. When at last we were able to give a blanket to each child, 200 more children arrived all at once after having been cut off for several days by the snow, and the problem started all over again.

For the Tibetans in exile, their children were all they had left, and they found it difficult to send them away, even though they could barely survive. But after a few months had gone by, many people got to hear of the marvellous work done by Tsering Dolma, and the children gradually left the camps of Jammu, Pathankot, Darjeeling, Sikkim and Nepal. A bus put them down in the little square of Dharamsala, from where they had to walk a mile and a half to reach Egerton Hall. Some were accompanied by their parents, who stayed just long enough to receive His Holiness's blessing before returning to road construction work.

My sister and I went to Simla. The British Save the Children Fund owned a magnificent building there at the top of a hill called Sterling Castle. There this organization provided another home for our Tibetan children which was called 'the Manor' and in the early 70s Miss Betts, an English nurse, used to work there, before joining us in Dharamsala.

I often took children to Simla who were particularly ill or weak, together with the young women who were to look after them. It was absolutely necessary to find people who spoke English to accompany the children. Our community counted amongst its members a certain number of girls, hardly more than 18, who had been at boarding school in India during the Tibetan troubles. Their parents, who were now exiles, could no longer pay for their school fees. Obliged to leave their schools, these girls volunteered to become interpreters for the doctors, nurses and the Tibetan staff looking after the children. Most of them abandoned all thought of further education. After talking to them, I considered it a privilege to be able to continue my studies. I was just over 20 and felt that, for them too, I was invested with a mission.

Tibetans who had already been living in India for several years also responded to the urgency of the situation by volunteering. I remember, for instance, a childless Tibetan couple. The man, Jampa, acted as an interpreter. The woman, Lhamo, helped my sister with administrative tasks and welcomed visitors to Dharamsala.

The news reaching us from Tibet was disastrous. The International Commission of Jurists had not yet published its second report, but we knew that China was perpetrating genocide in Tibet. His Holiness met refugees, heads of charities and people who arrived spontaneously to offer help. One of the first to turn up was Ruckmani Devi, president of the Indian Theosophic Society, whom I had met in 1956 during the Dalai Lama's journey through India.

I also remember a Hungarian woman painter, a friend of the Nehrus, who had lived in India for many years. One day this lady, who had a house in New Delhi, had saved a fawn, which she then offered to His Holiness upon her arrival in Dharamsala. The animal was still very young and had to be fed with a bottle. Amala and I fed him, and this occupied me considerably for several weeks. The fawn grew up to become the attraction of Swargashram. Every day, at about three in the afternoon, he began to dance about, much to the amusement of guards and visitors. His Holiness would roar with laughter.

The guards built an enclosure to protect the fawn from leopards and wild cats. In fact, there were many wild animals in the region and our dogs were regularly attacked by leopards. We had to protect the children especially. At night, when one of them asked to go to the lavatories outside the dormitories, an adult had to accompany him with a stick. We were particularly careful during the winter when the wild animals came down into the valley to look for food.

We loved animals in our family and His Holiness had always been surrounded by them. He often liked to talk about his fish at Norbulingka, as well as the parrots and peacocks.

A family that had recently arrived from Tibet gave His Holiness a magnificent black and white terrier. There was also the Tibetan Lhasa *apso* dog, which I had been given in Lhasa. So now the guards had to feed the growing fawn, the apso and the terrier. These animals were a source of comfort during difficult moments.

Every day, His Holiness received his teachers outside official visiting hours. I think that the Dalai Lama greatly looked forward to this moment because he had very close relations with them. For a Tibetan, his master of religious instruction is often more important than his parents.

When His Holiness prayed in the room next door, or if there were official audiences, we tried to keep quiet. However, at the start of our period of exile, we shared a normal family life in His Holiness's presence that we had never known before. Even though he usually took meals on his own, His Holiness would speak to Amala, my sister, my brother-in-law and me every day. When his timetable permitted, we all had tea together at about four in the afternoon. These were unforgettable moments.

My brother Gyalo Thondup set up a ping-pong table for the Dalai Lama. Tenzin Choegal played with him, sharing a moment of exercise and relaxation. His Holiness also played badminton on the large lawn behind the veranda. Even when things are difficult, the Tibetan character misses no opportunity to look on the bright side, and we appreciated all these moments devoted to sport.

On 21 October 1959, the Tibetan question was raised at the United Nations. A resolution, passed by 45 votes, with six abstentions, stated that:

> Recalling the principles regarding fundamental human rights and freedoms set out in the Charter of the United Nations and in the Universal Declaration of Human Rights adopted by the General Assembly on 10 December 1948.
>
> *Considering* that the fundamental human rights and freedoms to which the Tibetan people, like all others, are entitled include the right to civil and religious liberty for all without distinction,
>
> *Mindful* also of the distinctive cultural and religious heritage of the people of Tibet and of the autonomy which they have traditionally enjoyed,
>
> *Gravely* concerned at reports, including the official statements of His Holiness the Dalai Lama, to the effect that the fundamental human rights and freedoms of the people of Tibet have been forcibly denied them,
>
> *Deploring* the effect of these events in increasing international tension and embittering the relations between peoples at a time when earnest and positive efforts are being made by responsible leaders to reduce tension and improve international relations, [the United Nations]
>
> 1) *Affirms its belief* that respect for the principles of the Charter of the United Nations and of the Universal Declaration of Human Rights is essential for the evolution of a peaceful world order based on the rule of law;
> 2) *Calls* for respect for the fundamental human rights of the Tibetan people and for their distinctive cultural and religious life.

This resolution raised many expectations. In 1960, Tibet was once again placed on the agenda of the General Assembly of the United Nations. Helped by the Afro-Asian Council, the resolution was sponsored by Malaysia, Thailand, the Republic of Ireland and El Salvador. In the end, the session gave priority to the African question, each day postponing the Tibetan problem, and then finally simply adjourning it. From then on, China was free to pursue its policy of genocide with total impunity.

The announcement of this adjournment was a terrible blow, which partly destroyed the hopes which we had placed in the

United Nations. In spite of everything, His Holiness continued the struggle for his people.

In March 1961, a letter reached me from the school at Loreto saying that I had passed my final exam. Of course, I did not end my Indian school days at the top of the results list, but the main thing was to have passed. I must say that I was not particularly surprised: as I could not bother His Holiness with this kind of question, I had in fact already asked one of his tutors to do a divination and the result was positive. Reassured by my success, I slept marvellously. I was particularly happy because it confirmed the lama's prediction.

I immediately wrote a letter to my brother Thubten Jigme Norbu who was going around Europe looking for help for the refugees. He was at that moment in Switzerland, negotiating with the children's village of Pestalozzi in Trogen for them to take Tibetan children. He was also meeting a number of Swiss families.

Thubten Jigme Norbu was on very good terms with Charles Aeschiman, the director of the Atel company in Olten, in German-speaking Switzerland. The latter had decided to set up an organization for the adoption of Tibetan children. The Aeschiman family had already taken in two children and suggested to my brother that I stay in his house. In Dharamsala, the journey was discussed with His Holiness and the rest of the family and it was thought that a new experience could but benefit my future. The decision to leave was taken in April 1961, and I wrote to Charles and Gret Aeschiman.

Since His Holiness's exile, the status of the Tibetans in India had been rather special. As a political refugee, I did not have a Tibetan passport. Although it was possible for us to opt for Indian nationality, we considered it very important to retain our identity so that we should not be forgotten – and to show the world our determination. The Indian government once again proved to be extremely understanding in giving us an identity card that said 'Tibetan refugee resident in India'. I was given one of these cards. Then there was a short wait to obtain a visa, and several trips had to be made between Dharamsala and New Delhi. Charles Aeschiman intervened with the Swiss embassy and this helped things along.

The hour of my departure for Switzerland approached. Although I was enthusiastic about the prospect of a new journey,

I was very worried about all those I was going to leave behind. I had also inquired about the languages spoke in Switzerland. When I learnt that French, German and Italian were spoken there, I was seized by anxiety.

I comforted myself with the thought that about 20 young Tibetans had been sent to the children's village of Trogen. The Swiss Red Cross had also agreed to take in Tibetan refugees from Nepal and India. Two groups had already left, and with one of them was Champa, one of the interpreters from the Children's Village.

8

Studying in Europe

I was now 20. I had survived the first months of exile in Dharamsala, and had understood the importance of the political difficulties that endangered my country's survival. When I was a pupil at boarding school in Kalimpong, and later in Darjeeling, all our discussions had turned on Tibet. Similarly, no family meal or gathering passed without the Tibetan question being raised. In India, Gyalo Thondup, who was extremely preoccupied by the situation, felt compelled to act. And this feeling was shared by many other Tibetans living there.

I had in this way grown up in an environment where Tibet was people's main preoccupation. I now wished to finish my studies as quickly as possible in order to serve His Holiness the Dalai Lama. The more time passed, the more I realized how much help the refugees needed. My departure for Switzerland was in accordance with my family's wishes, but it was also an opportunity for me to increase my knowledge so that I would be in a better position to work for the Tibetan cause on my return.

In Tibet, women married very young; traditionally, young people could ask for one another's hand, but in fact marriages were most often arranged – and of, course, steps had already been taken by Amala concerning myself. My family had always allowed me a great deal of freedom; I was therefore responsible for my own actions and had to make my own decisions. For the time being I considered that other problems were more important. Amala understood this and told my suitors, or their families, that it was more important for me to finish my studies.

I approached the question of relations with boys in the same way as did all young girls of my age. Some schoolmates already had a boyfriend and we readily discussed their relationships. Once again, the nuns at Loreto showed exceptional intelligence. When we were between 16 and 18, they organized afternoon dances three times a year, to which the boys of Saint Joseph were invited. The nuns and fathers chaperoned us. These meetings were designed to teach us to communicate with members of the opposite sex. Of course, we had to behave correctly and there was no question of flirting.

With a growing number of young Tibetans studying in India, marriages for love became more frequent. This change in mentality developed particularly after 1956. In the early 1950s, most families had been forced, under Chinese pressure, to call their children back to Tibet. I had in this way seen all my schoolmates leave. However, in 1956, at the time of the Buddha Jayanti, many parents manifested their displeasure at attempts to impose a Chinese education on their children. Rather than recalling them to Tibet, they registered their children again for the missionary boarding schools. At Loreto and Saint Joseph, I saw again several of my old friends, including one of my best friends, Namgyal Lhamo, and her younger sister, Norzin Tsarong.

Certain families continued to consider arranged marriages as the norm. For Tibetans, marriage constituted a contract sealed in the following manner: when a couple was about to get married, an astrologer would first of all be called in. Looking at their birth dates, he could determine whether the future couple had compatible profiles. In the event of a favourable reply, the wedding was generally preceded by a period of engagement, varying from one to two years. Just before the ceremony, the young man's parents or uncles took presents to the future bride's home.

In Tibet, marriage is not considered a sacred act, but sometimes parents wish for the services of a lama. The rituals then take place in a room away from the rest of the house. The ceremony itself is organized in relative privacy, in the presence of parents and friends. At the time of the wedding, a contract is drawn up by the two families. It includes a list of the objects and

Lhasa, 1940. My first photograph. I am on Amala's lap, Pala is sitting beside her; to the right of Amala, my sister Tsering Dolma and a cousin; to the left of Pala, my brother Gyalo Thondup and my brother-in-law Phuntsok Tashi (Tsering Dolma's husband). Behind them are our servants.

Lhasa, 1940. Myself and Amala (detail of above)

Lhasa, 1950. Changtse-Shar, the family house in Lhasa

The Potala seen here from
our terrace

Lhasa, 1947. My niece
Khando Tsering and my
nephew Tenzin Ngawang.
I am on the right.

Lhasa, 1944. Myself between Amala and Pala, with brother Lobsang
Samten to the right and my niece, Khando Tsering

Lhasa, 1946. My cousin
holding my younger
brother Tendzin Choegyal
on her lap. I am on the
left. On the right are are
my niece Khando Tsering,
and my nephew
Tenzin Ngawang.

At school in Kalimpong, 1951. I am third from the left in the top row.

The hockey team at Loreto, Darjeeling, 1959. I am sitting first on the left.

Skiing at La Pelouse, Switzerland, 1962

(*Above*) My trip to Venice with Marina Lopez, 1962

(*Main picture*)
On the way to India in 1949. I am nine years old.

The family in Delhi, 1956. I am second from the left. Amala is next to His Holiness.

(*Right*) Lumbini, 1956. Nehru with Amala and some family members. I am on the right of the picture.

(*Left*) Delhi, 1956. Myself, Tsering Dolma, Indhira Gandhi, Amala, my brother Tendzin Choegyal and my niece (from left to right)

The first refugees in Dharamsala, 1960

Kulu, 1964.
Their parents are
building roads. They
are children of hope.

Bylakuppe, 1961.
Tibetan refugee
tents in the
settlements

(*Above*) Dharamsala, 1960.
Amala surrounded by
children at the nursery

(*Right*) Dharamsala, 1960.
Atchala, my older sister, with
the first refugee children

Basel, Switzerland, 1964.
Gathering of the first Tibetan children sent to Europe

(*Above*) Dharamsala, 1964. It is my duty to help the
refugee children.

(*Below*) With Gret Aeschiman in Olten,
Switzerland

6 July 1995. His Holiness the Dalai Lama's sixtieth birthday
(photograph by Tenzin Dorjee)

possessions brought by the boy and girl. When the bride is an only daughter it can be accepted that the boy goes to live with his wife's family. In the case of separation, each spouse takes back his or her possessions. If children are born from the match, the girls go with their mother, the boys with their father.

Charles Aeschiman and his daughter Danielle met me at Zurich airport, in October 1961. I was very surprised to see a Tibetan at their side. He was called Rakra Rinpoche and was in charge of the 20 Tibetan children taken in by the Pestalozzi Children's Village, Trogen. The Aeschimans gave us lunch at Zurich station, a new shock for me. I was struck first of all by the town's cleanliness, and my first European meal also seemed to me rather strange. Although Rakra Rinpoche explained the composition of the different dishes to me, I sometimes wondered what I was swallowing. All the same, I would have to get used to it. I found the bread excellent, however, and I thought with emotion of Amala who used to cook so well in our old house in Lhasa.

Rakra Rinpoche then took the train to Trogen, and we left for Olten in a chauffeur-driven car. On our arrival I met the rest of the family: Charles Aeschiman's wife Gret, and their two sons Jacques and Maurice (better known as Mops). Danielle was then 17, Jacques about 20 and Mops 12. Gret Aeschiman then introduced me to Tseten, their little Tibetan boy, and to Sonam and Nima, helpers in the Aeschiman family, whom I had met in Dharamsala and who had been sent to Switzerland by my sister six months earlier.

After a period of getting used to my new life, Charles Aeschiman took me to Trogen where I was able to meet the young Tibetans and Rakra Rinpoche. Then began the search for a school. As I had decided to learn French, our efforts were concentrated on the French part of the country. Gret and I set out for girls' schools in Montreux, Vevey and Lausanne. First of all she made me make several purchases, including a pair of high-heeled shoes, as I had arrived from India wearing my traditional Tibetan clothes and Indian shoes. I suffered enormously on the steep streets of Lausanne. After wearing these shoes all day, I would forget Amala's recommendation to change them in the evening, when the feet are swollen.

Gret Aeschiman considered that the establishments we had

visited were not suitable for me as the boarders were far too young, so Charles Aeschiman then telephoned a Catholic school in Bex, in the canton of Vaud.

The school of La Pelouse, a very small institution, had only 17 girls, from 11 different countries. On learning of Charles Aeschiman's request for a place for the sister of the Dalai Lama, I expect the sisters had to look in books to find out who he was. I therefore again packed my bags and set off for Bex, which is near St Maurice, accompanied by Gret and Danielle. The headmistress, Sister Mauricia, did not speak a word of English, but the initial contact was excellent, especially as my Tibetan clothes fascinated the nuns.

La Pelouse, part of an old farm, comprised two chalets. One housed the administrative services, the dining room and the nuns' rooms, the other the classrooms and our bedrooms.

I was to share a bedroom with Marina Lopez, from El Salvador. A little later in the day she introduced me to the other pupils: Alicia and Cecilia Herrera from Colombia, Janet Gardiner from Britain, Maura from the United States, Carmen from Mexico, Anna from Spain, Gaby from Switzerland, Monica and Hildegarde Schadler from Liechtenstein, Hannlore from West Germany, Marion from Holland, and Luisa from Italy. I hope that the others will forgive me if, for the time being, their names do not come to mind.

We were all there to learn French and therefore our lessons took place in Molière's language. In the morning we concentrated on grammar and history. Then came the other subjects, including history of art, taught twice a week by a lay teacher. To approach such a rich subject, ranging from the art of ancient times to modern creations, she showed us slides. With the help of an old gramophone, a nun introduced us to Mozart and Chopin.

In the summer, we played tennis or swam in the swimming pool. In the winter, we set off for the nearby ski resorts. At my first Christmas, Gret and Charles Aeschiman gave me all the equipment needed for skiing. During our time on the slopes, however, work was not forgotten. Sister Mauricia, who was at the same time an accomplished sportswoman, saw to that; we had to speak French all the time.

I was at La Pelouse to stay for a little over two years. Being the eldest of all the girls, I had the role of spokeswoman. St Maurice was three quarters of an hour's walk away, across beautiful country. Sometimes we took the bus or a taxi there to do our shopping. However, we were always accompanied by a chaperon who was meant to keep an eye on us. I was by now 22, Marina was 21 and the other girls between 18 and 20. One day, annoyed and profiting from my position as spokeswoman, I asked Sister Mauricia whether she had no confidence in us. That Sunday, as well as all the following ones, we no longer had our chaperon on our backs. Nevertheless, the nuns awaited our return and shook our hands. I found that hands were often shaken in Switzerland; in fact, the sister in charge of our rooms used this gesture to approach each of us before, breathing in deeply, singling out those guilty of smoking. Needless to say, some of us did smoke from time to time. We used to go to a teashop that served very good hot chocolate, and which was full of people smoking, so we used this pretext to defend those of our companions whose hair and clothes were most impregnated with the smell of tobacco.

The dining room had two tables. Sister Mauricia sat at one end of the largest, with the chaplain opposite her. We changed places each day and were madly happy when it was our turn to sit at the little table, where we could talk about anything we wanted. At the big table we had to keep up a conversation with Sister Mauricia and the chaplain about history, politics and music, all of it in French. Marina often came to my help, as with my rather sketchy French I found this exercise very difficult. After lunch, whatever the weather, there was always an hour's walk in the forest, or amongst the walnut, hazel or cherry trees.

In Kalimpong there had been priests from St Maurice. What a strange coincidence! As children, the one we had known best was Father Butti, who lived in a small farm close to the school and who sold us cheese and, more important, sweets on Sundays when we received our pocket money.

At Easter, or during the summer holidays, I sometimes went travelling. Monica and Hildegarde Schandler invited me to Liechtenstein, where their parents ran a hotel with a restaurant. In this Catholic family I discovered marvellous Easter customs. We sometimes played jokes on the customers. For instance, when preparing Hungarian goulash, Madame Schandler added

Indian spices, especially chilli that I had brought, making the dish very spicy. I visited various places in Liechtenstein with the Schandlers and several Austrian castles.

I spent most of my weekends with the Aeschimans in Olten. A strong friendship had grown between Danielle Aeschiman and myself. I did not, however, forget to visit regularly the Tibetan children at Trogen. More than 160 young Tibetans had now been entrusted to Swiss families, thanks to the efforts of the Aeschiman family. One day, Charles Aeschiman asked me to accompany him to the airport to greet a group of 40 children from Dharamsala. The families that would be adopting them waited with us.

I felt tremendous happiness at the sight of the children coming towards us. But suddenly this changed to intense sadness. Women were crying out: 'Where is mine? Where is mine?' The poor children did not understand what was happening to them. I suffered inwardly, although I knew that adoption was the best opportunity for them at that very difficult time. After lunch at the airport, the drama that I had been dreading took place. The children had to be separated and none of them wanted to leave their little friends.

I understood their distress. From now on they were going to be in families where nobody spoke Tibetan. Their expressions reflected the various stages of their terrible experience: Dharamsala, the nursery, then the departure (a real plunge into the unknown), a bus, New Delhi, the airplane for the first time, cars that they had never travelled in before and now people who did not understand them and who were going to take them away to live with them.

These families were marvellous; however, I had to recognize that, during the two and a half years I spent in Switzerland, there were certain children who adapted with difficulty to Western life. Some even had to be sent back to Dharamsala. At the same time, in spite of the difficulties these adopted children faced, because of the tremendous problems in coping with increasing numbers of children, and the need for them to receive better education, we decided to send children abroad but only in small groups with an couple to act as their foster parents. This way they could be together and also not forget their language and culture. Twenty children were sent to French Pyrenees and a group of six girls were sent to Belgium. Between 1960 and 1962, groups of children were sent to Germany and also to Britain to the Pestalozzi Children's Villages. We sent a number of groups to the Pestalozzi Children's Village at Trogen, Switzerland. These children did very well and over the years some of them have returned to India to work in the Tibetan settlements and communities.

In 1970, when our refugee situation improved and we were in a position to look after the children in our various institutions, we took the decision not to offer children for adoption, except in very exceptional cases where the child was an orphan, had no other family, and the adoptee family was close to a large Tibetan community. However, in the early sixties, the Tibetan government in exile was in an extremely difficult and helpless situation. But later, in 1975, on a visit to Switzerland, when I saw again the children who had been adopted, I had to answer an extremely delicate question: why had we given them up for adoption? I then had a strong feeling of sadness.

Adoption became for me an extreme solution, and today it is very rare for Tibetan children to be taken in by foreign families, except sometimes in Switzerland; but Switzerland is a very special case because there is a community of 2,000 Tibetans living there. The children are therefore not cut off from their roots. Also, the welcoming families there play a very important role, because it is they who choose the future adoptive parents, who must give every guarantee that they will provide the child with a real Tibetan culture.

From La Pelouse, I kept in correspondence with many of my friends from the days in Darjeeling. We had all taken different paths. The Princesses Shanti and Sharada had returned to Nepal. In one of my letters, in 1963, I had asked Shanti to help the Tibetans wishing to take refuge in her country. She, of course, exercised no direct political influence, but she promised to talk to her father. It was becoming difficult to exchange letters with my Burmese friend due to the growing communist influence in Burma. Namgyal gave me news of Darjeeling; my brother Lobsang Samten had returned from the United States, and he married my friend Namgyal Lhamo in 1963. Unfortunately I was unable to go to the wedding, but I was very happy that my friend was now a member of the family.

Tenzin Choegal, my youngest brother, was 13 when he arrived

in India. Amala sent him to North Point, St Joseph where he attended school. He sent me little messages. My niece, Khando Tsering, studied in London and my nephew, Tenzin Ngawang, at Cambridge.

Amala and my sister wrote regularly and I also received letters from His Holiness. He told me about my dog Tashi and his work. But all these letters finished with the same advice: finish your studies and then return as quickly as possible to help me and the Tibetan cause. When I was in Dharamsala, he had regularly listened to the BBC. He learnt English in this way, because he did not have enough time to learn with a teacher. He also read *The Vicar of Wakefield*, a classic of English literature. When he wrote to me in English, the letters had a very special sentimental value and I treasured them dearly.

Therefore, I was regularly informed of the situation of the Tibetans in India, of the nomination of the first people's representatives and of His Holiness's reflections on the need for constitutional democracy. He spent two years working on this project, first circulating the draft to the Tibetan people for their opinions and finally promulgating the draft future constitution on 10 March 1963. These letters re-affirmed my determination to serve the Tibetan people myself. The much-awaited moment approached, and I was completely aware of my family's difficulties in India.

In the end, the two and a half years in Switzerland, followed by seven months in England in 1962/63, went quickly. But I had benefitted so much from this time in Europe.

Still dressed in my traditional Tibetan clothes, I went to Paris where I spent a week with Danielle Aeschiman who was studying at the Sorbonne. She had a room on the boulevard Saint Michel and had rented another for me nearby. Every morning, she accompanied me as far as the Louvre; at lunchtime we would meet up again at the museum coffee shop and in the evening I waited for her outside her classes. I loved the museums and spent unforgettable hours contemplating the paintings of the Impressionists and admiring tourist sites such as the Eiffel Tower.

One evening we decided to take a taxi and go to the Moulin Rouge, just to have a look. The driver was a bit embarrassed and cast anxious looks into the mirror, probably wondering where we came from, with myself dressed in a chuba and Danielle looking even younger than her 20 years. Suddenly the driver said to us: 'You must not go out this evening. Something terrible has happened. General de Gaulle has died and there will be trouble in the streets of Paris. It would be better for you to go back home.' The next day, Danielle came to breakfast and told me laughing that the General was in fine health! The driver's concern made him appear charming.

Marina Lopez and I wanted to take the bus to Lugano and see some of Italy: Florence, Rome, Pompeii, Sicily. With the interpreter, we were the youngest. The other tourists were elderly people from Germany, Belgium and the United States. In Florence, Marina lost her temper. As usual, I wore a chuba and, outside a shop or a restaurant, a crowd would form around me. The Italians did not hesitate to stare at me and examine me from head to foot. Marina dragged me into a shop to buy a skirt, jacket and shirt. Dressed in this way, the Italians just took me for another ordinary Japanese tourist.

Although I was far from my family throughout these years, I still felt the influence of Buddhism in the depths of my being and in all my actions. In India, as I have recounted, I discovered another religion, Catholicism. However, even when confronted by strong missionary conviction, such as that of Sister Antoinette, because my Buddhist roots were sound, my faith only increased. In chapel or church I recited 'Hail Mary' or 'Our Father' with all the other little boarders but, from the age of 12, I also recited mantras.

In fact, my spirituality developed under the influence of the nuns. As I was the Dalai Lama's sister, they no doubt expected more from me in this area than from my companions. When talking about His Holiness, one first of all thinks of the monk, the spiritual leader; his temporal role does not immediately come to mind. Moreover, I am convinced that all religions stem from the same essential base; I have therefore never found any particular difficulty in living with girls of different religions: Muslims, Hindus or Catholics. In my opinion, goodness, compassion and the desire for justice and love are universal values that go beyond all frontiers. I would also add truth to this list. These values form the basis of my education and are at the heart of Buddhist teaching.

These notions, which had been instilled in me since my

earliest years, did not, however, totally satisfy me. I wanted to deepen my knowledge of the great Buddhist principles. In 1970, while I was in charge of the children's village in India, I felt the need for a break in my working life. I took part in a 12-day seminar where a lama gave Tibetan teaching, translated into English by an interpreter. Still very young, I sometimes found it difficult to take everything in. Unlike Catholicism, which is simply a matter of faith, Tibetan Buddhism works by questioning, and certainly does not lead to blind faith. It is essential to find a good teacher and to know him well. Dialogue with a good teacher will dispel any doubts you may have.

In an age where science and technology triumph, Buddhism is certainly the most attractive religion for men and women of all countries and origins. Many Catholics and Protestants do find it difficult to obtain satisfactory answers to the questions that preoccupy them. When we are told that Catholics go to heaven and everyone else to hell, should we believe this without raising the slightest objection? Is it possible to so easily accept that we either find everlasting happiness or burn forever in vengeful flames?

I find great comfort in the Buddhist concept of responsibility for our own actions. If we follow a positive path, something good will come of it; if our behaviour is negative, we will pay for it. However, the negative approach is never definitive because Buddhism implies the possibility of constant evolution. For example, if you plant bad seed, your harvest will not be a good one. Nevertheless, we know that if you plant good seed in the same soil, a good harvest will follow. In this way, responsible for our actions, we reap what we have chosen to sow.

Unlike certain companions who felt confronted by a real dilemma and ended up converting to Catholicism, I felt that my faith in Buddhism was strengthened by the years spent at Loreto.

Life at the convent had influenced us all. Books were censored. Hemingway's *A Farewell to Arms* was not allowed in the school library. But I had discovered a book by Charles Dickens that told the story of a man and his double during the French revolution. One of them was French and the other English. Both loved the same woman and, besides, they were friends. The French aristocrat was about to be guillotined when the Englishman decided to take his place in order to save his friend's life. It seems strange remembering all these things. Our choice was not limited to the classics of English literature. We also secretly brought Mills & Boon romances to read at night in bed by torch light.

At La Pelouse, the nuns regularly showed us films, but they were just as strict. As soon as somebody was going to be kissed on the screen, a nun placed her hand over the projector. At the time, Elvis Presley was every young girl's dream. One day, my friends dragged me into a cinema in St Maurice where Alfred Hitchcock's *Psycho* was showing. It contained lots of blood and murders; in fact, everything that horrified me. I left the cinema in the middle of the film, forcing my friends who were enjoying the film to leave with me. I was just over 20 and had very old-fashioned ideas. Several years later, when discussing with some old friends our boarding school education and the possibility of sending our children to such an institution, we all replied in the negative. We all felt that we had been overprotected, and that this kind of education was no longer suitable in the 1970s and 1980s. Of course, at the time we were not aware of this. However, a wall enclosed our schools in both Kalimpong and Darjeeling, meaning that we had no significant contact with the outside world.

Towards the end of my stay in Switzerland, my French was still only very average. Gyalo Thondup came to see me at the Aeschimans and it was decided that I should go to London to take a secretarial and office management course before my return to India. I was very sad to leave the Aeschimans.

Gyalo Thondup had a lawyer friend, D K Sen, who arranged my stay in the English capital. Mrs Saul Dailey, the Secretary to the Tibetan Society, agreed to take me in as a paying guest. I went to live in her house in May 1963. I was enrolled at Mrs Hoster's College, a girls' school near the Natural History Museum, in South Kensington, for lessons in English history, typing and shorthand, a subject in which I was not very gifted.

The day after my arrival, D K Sen accompanied me to the college to show me the way and I took the underground for the first time. How different it was from Switzerland! London seemed so noisy and dirty. But I could once more express myself without the slightest difficulty and see again some of my school friends from Darjeeling. Duengkeo Kosin, the daughter of a distinguished Thai lawyer, was now studying law in London and her mother suggested that I come and live with them, in the spare room of the flat to which they were about to move, just round the corner from the school.

Every week, D K Sen invited me to lunch. I told him about my impressions of college and my life in London. I had met Lady Alexander Metcalf, the Director of the Save the Children Fund, who was actively concerned with Tibetan refugees in India. At her suggestion, Harrods department store had 400 chuba made, which they donated, and a shoe factory gave 1,000 pairs of new shoes for the children. I spoke to D K Sen about my plan to move in with Duengkeo and her mother, because I felt rather lonely at Mr and Mrs Dailey's. But D K Sen refused. He wanted me to get used to British life. The situation improved a bit when Mrs Dailey took in a Scottish girl, Fiona Hunter Russell, a classmate. But Fiona only remained for six weeks. Then my decision became irrevocable and I went to live at Duengkeo Kosin's.

I felt very happy in South Kensington with Duengkeo and her mother, whose friend also lived there. The couple were the Thai bridge champions and had succeeded in getting into the very exclusive St James's Club. They lived by their skill and were obviously doing very well. On their very frequent victory days, we went out to a restaurant.

Duengkeo Kosin's mother asked me to do her a special favour: feed the cat, a very beautiful Siamese. I prepared his meal every evening and gave it to him the next morning. The animal proved to be very difficult and refused to eat any meat that he considered to be over- or under-cooked. I therefore learnt to cook meat perfectly, thanks to the cat!

Just as I was about to leave London for the United States, and only awaited my visa, I learnt of President Kennedy's assassination. I was very shocked. He symbolized a new generation of politicians and had raised enormous hope amongst the young.

I went to the American embassy three times to try and obtain the famous visa. But apparently my status as a Tibetan political refugee in India did not inspire the embassy official with much confidence and he kept on asking me for more papers. Until then I had not declared my identity as the Dalai Lama's sister. But, sensing a refusal, I decided to tell him who I was; he made me wait for a quarter of an hour and then returned with the visa.

In the United States, I went on a journey that took me to

Seattle, San Francisco, Los Angeles and New York. Legjin Tsering, who was studying at Washington University, accompanied me as far as the Mexican border. There I met Mr and Mrs Toulouse who looked after Tibetan refugees in Seattle, Mr and Mrs Fields from California, and Mr and Mrs Redding, two missionaries.

I felt extremely moved on seeing Thubten Jigme Norbu again as I had not seen him for a long time. I spent several days with him and his wife, Kungyang La.

On my return journey to India, a halt in Vienna allowed me to pay a visit to Lobsang Samten and Namgyal, who were soon to run the Tibetan Office in Geneva. Heinrich Harrer had an exhibition of wonderful material about my country there. Namgyal and I had a lot to tell one another after a three-year separation and I spent a week with her and my brother before catching the plane to New Delhi.

PART II

1964–1979

9

The Death of Tsering Dolma

It was mid-February 1964 and I was impatient to return to Dharamsala. As a student I had studied and travelled a great deal and met many people who felt concern for the Tibetan question. However, I was not really satisfied by the progress I had made. Although I had only acquired some knowledge of French and certain secretarial skills, I did not really want to embark on further long studies. A degree would only have meant something to me if it had brought me nearer to my objective, one that had remained unchanged since I was 16: to help His Holiness the Dalai Lama.

The journey from Zurich to New Delhi seemed endless and I found it difficult to contain my excitement. I was already looking forward to celebrating the Tibetan New Year with my family. Gyalo Thondup and Diki Dolkar came to fetch me at the airport. They now lived in the Indian capital with their children. Amala was spending a few days with them to take a rest from the intense cold that descended on Dharamsala at that time of the year.

Around the end of February, Amala and I took the train to Pathankot, where the Private Office had sent a car to fetch us. On arriving in Dharamsala, we prepared khatas. His Holiness received us almost immediately and gave us his blessing. It was a moment of crucial importance for me. His Holiness considered that the hour had come for me to serve the Tibetan cause. He asked me to tell him how I would like to do this. When I suggested secretarial work, he explained that he already had English-speaking people around him. In his opinion, I would be of much more use in the children's village.

The situation in the village had considerably improved. Tsering Dolma now had an office, even though it was only a narrow room, with a typewriter and a few chairs. Kelsang La, a young Tibetan girl who had been a pupil at Kalimpong, dealt with the correspondence and projects. Most of the letters consisted of requests for help to charities and different Indian institutions, for the children were still arriving in ever greater numbers. The Indian government had again been very generous in setting up refugee camps near the borders, such as the one at Buxa. This camp took in monks, and the students there were able to study under the guidance of masters who had, like themselves, succeeded in fleeing the Chinese repression.

At Buxa there were also refugees in transit, who were then directed towards other camps. Many Tibetans had also managed to reach Sikkim, where they were now building roads. However, most of them tried to reach Dharamsala. When they heard about Tsering Dolma's work, they wanted to place their children under His Holiness's protection and receive his blessing before leaving to look for ways to survive.

A new building called Kishore Nivas had been given to the village in 1962. But after only two years it became impossible to house all the children there. The youngest remained at the nursery, while those who were already eight waited in a temporary school before going on to the schools set up by the Indian government.

There were more than 800 children in the village at that period. The conditions there came as a great shock after my comfortable time in Switzerland, Britain and the United States. The bungalows were full to bursting point, mostly with babies needing care and attention. They were suffering from malnutrition and, because of the overcrowding, several illnesses broke out, mainly eye and skin infections. Almost all the children had diarrhoea. They had just crossed the Himalayan mountain range in terrible conditions. On reaching the border, the elder ones had gone on to Dharamsala by bus or, most often, on foot. They were sometimes saved from death by other refugees who found them exhausted and famished by the side of the road. So much hardship caused serious trauma and there was a particularly high mortality rate among both children and adults.

The refugees had left everything behind them in their flight from the Chinese atrocities. Many had seen their parents die or taken away from them. Some had even had to kill their parents during *thamzing* sessions. Others had been bitten by wolves or buried beneath the snow. On their arrival, many had to have an arm or leg amputated due to frost bite.

In our work, we had not only to care for bodies, we also had to alleviate terrible psychological suffering. At night, the poor children had horrible nightmares. The foster mothers remained at their sides, giving them more attention than the other children. The doctors and nurses were overworked and Kelsang La did not know what to do next. My sister began work at dawn and finished after nightfall.

As we knew almost nothing about these children, I decided to question them. I talked to them and, of course, comforted them too. It was necessary to find out where they came from, to learn whether they had brothers or sisters, aunts or uncles, and if their parents were still alive in Tibet or had tried to flee with them. They found it very difficult to talk. In fact, all these children were living in a waking nightmare and it would take them a very long time to come out of it.

Many charities and generous people came to our help. Voluntary workers arrived from all over the world. It would be impossible to mention them all. The Swiss Red Cross continued to do extraordinary work, for instance training young Tibetans to work in the newly built dispensary and laboratory. Then there were the Save the Children Fund UK, Care United States, Swiss Aid to Tibetans, American Emergency Committee for Tibetans, the Tibet Society of Great Britain and the Tibetan Refugee Aid Society of Canada, not to mention people such as Doris Murray from England and Josy Harder of Switzerland, who showed exceptional devotion. We also received help from Australia, New Zealand and many European countries, not to mention individuals such as Eric Muhlmann and nelly Kunyi.

In spite of all our efforts, the conditions in the village improved little, although we could now send the children on to the schools more quickly; Conium House, Egerton Hall and Kishore Nivas were still overcrowded. The temporary school played its role but was also almost full. It should be remembered that Dharamsala is at an altitude of over 6,000 feet, and ithe region receives the second highest rainfall in India. The children slept on the bungalow floor, which luckily was made of wood. Though an ordinary blanket on the floor was sufficient for most of the year, in the middle of the winter, with temperatures below zero, there were daily tragedies. Stoves had been installed, but we lacked fuel.

My sister and I would leave the bungalow at dawn, arriving at the village at about half past seven, work all morning and, after a quick lunch, return to our tasks until late at night. Two or three times a week I would accompany children to the hospital in Lower Dharamsala. A German charity had given us a car which served as transport for the many emergency cases. Sometimes a Tibetan nurse would accompany us and I was in permanent contact with the doctors. I also sometimes went shopping at the local general store.

A month after my return to Dharamsala, Gyalo Thondup suggested that I go to New Delhi to take my driving test. I obtained my licence without much difficulty, but I felt slightly anxious about driving in Dharamsala. It had been quite an experience driving in the wide congested streets of the capital, amongst the carts, rickshaws, buses belching fumes, and nonchalant cows, but the steep, narrow road with hairpin bends between McLeod Ganj and Lower Dharamsala seemed to me unimaginably dangerous.

One morning, as Tsering Dolma had stayed behind to work in the bungalow, I had to go to the hospital. I asked the driver, a former bodyguard to his Holiness, to let me drive. Everything went fine until the first bend where I did not brake hard enough and the car went off the road, rolling over three times. The shock forced the door open and I was thrown out. As I fell, a piece of metal struck my head and I fainted.

Luckily my passenger got out of the car unharmed. As I always carried an enormous pile of documents around with me, his first reaction was to save the papers which had been scattered all over the hill and which had each child's details noted on them. Then, after calling me several times, he went round the car and discovered me trapped under the chassis. I was still breathing. He was able to push the car off me, saw that my face was covered with blood, got me out, dragged me with difficulty to the side of the road and carried me back to the bungalow. Amala uttered a shriek of horror at the sight of my gaping head wound which was bleeding profusely.

After checking that I had not broken anything, the Swiss Red Cross doctor bandaged my head and decided to take me to the hospital at Ludhiana, five hours' drive from Dharamsala, which was run by American missionaries and had an X-ray room. I swallowed a large quantity of analgesics and the doctor settled me comfortably in the Mercedes that the community of Tibetan refugees in Switzerland had just presented to His Holiness.

To start with, the pills enabled me to sleep, but the end of the journey was much worse as my head and back were hurting badly. As soon as I arrived I was taken into the emergency ward. My head, neck, and spinal column were X-rayed, revealing a series of injuries to the vertebrae. I had to be put in plaster. The head wound required stitches and the American doctor wanted to shave off my hair. I refused, which created a long and tiresome discussion that I won because, in the end, he only shaved the area around the wound. I ended up spending six weeks in hospital.

I had made a new friend in Dharamsala: Bina Cumming, a voluntary worker who did not speak Tibetan. She decided to come to Ludhiana to keep me company. The nurses gave her a bed next to mine. Bina washed my hair carefully and pushed me around in a wheelchair. We visited the Tibetan patients in the hospital, especially the children. I was not particularly docile, often refusing to take the medicine which the doctors prescribed to calm the pain, which at times became unbearable.

I was at last able to return to Dharamsala, although I continued to be in pain. Amala decided to consult Dr Yeshi Dhonden. This was my first real contact with Tibetan medicine and its practices, which are influenced by Buddhism. Yeshi Dhonden asked me a few questions, examined my eyes, tongue and urine. Then he took my pulse, a very important method of diagnosing. He placed three fingers on the radial artery, beginning with the right wrist and then taking the left one (with a man he would have begun with the left wrist). I felt him exercising different pressures. He explained that in this way he was able to detect any problems in the skin, flesh or bones. Dr Dhonden impressed me enormously. He made up some medicines which he said would bring about a fairly rapid improvement in my condition. Before leaving the hospital at Ludhiana, I had asked if there was anything else, apart from analgesics, for alleviating the pain; the doctors had replied in the negative. Yeshi Dhonden had demonstrated that this was not so.

After about ten days I felt better and, above all, no longer had back or head pains. I felt terribly guilty because my sister had to take on a great deal of extra work because of me. By the time I was once more able to be of use, it was nearly 17 May, an important date for the Nursery for Tibetan Refugee Children as it was its fourth birthday. The nursery had grown to the extent that it was now a real children's village.

His Holiness used to receive a great many foreign visitors. In the evening he would tell us about his conversations. One day, the priests of the Jesuit college of St Joseph came to Dharamsala; among them was Father Stanford, who had been my nephew's headmaster and who also knew me very well. When I had my car crash, he had expressed his concern to my family. He asked me if I had driven again since then, adding that if I waited any longer I would probably never dare to. In fact, I did not drive at all. Even today, I do not feel secure in a car if I do not know the driver very well.

Tsering Dolma had started to complain of pains in her legs, but nevertheless refused to use the car at her disposal, saying that this would save petrol. In spite of her more and more obvious suffering, she continued to leave the bungalow very early in the morning, going round the village on foot and returning late in the evening. She devoted her life to the children and paid little attention to her own health. In the evening, a servant massaged her legs at length and begged her to consult a doctor. Tsering Dolma eventually agreed to be examined by a Belgian woman, Dr Cécile de Swemmer, who worked at the Ludhiana hospital. Suspecting a uterus problem, she asked my sister to go to New Delhi as soon as possible to undergo additional tests, but she refused to go.

His Holiness, accompanied by Lobsang Samten and his bodyguards, spent a lot of time in the village. The Dalai Lama was like a father to all the children. He spoke to them, saw how they were getting on with their Tibetan writing and always told them that they were the 'hope of Tibet' and the 'seed for the future Tibet'. When a new group of children arrived, my sister took them to have an audience with His Holiness, who explained to them the importance of education and the rules of hygiene that had to be respected to remain in good health. I was always astonished to see how serious the children were after meeting His Holiness, as if they now felt invested with a mission. Most of them still remembered clearly the horror and suffering that they had been through and knew that they no longer had a country.

We planned a large celebration for 17 May 1964 in His Holiness's presence, with representatives of the Indian government and many other guests. The festivities were to last for three days. The children learnt dances and folk songs for the occasion.

As was the custom, we organized a huge picnic near Dal Lake, which at that season was nearly dry. The site, surrounded by forests, was magnificent. A tent was put up in a clearing for His Holiness, as well as other tents for the dignitaries and guests. Speeches were, of course, given. The children gave their performance and we then distributed sweets. It was a marvellous day for the heads of the village, the nurses, and all the voluntary workers and staff sent by the charities.

His Holiness mixed with the children, drinking tea and tasting their dishes and looking at how they were prepared. Games were organized, including sack races and skipping. The nurses also joined in and the children shouted encouragement to their foster mothers. The ground resounded with cries of joy.

Tsering Dolma had a tremendous time playing basketball and volleyball. Nobody could imagine that she was seriously ill. When, however, at the end of the three days of festivities, it was time to start work again, my sister remained in the bungalow. His Holiness forced her to go to New Delhi to have a complete medical examination, at the same time reassuring her that everything would be looked after in the village. He said that Kelsang La would help me and that I was very responsible.

Tsering Dolma and her husband Phuntsok Tashi set off for the Indian capital, where Gyalo Thondup and Diki Dolkar met them. His Holiness's secretaries wrote to my nephew Tenzin Ngawang, who was at Cambridge University, and to my niece, Khando Tsering, who was at school in Switzerland. Gyalo Thondup decided that it was best to entrust my sister to some doctor friends who had lived in Calcutta since the late 1950s. They caught a plane there, and then, several days later, we learnt the terrible news: Tsering Dolma was suffering from cancer.

She needed to be operated on immediately. His Holiness was informed immediately and advised sending our sister to

London. She left for England in October. Tsering Dolma survived the operation, but medical attention had come far too late. She died in London in November 1964, aged 44. Her husband and two children were with her when she died.

The news hit Dharamsala. Tsering Dolma had devoted her life to the children in exile. She had created from scratch the structures which had enabled hundreds to avoid almost certain death and, after the first urgent medical care, to receive little by little a sound education in a climate of love, tenderness and understanding.

Faced with death, Tibetans remain practical. The body no longer has much importance after death, except in the case of an important lama, a rinpoche. Because of the wood shortage in many regions of Tibet, only very important people were cremated. Most bodies were cut into pieces and fed to the vultures – the last act of a compassionate person. The thought of our bodies being fed to animals after our death did not worry us. Some bodies were thrown into a river or lake to feed fish.

To bring Tsering Dolma's body back to Dharamsala was out of the question. After her cremation in London, her ashes were brought back by my brother-in-law, Phuntsok Tashi. The astrologer made a pronouncement and we began the rituals that marked the beginning of 49 days of mourning, carried out by the entire population of Dharamsala. The butter lamps burnt continuously. Every seven days new offerings were made to the deceased. As Tsering Dolma's soul was still near to us, we offered it tea and food as a sign of respect. At the end of the period of mourning she would be reborn elsewhere. We performed pujas, and then gave khatas before receiving condolences.

Normally, the deceased's ashes are dispersed in the mountains or in a river. We took the unusual decision to preserve Tsering Dolma's ashes in an urn in the Tibetan Children's Village. Perhaps one day, when we return to Tibet, we will take them with us.

During the days that followed my sister's death, I felt completely lost. I was 24 and very heavy responsibilities weighed on my shoulders. It did not occur to me to avoid them, though. Every day there were new challenges to be faced: food, blankets and clothes to be found; cases of chickenpox or other infections to be dealt with and new children kept pouring in. I knew that the entire family expected me to take over from Tsering Dolma as quickly as possible.

Fortunately, His Holiness still lived in our bungalow. When I returned in the evening, the audience room was full of people. His Holiness gave unsparingly of himself to preserve the Tibetan culture. The government in exile also worked very hard. Besides education, priority was given to the Department of Home which was attempting to conduct a census of all the refugees. A Department of Religion and a Security Council in charge of the protection of the Dalai Lama had also been created.

Even though we were still all living together in the bungalow, Tsering Dolma's death left an immense emptiness. At 64, Amala continued to look after His Holiness. She also spent a great deal of time praying and was even learning to read so as to be able to read prayers; she had also asked me to show her how to sign her name in English. Amala was a good pupil, assimilating these new tasks with considerable ease.

In spite of all the work, I continued to correspond with my friends. I wrote to Heidrun Bartch, a German school friend, and she came to spend six months helping us. Legjin Tsering was then staying in the United States; I told her about my difficulties and she too came to join me. She stayed with us at Swargashram, which we called the Palace, and helped with secretarial tasks in His Holiness's Private Office. With a degree in economics, she could correct the reports prepared by the Tibetan civil servants for the Indian government and various charities. In the evening, she taught Amala English. My mother spent long hours walking in the nearby forest. When she returned, she would tell us about who she had met and what she had seen: her conversation with a shepherd, the liveliness of a snake, the passage of a group of monkeys. She loved to picnic with an aya who spoke Hindi. Amala would often come to the children's village and talk with the little ones and the staff and hand round sweets. The children always looked forward to His Holiness's and Amala's visits.

Of course, Amala also kept His Holiness company when he managed to take a few moments' rest. In spite of all the visits and his many concerns, he still managed to study Buddhist philosophy with his tutors. When we wanted to talk to him, we just had to push the door open. After my sister's death, I often turned towards His Holiness for advice or help in making the right decisions. Although sometimes he must have had enough of my coming in to ask for yet more advice, he never showed it. The children's wellbeing was very important to him.

There were then 100 Tibetans working in the village. I was very grateful to Kelsang La, my sister's secretary, for her remarkable work. I had acquired very theoretical notions of secretarial work, but now I mainly had to resolve human problems. Though I had to make all the decisions, I learnt a lot from Kelsang La, even though she was two or three years younger than me.

Everyone worked without stopping and the nurses did not know which way to turn. The teachers did their best to ensure that proper teaching was given. We suffered, however, from the inadequate size of our buildings. The children were accommodated at Conium House, Egerton Hall, Kishore Nivas or Kashmir Cottage.

I must say that I had much more difficulty dealing with the adults than with the children. I discovered the complexity of personal relationships. I spoke about this to His Holiness, because I could not understand how adults could argue in the presence of these children who had so much need of help, love and understanding. His Holiness reassured me, saying that if everyone was perfect, our existence would have no justification and we would have no place in the world.

I have never forgotten His Holiness's answer. In a few words he had summed up the essential message of Buddhist teaching. Some people suffer more, others less. Reality can be difficult to face, or not so difficult; but the degree of difficulty we experience is determined by the acts of our previous existence. We therefore live according to our karma. Some people find this easy to understand; others, even after lengthy explanations, cannot understand.

I managed to deal with differences of opinion, in spite of my youthful impatience. I considered that it was not enough to work from nine to five, because the children required a continual presence. When a charity or representatives of the Indian government asked for information on any of the children, or wished to know about a project's budget, a delay was unacceptable. Help, of which we had the greatest need, depended on our replies. Kelsang La and her two brothers, who had just graduated, sometimes stayed behind with me very late working on these urgent matters.

The children continued to flow in. I therefore decided to

reorganize the village to cope with the 800 children who now lived there. One day, some voluntary workers came to see me. They were exhausted and raised a crucial question: 'Pema-la, we can't manage any more. Every day we have to deal with about 15 children called Tenzin, 20 called Dolma, 30 called Tashi; how can you expect us to cope?' Doris Betts, an English nurse, suggested giving a number to each of the children and making a kind of identity card which could easily be worn around the neck at all times. We therefore bought some very thin aluminium sheets that we then pierced and engraved. Number 1 now lives in Switzerland and Number 2 in Australia; they are both now nearly 40. Each card had inscribed on it the child's name and also that of his parents and where he came from. A copy was kept in the dispensary. The Swiss doctors and some of the nurses did not like the system; I explained to them that at least it would avoid vaccinating the same child twice or giving him unsuitable medicine.

Of course, implementing this card system was no small matter. It took us ages because everything had to be done by hand. Every day we took 15 children, looked up their details in the files and transferred the necessary information, in English, onto the cards. The work of the nurses and doctors of the charities was in this way made much simpler.

By 1965, after five years of exile, Dharamsala was much transformed. The days of the deserted-looking town already seemed very far off. On our arrival, the Indian authorities had requisitioned several buildings to rent to Tibetan refugees. The government in exile had then fixed three priorities: to find shelter for everyone, to provide food and clothing, and to provide work. It did not matter if several people were living in the same room, if tents had to be shared or if civil servants had to work in offices that were much too small. The Tibetan rehabilitation plan for refugees did not aim to provide permanent facilities. We did not talk about permanent buildings because, for one thing, they exceeded our means, and, more importantly, we hoped that the exile would not last. Our only concern was to meet everyone's needs and to obtain sufficient food and medication for those who were ill. The first building, built at the end of 1964, was a children's hospital.

10

The First Sponsored Children

During the winter of 1964/65, 134 more children arrived from Nepal. Exhausted by their journey, they were practically all suffering from gastroenteritis. Ten children had died on the way. As there was no more room in the village, we had to rent some empty houses in Lower Dharamsala for them.

After examining the children, the Red Cross doctor asked us to buy some glucose as quickly as possible. Unfortunately, we did not have the necessary equipment to put each of them on a drip. I asked the foster mothers and the voluntary workers to help me. Some of them prepared a mixture of black tea and glucose, while others made the children drink this strange mixture very slowly from a spoon. The children suffered dreadfully from stomach cramps, and there was nothing worse than having to listen to their cries of pain, especially as we could do nothing to alleviate their suffering because we were so short of resources.

It was even more difficult to imagine what their mental sufferings could be. In Tibet, they had heard adults talking about the terrible fate of their neighbours, friends or even people they did not know – but all Tibetans. The children understood that they were fleeing from an increasingly dangerous situation; at the same time, they realized that they now had nothing. They were trudging like robots towards an unfamiliar destination. It took them several weeks, sometimes several months, to once again enjoy life.

I took the new arrivals for an audience with His Holiness, as Tsering Dolma had been accustomed to doing. I was amazed by their extraordinary eagerness to learn. Even at six or seven, they already had an acute sense of their own responsibilities.

Only very few of us were qualified to teach Tibetan or the prayers, dances and folk songs. Even fewer were able to teach English to 'my' children. We still did not have any classrooms so lessons took place outside on the slope of the hill. When it rained, the children took shelter on the veranda or, if there was not enough room, under the huge trees, where they also sat in the summer to shelter from the strong sun. The teachers took the children outside in groups, carrying under their arms chalks and a piece of material which, unrolled and fixed to a tree trunk, served as a blackboard. The village buzzed with life.

There were three different reception centres for the children which helped in organizing our work. However, as I have already mentioned, there was a shortage of teachers. During my sister's time, a request had been sent to the Indian government and they agreed to pay some of the teachers' salaries. And so, to the Tibetan teachers and the handful of volunteers who taught English, were added teachers who taught Hindi to the children.

The dispensary took in the sick, but it was always overcrowded and the staff were overworked. The Swiss Red Cross doctors remained on average for two years, rarely longer. Those who spent a year with us, left as soon as their replacement arrived in Dharamsala. Sometimes they prolonged their stay by an extra month, telling the new team about the most common illnesses and how to look after the exiled children. In the early days, the Swiss Red Cross delegated two nurses, the Save the Children Fund, UK made funds available with which to build a hospital, and Swiss Aid to Tibetans made donations for a new dormitory. But in spite of this growing international mobilization, we still did not have enough room.

By 1965, over 85,000 Tibetan refugees had arrived in India. His Holiness requested the Indian government to allocate some land for them on which to resettle. Hundreds of Tibetans left the roadwork camps to go to different regions of the country where the State government had most kindly given land for the resettlement of the Tibetan refugees. Most of the land that was given was forest so the first thing that our people had to do when they arrived was to clear away the dense jungle. They dug wells and built houses. Life was not easy and they had to work hard; on top of this was the hot climate which they had to get used to. Having always lived high up in the mountains, it was most difficult to adjust to this new situation and many of our people lost their lives as they could not acclimatize. The refugees were divided into 'families' of five people. Each group of five people received a house with three rooms and about five acres of land. This system was followed in nearly all the settlements. In some of the settlements there was some arrangement for schooling the children and so they were able to join their parents, but mostly the parents who joined these settlements left the children in our care. Therefore, the number of children rose constantly and the need to feed and clothe them was a terrible worry for us all.

As the years went by, new difficulties arose, but everyone still hoped for a rapid return to Tibet. This conviction enabled them to endure all kinds of suffering and to survive in very difficult conditions, but it also created situations that counteracted the projects set up by the government in exile in liaison with the Indian authorities. The immigrants sent to the settlements imagined that they would be staying there for only a limited period of time and thus, it must be said, did not do very much to improve their living conditions.

When the Indian or Swiss agricultural experts showed them what sorts of fruit trees would be best for their land, the refugees asked questions like: 'How long does it take for a banana tree or a coconut tree to give fruit?' When they were told that it would take from five to seven years, the Tibetans burst out laughing, explaining that they would not be around then to taste the fruit.

Seasons succeeded one another. His Holiness continued to try and find a solution to the Tibetan problem, but every day conditions in Tibet went from bad to worse. The obvious had to be accepted. Our immediate future was going to be abroad, in India, Nepal and Bhutan. We slowly realized that we would have to build a strong base in exile in order to preserve our culture, religion and identity, and in this way prepare for our eventual return to Tibet. Education was one of our priorities, economic development in the settlements another.

The government bodies and charities gave us a lot of money. These sums usually went through the Central Relief Committee for Tibetan Refugees, set up by Mr and Mrs Achariya Kripalani and Kaliyan Sen Gupta. Tsering Dolma had made many contacts that were now bearing fruit. When I took over responsibility for the village, I kept in touch with these organizations, besides writing to many new organizations and people whom I had met during my studies. In order to deal with the cheques that were now regularly sent to me, I opened an account in the name of the Nursery for Tibetan Refugee Children.

One day in 1965, the Indian Ministry of Eternal Affairs summoned me to New Delhi, together with Mrs Taring who ran the Tibetan Home Foundation in Mussoorie. The visit began in a disagreeable manner. The official explained to us that we could not receive funds directly from the donor agenices except for small token donations. I replied that these sums hardly ran into hundreds of dollars. They were usually small amounts sent by individuals, most often my friends, that varied between 10 and 100 American dollars. The official persisted, though, asking us to do things in the proper manner to avoid personal liability and possible harm to the children's village. Our meeting ended with my saying, 'If it's illegal, and if this creates problems, you'll simply have to put me in prison.' I returned to Dharamsala and continued to have the money put in the nursery's account.

Our efforts began to bear fruit. Individual contributions began to arrive in greater and greater numbers. Every day I sent reports describing the condition of the children at the village to people likely to give us help. I had seen how the Pestalozzi villages worked in Switzerland and Britain and this gave me the idea of creating a system of sponsorship for the children. Since 1960, Mrs Muhlmann, who lived in Hawaii, had sent us 100 dollars every month. I kept up a regular correspondence with her, telling her about our projects for the village and all the problems that needed to be solved. I fixed the amount for sponsoring a child at 10 dollars, a fairly large amount in India at the time, which would enable the child to be fed, clothed and educated.

Kelsang La and her brothers prepared files with photos of the children and their personal stories. I sent them to Mrs Muhlmann and many others, most of whom agreed to find sponsors. I also told her that I wanted to save her monthly contribution, as well as the other donations we received regularly. Our intention was to build a small bungalow for the sponsored children rather than a dormitory. The first house, costing 20,000 rupees, was built in

1966 and inaugurated on 17 May 1967. Twenty-five children were able to live there. This was so different from the dormitories where more than 100 children lived! This 'home' system worked wonders and enabled us to create a family atmosphere around the children, who continued to suffer from emotional trauma. A new life, in a home, with a foster father and mother to care for them, and brothers and sisters to share this home with. This could only help to heal their mental anguish and so I relentlessly continued the effort to build more homes.

One of the women who was looking after the children died two days after she had given birth to a son. The baby's father, Aku Tobgyal, used to work in the nursery doing all sorts of jobs, taking the children for walks in the forest, teaching them folk songs and dances. He was really fond of the children and they all loved being with him. Tobgyal was heartbroken at the loss of his wife and now, in addition to his very busy job, he had to take care of the baby. This was quite impossible. He did not know what to do and so, as good fortune would have it, Juliet, our English nurse who had been sent by Save the Children Fund, UK came to the rescue and took little baby Tenzin Chokla to live with her in her small quarters. She doted on him, watching over him as if he were her own child and buying him a pretty little basket that she put in her room. I was away from Dharamsala when the mother had died, and my sister was still alive and looking after the nursery. Everyone was very amused to see Juliet with her adopted baby. Time went by and then, one day, Juliet announced that she was leaving. She was going to marry an Indian army captain whom she had met in Dharamsala. Tenzin Chokla was by then six months old and it was impossible for her to take the infant with her.

In the end, I decided to look after him myself. I spoke to Amala about it first, explaining that the baby had never known the dormitory, and giving her the reasons for my attachment to him. Amala accepted my idea and helped me to prepare my bedroom. At home, everyone, including the servants, Amala and my sister, looked after the baby. Even so, Tenzin Chokla would cry every night at about two or three in the morning. As I was worried that he would wake His Holiness, I had to get up and take him in my arms and give him a bottle. If it was fine, I would walk him on the veranda, murmuring tender words to him and humming Tibetan songs.

I became more and more attached to this baby, who became the star of Swargashram. The bodyguards played with him in the garden and even His Holiness, whenever he saw him, broke into the marvellous laugh that is familiar to everyone today. Tenzin Chokla took his first steps with me. One day, after my sister's death, when he was nearly 18 months old, Amala said to me: 'You must be sensible. You can't keep this child here. He's got a father and he must get used to living with children of his own age. And then you must also think about your own life. You will also marry one day and have children.'

Amala's words were full of good sense. It nevertheless hurt me a lot to give up Tenzin Chokla. The morning that I took him to the nursery, his father was very happy to see him back again. That evening I cried with sadness, missing him terribly. I made up for this absence by going to his dormitory every day to look after him. After a few days had gone by, I could see that in the end he was really very happy to be with the other children. This did not prevent me from spending a little more time with the toddlers in his group, though.

His Holiness continued to receive many visitors in Dharamsala: Indian government officials, foreign representatives, or people who came just to offer him their support. The government in exile was completely overworked. The Tibetan situation was inevitably raised during these audiences. When His Holiness had tea with us or, on Sundays, a meal, I could feel that he was deeply hurt by the atrocities of the Chinese communists on the Tibetan people.

Sometimes he left the 'palace' for a long walk, surrounded by bodyguards. He loved these mountain walks which gave him an opportunity for reflection. Sometimes Amala and I would go with him, but he walked much too fast for us. He would reach the top of the hill in two and a half hours, a good hour before we did. He liked to spend ten days up there at a place called Truind, or at Dharamkot; however, this did not mean that he was not kept fully informed. Each morning, at about ten, and each afternoon at about four, he talked with his private office by walkie-talkie and, if there was anything urgent, immediately went back down again.

I found it very moving to be up in the mountains with His Holiness. Those times were very special, and would not have happened if we had been living in Tibet. I managed to confide in him a lot and we talked about my work, the growing housing problem, the first sponsorships – and about the future.

After Tsering Dolma's death, my brother-in-law came to live with our family. It was then that I first mentioned the possibility of my marrying. Amala considered that as it was my future that was in question, the choice was entirely mine to make. Young men had already been to the house to ask for my hand, but Amala invariably gave them the same reply: that the decision was mine.

John and Didi Toulouse were then living in New Delhi, where they ran a support group called the American Emergency Committee for Tibetan Refugees. They regularly came to spend a few days in Dharamsala with their friend, a nurse from Switzerland, working for the Swiss Red Cross, called Josie Harder. She would prepare an excellent raclette with the cheese that she brought in her luggage. She also cooked rostis. There was another nurse, Doris Betts (Save the Children Fund, UK), who at 50 was a real live wire. Doris considered that the young voluntary workers, who came in ever greater numbers from Switzerland, Canada, Britain and Australia, had the right to have fun. So three or four times a year, she organized parties late in the evening when work was over, in the meadows next to Dal Lake, for around 20 young people. Some of the other slightly older Tibetans did not really approve. We gave them chairs so that they could chaperone us during our amusements, while at the same time saying a few mantras. Doris organized the games and, at the end of the evening, we danced. I particularly enjoyed an American dance that resembled the Tibetan dance called *gorshe*.

Josie had become John and Didi Toulouse's accomplice and was forever telling me that I should be careful not to end up an old maid. One day, Didi rang me and asked me to come to New Delhi as fast as possible. This was impossible, though, because of my work. Didi then turned to Josie, who had come to see me, and insisted that I accompany her to the Indian capital to buy some medicine.

The operation was masterfully prepared. On my arrival in New Delhi, John and Didi announced in unison: 'We've found you a husband at last!' At dinner that evening I met Lhundup Gyalpo again, whom I had known since my childhood in

Darjeeling. At St Joseph, his brother had been one of my nephew's best friends. After this evening with our friends, Lhundup Gyalpo asked to see me again. Didi did not stop tormenting me: 'Hurry up, or otherwise someone else will take him.' Lhundup Gyalpo came from a Kham family who had lived in Lhasa before the Chinese invasion, trading between India and Lhasa and also with China. At the time of our meeting, his father lived in Kalimpong and his mother had just died. Lhundup Gyalpo, two years my senior, worked for an organization called TIRS (Tibetan Industrial and Rehabilitation Society). Set up by a New Zealander, it helped refugees to start craft companies with funds from Australia and New Zealand. Before that, Lhundup Gyalpo had had to leave school early as his family needed him as an interpreter. Later on he was able to continue his studies in Britain.

Lhundup Gyalpo's brother, who had just returned from Germany where he was studying, accompanied him to Dharamsala to ask my mother for my hand. Gyalo Thondup and Diki Dolkar also met Lhundup Gyalpo and gave a generally favourable opinion of him. I set off for Kalimpong, where our wedding was celebrated on 13 November 1965.

We spent less than a week together in New Delhi. After discussing how we should live together after the wedding, we had to admit that it was impossible to live as newly-weds in the family home at Kalimpong while so many Tibetans were suffering. We chose to put our work first, which meant living separately for several months. Lhundup Gyalpo therefore remained in New Delhi and I went back to live with Amala.

Nothing really changed in my life in Dharamsala now that I was married. I got on marvellously with Amala and I was particularly spoilt by my brothers. All the same, I had a very difficult character! For instance, when Amala cooked a dish that I thought not quite perfect, I always pointed it out to her. At work, I always wanted things to happen very fast. Amala said that my behaviour risked hurting people and that, because of my impatience, it could be humiliating. For example, when I asked a servant to do something, I often found her too slow and usually ended up doing it myself.

Sometimes, I must admit, I was just simply disagreeable. One day, when we were overwhelmed by work at the office, I asked for some information on one of the children. An elderly man, whose job it was to write the children's names and story in a huge book, began to search. I tore the register from his hands and began anxiously to look for the name myself. Not finding it any easier to discover, I went up to the poor man and gave him a great whack on the head with the book.

As I never hid anything from Amala, I told her about this incident and she immediately reprimanded me. One evening I met one of the oldest members of the Kashag, then in charge of Religious Affairs, at home. Amala had probably spoken to him about my behaviour towards the people who worked with me. We had a long discussion. One of his sentences is engraved on my memory: 'You are Jetsun Pema and you have your own personality, but never forget that you are also the sister of the Dalai Lama. Under no circumstances do you have the right to cause him discredit.'

After this, before making a remark to one of the foster mothers, I first of all imagined the tasks that they had to accomplish in the home. Every day, they each had to wash, dress, and feed 50 children aged between six and eight. This was a very tough job.

Amala thought that now I was married, I should learn to cook. I already knew how to embroider and knit: now it was the turn of the stove. My mother decided to begin with the preparation of different noodles. She explained why it was preferable to use a board rather than a bowl, and that in Amdo, one made a hole in the middle of the flour and slowly poured the water in. Putting Amala's advice into practice, I poured the water into the flour. Unfortunately it went everywhere and it therefore seemed to me wiser to use a basin. The dough would be poorly kneaded, replied Amala. Finally, seeing that I was not really ready for this task, she gave up.

From 1965 to 1970, the fate of the refugees remained precarious; my family's future was also uncertain, even though in many ways we could consider ourselves privileged. All the jewellery of Amala and Tsering Dolma had by now been sold. Our material needs were not great, and when we thought about the condition of our people, our own condition was of little concern to us. Gyalo Thondup gave a little money to Amala. Living together in the bungalow, we mutually sustained one another. How could we possibly lose confidence when His Holiness confronted all his people's ills with such remarkable courage? He continued to console the new refugees who came to recount the horrors that their families had endured.

The first 25 sponsored children were settled in the home that had been built for them. On 17 May 1967, His Holiness inaugurated this new building that was so full of promise for the future. All the children kept up a correspondence with their sponsors, the content of which evolved from month to month. To start with, they sent drawings that related to their life in Tibet: farms full of animals, prayer flags, nomads' tents, and yaks amidst the snow-covered mountains. Little by little, the children began to draw houses with flowers; sometimes they wrote a few words. Then, small drawings of a tree or a bunch of flowers illustrated a few sentences such as: I am called ..., my age is ..., I am in such and such a class. The sponsors were delighted to receive these letters. Two or three years later, the letters began with 'Dear sponsor' or 'Dear sponsor family'. Of course, this progress motivated the families even more. Through the child's story, they now began to have a fairly precise picture of Tibet. When sponsors talked about their role to friends and colleagues, many others decided to become sponsors. Thus, within four years, we went from a handful of generous sponsors to several hundred. For our children, who were mostly orphans who knew nothing of the fate of their parents, it was important for them to be able to say: 'Somewhere in France, or Germany, or Switzerland or the United States, a family or somebody is concerned about my future. There is still someone who fond of me.' This gave much hope and security for the children and this also created international understanding. Most of our sponsors for the children were not rich people but they were all people with a big heart and who felt deeply for our children. Many sponsors had to make sacrifices to send their sponsored child the money each year. There were many sponsors who continued to help their children for 10 to 15 years. We have sponsors who have been sponsoring two generations of children. We are very much indebted to them and our sincere gratitude goes out to each and every one of them.

We had settled on a budget of 10 dollars per child per month to be used for food, clothing and education. However, to start with we had many more children than sponsors and the money was used for everyone. Every day it was necessary to negotiate for rations of rice, flour and other foods with the head of the

Indian camp. This was when I learnt to delegate responsibility. The effect was immediate: I had a little less work and those around me were much more motivated.

Once the first home was built, I wrote to various organizations to ask for their help so that we could build similar houses. But it was necessary to buy land for such projects. In 1966, His Holiness made a first contribution of 25,000 rupees and the Norwegian Refugee Council gave the remaining 100,000 rupees. Forty-three acres were bought, in the Dalai Lama's name, from a family called Suri who lived in Nangal. As soon as this transaction became known, numerous organizations gave their financial support for the construction of further bungalows. On each occasion, the children organized a celebration and, on 17 May 1970, the anniversary of the Nursery for Tibetan Refugee Children, His Holiness came to inaugurate the new homes. The scarcity of water was yet another problem. We were able to install a water connection exclusively for the use of the TCV from a water source on the mountainside – a distance of about 8 kms. It was no easy task since all the pipes had to be carried up the mountain individually by our own staff.

We were now confronted with a new problem: the overcrowding of the boarding schools that the Indian government had made available to us. I therefore decided to expand the teaching facilities in Dharamsala by arranging for the classes, which at that time ended at the sixth form, to continue. It was necessary to improve the standard of teaching. We were joined by monks and also by young men who had just graduated and whom we quickly trained.

Little by little, our education system improved, but it was still inadequate. More and more foreigners began to be interested in our children and to sponsor them. In the late 60s and early 70s, sponsorship enabled us to obtain more funds to give the children a modern education, albeit one grounded in Tibetan culture and religion. In fact, this was our first priority.

In Tibet, the schools had not developed a regulated system of education. It was an entirely new concept for us and, I must admit, I worried about it a lot. I was neither a specialist in education nor a trained teacher. I therefore once again decided to turn to the Indian government for help. They consented to open a new grant-in-aid facility and also sent us a headmaster. Our aim was to develop a Tibetan education for our children that would preserve their identity so that later on they could be proud of their roots and religion.

In any case I eventually came to terms with the idea of the new headmaster's arrival, because our need for money was so great. A Muslim from central India arrived at the beginning of 1969, and rapidly transformed the school into a rigid, strict organization. I had always believed that children needed a certain amount of freedom, and the more time went by, the more this situation made me unhappy. I was convinced of the absolute necessity for an independent school.

I asked the headmaster to give us a day's holiday so that we could celebrate the Tibetan festival Prayer for Peace, which falls on the fifteenth day of the fifth month of the Tibetan calendar. He refused, saying that the day was not an Indian public holiday. He said that there was no reason why he should comply with this request and that we should strictly follow the decree that applied to all schools on Indian territory. I was very shocked by his reaction and disliked this man who did so little to promote our culture. This headmaster also recruited Indian teachers, and so more and more we came up against a complete lack of sensitivity towards our circumstances.

We received a lot of tinned food, most of which contained pork, which was not acceptable to Muslims. A serious language difficulty was another problem. The headmaster did not know any Tibetan and the foster mothers in my team did not speak English. The difficulties accumulated and I did not know what to do. The day of the Muslim New Year, a foster mother arrived in the office in tears, terribly shocked. She had just seen the headmaster slitting a goat's throat under his veranda; its cry of agony had startled the whole village. The sight of this poor beast, with its throat slit and the blood spurting, was unbearable to her. My explanations to the elder Tibetans had no effect. There was only one course of action: relations were severed with the headmaster. Faced with an atmosphere that had now become too charged, he asked for a transfer, which he obtained without difficulty. In 1971, a second headmaster, also Muslim, but younger, was appointed by the Indian ministry. We had much less difficulty in working with him and in exchanging points of view. He even agreed that we could conduct interviews before the appointment of an Indian teacher. To this end, we drew up a questionnaire for each candidate; this was, of course, completely illegal. These questions allowed us to have an idea of their feelings towards Tibet and its culture and religion.

By now, 3,500 children had passed through the Nursery for Tibetan Refugee Children to attend other schools, or to be adopted. A growing number of them were sponsored and the financial situation of the village improved considerably. Although the provision of adequate food and clothing remained one of our main priorities, the children's future would depend on their receiving a modern education.

We now had sufficient funds to envisage taking on more responsibility and directing our own destiny. Therefore, in 1978 I wrote to the Indian government to say that we no longer needed the headmaster. When the headmaster was withdrawn the India government also stopped the grant-in-aid money. Before taking this decision I had talked to everyone. They all agreed with me, even the Tibetan teachers paid by the Indian government whose salaries would drop considerably. From now on, we were free to develop our own educational programme for the Tibetan children.

To give children an education steeped in the religion, language and history of their country was not an easy task, even with our newly acquired independence. And because Buddhism is not just a philosophy, but also a way of life, we could not consider teaching it in the same way as we had in the past when we were still in Tibet. We took the children to visit temples and sometimes important lamas came to teach them certain aspects of our religion. The monks explained the essentials of Buddhism and taught them how to put these into practice. It was no longer a matter of learning a sacred text by heart and reciting it in class the next day, but of understanding the prayers. It was important to tell the children why a particular prayer to the goddess of wisdom enabled merit to be accumulated for a future life, or how a mantra could stimulate the mind. The children benefitted much from this and we were very pleased at their progress.

We taught the law of karma to the youngest children from their earliest schooling on. The monks taught them the story of the Buddha: 'Siddhartha Gautama lived in the north of India in the sixth century BC. His father, Suddhodana, reigned over the kingdom of Sakya. His mother was the Queen Maya. At 16 he married the beautiful young princess Yashodhara. They lived a luxurious existence in a palace, free from all worries. One day, going out secretly with a servant, he met in succession an old man, a sick man, a funeral procession and an itinerant monk. Revolted by human suffering, he decided to search for ways to overcome it. At 29, just after the birth of his only son, Rahula, he abandoned his kingdom. Becoming an ascetic, he wandered around the Ganges valley for six years and met masters of all the religions, which he studied and practised one after another. None of them enabled him to find peace. Meditating under a tree, known ever since as the Bodhi Tree or Tree of Enlightenment, at Budh Gaya on the banks of the river Nairanjana, Siddhartha attained enlightenment. From that day onwards he was known as the Buddha, that is to say the Enlightened One. He was then 35. He transmitted to the group of five ascetics who accompanied him the teaching that would enable them to attain enlightenment. Then, for 45 years he taught everyone, from kings to beggars, the correct path to follow. He died at the age of 80 in Kushinagara, leaving behind the keys with which all people would free themselves from all servitude. His final piece of advice was: "Be your own lamp."'

As the children grew up the monks went into more detail, explaining to them for instance the Four Noble Truths, a teaching that Buddha discovered when he was enlightened and which contains the heart of his message: 'According to Buddha, man is his own master and no higher being or power exists to control his destiny. Through his personal effort and his intelligence, man has the power to free himself from all servitude. Each person's emancipation depends on his understanding of truth. Everyone is therefore responsible for his own happiness and unhappiness; but he who is able to discover the real nature of the connections that co-ordinate the infinite pattern of cause and effect, will have broken the internal circle and be delivered.'

During the celebrations, the children said prayers at a ceremony in a temple or simply on the school veranda. In this way, they gradually developed close ties with our culture and religion. However, unlike us and our grandparents, they had monks who took time to explain the treasures of Buddhism to them. By putting these teachings into practice, the children came to understand the importance of not stealing or lying. If one day you visit our school at Dharamsala, do not be surprised if you see a small child save an ant that is about to drown in a puddle or pick up a worm lost on the road and bury it in the ground again. That is also part of Buddhist teaching: do not kill, be good to all forms of life.

In spite of this, it is not easy to put religious principles into practice. Today, we are still trying to find an appropriate textbook with prayers and parables so that the Buddha's message can enlighten the children's sensibility.

We still follow the curriculum laid down by the Indian government. We want to give an education that has official recognition so that the children leaving our schools can go on to study at universities in India or the West. Ever since the day when I decided to make our schools independent, we have tried to liberalize our education system, but have nevertheless remained under the tutelage of the Central Board of Secondary Education (CBSE), Delhi which also controls the books we use. There appears to be little flexibility within this system, but in fact that first examination does not take place until the child is 15 or 16 years old. Between pre-primary school and the ninth form, we are free to make the best use of our time. During these first years we concentrate mainly on teaching the history and geography of Tibet, as well as our traditions. Most of the children are orphans and even the others have usually heard only a few tales from their parents. Since 1986, the classes have been held in Tibetan, up to the fifth form. The other subjects taught are mathematics, social sciences, English as a first language, Tibetan as a second language and Hindi as a third. In infant school the children learn English and Tibetan, and Hindi is taught from the third form to the eighth.

11

I Become 'Amala'

Our life in Dharamsala was becoming organized. The village was opening up to the world. The ghost town we had discovered on our arrival in 1960 had been transformed and a new town seemed to be rising, phoenix-like, from the ashes. The Tibetans even began to open restaurants and set up new stalls. Everyone tried to manage as best they could, their objective being to survive exile. As for the government in exile, it was extremely active.

I now had two little girls, Tenzin Choedon, born in 1966, and Kelsang Yangzom, born in 1968. My mother looked after Tenzin most of the time, because two weeks after giving birth I was already back in the office. One day, my daughter wouldn't stop crying. We had no powdered milk, so Amala gave the baby her breast to calm her. As she did not have any milk, she said to me: 'My breasts no longer give milk, even though I raised 11 children!' Amala hoped to calm the infant's cries, but her breast rapidly began to hurt. She then decided to try a biscuit soaked in tea. To my great surprise the baby accepted this food without difficulty and was then quite calm. When she was three months old, I took Tenzin to work with me and she would lie in a cardboard box near my desk. She grew up in the midst of the Tibetan children's village and was like a mascot to us.

Amala was away during my second pregnancy. She spent nearly a year in Switzerland with my brother Lobsang and his wife Namgyal Lhamo before going to the United States to see Thubten Jigme Norbu and his family. On her return I went to meet her in New Delhi and she embraced my second child, Kalsang Yangzom.

I still wrote regularly to my friends. Legjin Tsering stayed for some time in Dharamsala. She was of invaluable help to me. Heidrun Bartch also came to stay, spending six months in the village in 1968, dealing with administrative tasks and teaching English. I greatly appreciated her presence, because we could talk about all sorts of things including memories of boarding school at Loreto Convent in Darjeeling.

One morning, when we were preparing a brochure for which she was taking the photographs, Heidrun came to see me: 'There is marijuana growing all round Dharamsala and I want to try it.' To dissuade her, I cried: 'It's dangerous. You have no idea what will happen to you.' My words did not have the slightest effect, though. The following morning, as Heidrun did not come into the office, I went to Home Number 2, where her room was. Lying in bed, covered with spots, she explained what had happened. She had picked some marijuana leaves and brewed them in a teapot: 'I swallowed this horrible mixture and suddenly felt awful, with a nasty headache.' She never touched marijuana again.

Heidrun had a talent for drawing. One of the windows of her room looked out on the children's room and one day she said to me: 'It's really not very agreeable to feel spied on.' After we had boarded the window with a plank of plywood, she remarked: 'Before, the children looked at me all the time; now, I've got this horrible piece of wood.' I replied: 'Why not paint it, or decorate it with a drawing?' She got started immediately. Every evening, she shut herself in her room and, whenever anyone visited her, hid her work under some material. Two months later she announced: 'I've finished! You can all come and have a look.' Heidrun had drawn the Potala and all around it had pasted posters saying 'Chinese, go home!' After Heidrun's departure the drawing remained in the window for a long while. When she got back to Germany, she met and married an American soldier and they went to live in South Carolina. I saw her again in Dharamsala in 1991. She introduced me to her son Ryan, then aged 12. When he saw a Lhasa apso, he asked his mother if he could take one of these dogs back to the United States.

Some of my friends from La Pelouse sponsored children. One of these friends lived in Liechtenstein and asked me for details on five of the children. When the time came to decide which one to sponsor, her husband thought that it was impossible to make a choice, so they sponsored all five. In 1993, my friend had sent her daughter, Tania, who spent several months looking after the infants. Her boyfriend, Markus, was very good at carpentry and repaired the cupboards and beds in the homes. Tania is now learning Tibetan and studying to be a journalist.

His Holiness was an example to all of us. His life was devoted to the Tibetans. Every day, he got up at four, prayed and meditated. After breakfast, he dealt with government business, then, in the afternoon, he gave audiences. I tried to be worthy of him and to give all of myself in my work for the children.

His Holiness was surrounded by all sorts of people on official business. I was lucky to associate with him in private and I was amazed by his energy. Once he was through with his official business, he would study English and kept himself constantly informed. He was very fond of scientific journals.

I remember Amala giving me a beautiful watch. When it stopped working, I took it to His Holiness, asking him to repair it for me. In opening the watch, he probably did it more harm than good, but the Dalai Lama is fired by the desire to always understand everything, including the workings of objects such as old watches, cameras and radiocassettes. President Roosevelt had given the thirteenth Dalai Lama a pocket watch with a very complicated movement; when he was still in Lhasa, His Holiness had taken it to pieces, but had not been able to put it together again. As for my watch, in the end I took it to be repaired in New Delhi.

Towards the end of the 60s, His Holiness assumed very heavy responsibilities and we had little time in which to talk. Today, an efficient organization has taken over much of the more urgent work. Nevertheless, the Dalai Lama did have time to find a pretty name for my first daughter, just after she was born. As my second child's birth approached, I thought that the time had come for His Holiness to move to somewhere more peaceful. He needed calm and solitude, and at Swargashram this was not always possible with so many toddlers around. So, in 1969, His Holiness moved into his present residence, a bungalow that had been found and restored by the government. It was neither grandiose nor majestic, just a simple place in which to meditate and work. An office and audience room were added. It overlooked a magnificent garden on a slope of the hill, where fruit trees and flowers had been planted.

His Holiness loves gardening and, when he has time, tends his plants. He was particularly fond of the orchid bulbs some Tibetans had given him. These do not like the cold so he had asked for a greenhouse to be built. The Dalai Lama also fed the birds which came and perched on the edge of his window. When I went to see him, my children were enchanted by the sight. There were a lot of nests in the garden and His Holiness also looked after any wounded birds that he found there.

Once a month we went to his new residence and Amala baked him his favourite bread or prepared a dish. When Lobsang Samten was present, they would talk for hours about the events in Tibet and the refugee communities.

His Holiness did not have any pets at this time. Several years later I brought a little rabbit back from Kulu for my eldest daughter. I was already living in the house where I live today. When Tenzin saw the animal she said that she wanted to show it to His Holiness. So, one Sunday, she set off towards the residence, a basket under her arm. His Holiness asked what was in the basket and Tenzin proudly produced the rabbit. His Holiness burst into laughter: 'He's very beautiful! I would love to keep him.' Without a moment's hesitation, Tenzin gave the animal to her uncle. This spontaneous gesture filled me with joy. Any Tibetan could have made it as it was so natural to give a present to the Dalai Lama. The animal lived for nine years. It was a rabbit with an exceptional karma, because it spent the winter in His Holiness's bedroom, sheltered in a comfortable rabbit hutch. When the weather was fine, His Holiness or the bodyguards would take it for a walk in the garden.

My family was very important in my life. I was lucky in having an exceptional mother and adorable children. My husband, Lhundup Gyalpo, worked in Bangalore. But I put the Tibetan children and my people's cause before my personal interests, and my daughters and son grew up fully aware of this choice; but I always devoted the little free time I had to them.

His Holiness had promulgated a draft democratic constitution for the Tibetan people in exile, with the hope of putting it into practice once back in Tibet. As for me, I tried to be democratic in my daily life, especially in the children's village. I considered that it was essential to promote team work. New ideas on education were fiercely argued at our meetings, where we also discussed the building of new classrooms and how the money that was arriving in ever larger amounts should be used.

I had to be very firm with the older people who could remember their arrival in Dharamsala and who had lost all they owned on the way. They would feverishly accumulate little stores in the school larder and in the treasury, while I on the contrary always preached that we should give as much as possible to the children. When there was a little left over at the end of the accounting year, I always tried to buy new clothes and more nourishing food. It was my opinion that if one day we found ourselves in serious need of money, donors would come to our aid. If we kept these reserves, the donors would lose the sense that their donations were being used well.

Although I was not always satisfied with the way work was done, I now managed to control myself and no longer lost my temper. After all, I had to show an example to my own children and the children of the village. Before taking a decision about allocating work, I always asked myself: 'What would I do if this decision concerned my own son or daughter?' Children are very sensitive beings and they often make very accurate judgments about the people who look after them. Becoming a mother also creates an enormous change in a woman's life, and it certainly had an important effect on my emotional and intellectual development.

On my return from Switzerland, the village children called me 'miss', whereas they called my sister 'Amala'. It was quite a shock the first time I was called Amala, by a 13-year-old boy. I later had the same feeling when my great-nephews pronounced the word 'mola', grandmother. To start with I felt a bit embarrassed, but I later learnt to value this precious link that bound me to all the young refugees.

The ultimate aim of all Tibetans is to return to Tibet, especially of those who, like myself, were brought up in India. We look after the children and prepare them to take on their responsibilities in a Tibet that we believe will once again be free. The young are the seeds of the future. The most important aspect of our mission in exile is to give the children a Tibetan education and teach them our language and culture. If we do not do this, we will not fulfil our duty and assure the survival of our nation.

His Holiness's presence at Dharamsala, since 1960, has relit the flame of hope, a flame that will never go out. He illuminates our path towards Tibet.

1971 was an important year. The Nursery for Tibetan Refugee Children was registered under the new name of the Tibetan Children's Village (TCV). The teachers used the Montessori method, which gave pupils freedom of action under their adult guidance. The children thus received a varied and complete education between the ages of three and six.

I refused to place the children in soulless dormitories. In order to create a family atmosphere around them, we took care to house together refugees of different ages, so that the oldest could look after the youngest. In each home, a foster mother and father, or sometimes just a mother, were in charge of about 25 children, who spent an average of six years in the home.

To start with, meals were cooked in a kitchen used by the entire TCV. Little by little, each home had a kitchen, and the children would help their foster parents with peeling vegetables and the preparation of certain dishes, with the exception of rice or the main course. In this way, as time went by, the homes became more and more independent. But the essential problem of organization still remained to be solved. We had to teach the adults to once again run family life. Most of the help we received was in kind. We handed these foodstuffs over to the foster parents, with a small amount of money to buy the children's toiletries and other items needed in the home.

Later, when the financial situation of the TCV improved, pocket money was distributed to the children so as to give them an idea of the value of money and teach them how to manage a budget.

Confronted by our growing numbers, we were forced to take the decision to put two children in each bed. In many of our Tibetan settlements in different parts of India, the Tibetan population suffered much from tuberculosis. Young parents succumbed to the terrible illness, leaving small children behind them. Faced with these new difficulties, it was necessary to respond very quickly, and we opened a home specifically for these little babies.

At my request, Heinrich Harrer had asked Dr Hermann

Gmeiner, the president of SOS Kinderdorf, to help the Tibetan refugees. Dr Gmeiner was a remarkable man, believing strongly in the virtues of tradition, language and religion. He thought that a child should never be uprooted and he favoured the creation of villages in all countries where there was a need for them. Shortly after the Second World War, he had created villages in France, Germany and Austria for the children of war victims. Dr Gmeiner categorically refused to bring Tibetan children to Europe, but he sent us a nurse, Sister Ursula, who had worked in India for a long time. Her mission was to look for a place to build a children's home. I convinced her that our case was the most urgent.

Sister Ursula sent her report to Austria. This was followed by a visit from Dr Reinprecht, Dr Gmeiner's assistant. Faced with the enormity of the problem, he quickly understood our difficulties and felt for our children's needs. He immediately had the necessary sums sent to build the new houses. Our situation improved daily and SOS Kinderdorf also agreed to sponsor children. Sister Ursula remained with us until 1974, moving into a home and helping us in the office. On 10 January 1972, the Tibetan Children's Village was formally affiliated to SOS Kinderdorf International, Vienna, Austria.

Dr Gmeiner's association proved to be very strict about the management of donations. To start with, the money went through the SOS office in New Delhi. When Dr Gmeiner had seen for himself that we also had very strict procedures, he allowed us to receive the funds directly; this made us autonomous and it became easier to react to events. It was also a tribute to the quality of our work at the TCV.

By 1975 we had 29 homes and the children were no longer forced to spend the night in immense dormitories. We planned to house 20 to a building. Thanks to grants from the Indian government and other sources, life in the settlements also improved. Day and boarding schools were built. We mainly took in orphans, but we sometimes accepted children with one remaining parent.

As we were receiving more and more babies, we were forced to create a special environment for them. We were then able to take in infants up to the age of three. The babies needed a lot of health care and continual attention. Sometimes groups of them arrived suffering from malnutrition or requiring intensive treatments.

In the early days, we used to place children aged between three and a half and fifteen together. We soon saw that this was an error: the wide spread of ages created dissension. We then decided to open four homes for children between the ages of three and a half to nine or ten.

Aiming all the time to improve everybody's daily life, we organized meetings between teachers and the foster mothers and fathers so as to find the most appropriate solutions to our problems. We decided to first group the oldest boys together in the same building. The foster mothers, who were often illiterate, found it very difficult to look after these adolescents and were unable to help with their homework. We therefore had the idea of opening a kind of youth hostel, and were helped with this new scheme by SOS Kinderdorf. The first hostel was for the boys and 60 adolescents from the ninth form onwards. As a result, the problems in the homes diminished. The eldest girls helped the foster mothers more: they learnt to cook, did the washing up and looked after the little ones.

Each year, we upgraded the level of our school curriculum. Our school sought affiliation to the Central Board of Secondary Education, Delhi and got its recognition in 1976. In 1978 the first batch of 18 students appeared for the Class Board exams and they did very well. We were very pleased with these results. Since 1971, the Government of India stopped the subsidy and no new teaching staff were appointed. The sponsorship system that had been developed over the years enabled us to recruit our own staff, to pay them, and even to help the children who were not sponsored.

A new programme was introduced called 'Tibet: Our Country'. We asked the children to do research, and then for a month they made models and masks and wrote essays on their country, helped by the teachers. The subjects were very varied: the monasteries of Tibet, the life of the nomads and farmers, traditional costumes, wildlife and flowers. At the end of the month, we organized an exhibition at which all the children showed the fruits of their research. This highly stimulating programme gave the children the opportunity to carry out their own research on their country in the library or to meet older people and talk to them about the traditions and daily life in Tibet. We gradually got together a large collection of objects to do with Tibetan culture and, over the years, the exhibitions became more detailed and interesting.

To avoid daily life at the TCV becoming monotonous (some of the children had already been living there for eight or nine years), we introduced new activities: elocution contests, acting, poetry reading, traditional dancing and debates in Tibetan or English on subjects of general interest. If a child was caught smoking, we immediately organized a debate: 'For or against smoking?' These activities also served as a diversion for the village staff and teachers.

By now, most of the children at the school were teenagers. During Tsering Dolma's lifetime, some of them had even become craftsmen. Foster mothers, who were now getting old, and for whom it was too tiring to look after the children, kept themselves busy by reusing the wool from the children's old pullovers. They washed the wool and dyed it again and used this wool to weave some colourful little mats for the children to sit on. Nothing was wasted and we made use of all sorts of things which ordinarily one would throw away. To preserve the arts and crafts of Tibet, craft centres appeared within the various settlements and also in our Children's Village in Dharamsala.

Certain pupils, after completing their studies, learnt tapestry weaving techniques, *thanka* painting or how to make traditional garments. The first batch of craft trainees completed their training in 1979. It was an important programme for us, because it developed our know-how and helped us to preserve our culture. It also enabled the young to become independent and self-reliant. The first batch refused to leave the village and stayed on to help develop the Dharamsala crafts centre, which was set up at Kishore Nivas. When the sponsors heard about this activity, many of them purchased items made by the trainees.

Life was organized in a similar fashion in the settlements. I frequently went to those at Mundgod and Bylakuppe, South India. Each settlement was like a mini Tibet of about 2,500 acres in which 2,500 to 10,000 refugees lived. As far as the eye could see there were Tibetans living in Tibetan style. I found it very moving to hear our language being spoken. In the middle of a foreign country, the very distinctive atmosphere of our nation survived. The inhabitants had placed decorated altars inside their houses, with tapestries like the ones I had known in my childhood.

Most of the Tibetans living at Bylakuppe and Mundgod had been nomads. They had to be taught how to manage their food supplies in a settlement and were confused by the idea of a budget. They did not know how to cultivate the land but, being hard working, they learnt quickly. Today, Bylakuppe has a record maize yield.

Having being settled for over 30 years, the families had naturally grown and new families had formed. But although the population had increased, the amount of land available had not grown. A certain number of refugees set themselves up in craft trades. In 1974, I went with my husband and three children to Goa, where we met Tibetans who sold sweaters. They traded in Bombay and the other big cities where large numbers of tourists were to be found.

I thought about how the situation had changed since the first six or seven years of our exile. At that time the refugees had said: 'Next year, we will be back in Tibet.' With the passing of time, the families became more and more integrated in the life of the settlements. They had been given land on which they had built homes and had given birth to children. One harvest had succeeded another. Even so, everyone's main objective was to return to Tibet.

In the 1980s, the Tibetan villages swarmed with bicycles and motorcycles, even the monks used them. On Sundays, the Indians who lived nearby came to sell their fruit and vegetables at the very lively markets. Without knowing it, the Tibetan exiles were becoming physically integrated with their surroundings. Their thoughts, though, remained directed towards Tibet and the wonderful day when they would once again return to their country.

The largest of the 56 colonies was to be found in the south of India, more than 1,500 miles from Dharamsala. So as to maintain better co-ordination and understanding amongst our community, from the early 1960s onwards the government in exile organized an annual meeting of the representatives of the different colonies, the people's representatives and delegates from various other organizations. We gave reports on our respective work. These were followed by debates, which were often very animated, and we really had the feeling that, even outside its frontiers, Tibet still existed. These meetings brought about 350 people together. They were sometimes presided over by His Holiness, who paid close attention to the different points of view that were expressed.

I was nearly 40. My children were growing up but I was still very close to them. On Sundays or during the holidays, we would often go for long walks in the mountains or the nearby forests. Sometimes their schoolmates would come with us for a picnic. When I could get away from my work for a while, we would visit Gyalo Thondup and Diki Dolkar, who still lived in Delhi. I also enjoyed moments of relaxation at home, reading a lot, especially detective novels, and listening to classical music.

Sometimes I went to see hermits, who lived high up in the mountains and whose arduous life was entirely devoted to prayer and meditation. I would bring them provisions for the winter months: a bit of tsampa, butter, bread and incense. I also brought them a little money so that they could go on the great pilgrimages to sacred places in India or Nepal. In all, there were 20 hermits living in the mountains above Dharamsala. Today, there are over 70. My children often accompanied me, and before exam results the students would ask a hermit to give a divination. Meeting and talking to the hermits was very soothing for one's mind and we did enjoy this very much.

Naturally, I often went to see His Holiness as well. He had now been head of the government for over 40 years and had very heavy responsibilities. As a mature man he still retained all his youthful enthusiasm and still believed in the virtues of negotiating with communist China, particularly after Mao Tse-tung's death in 1976. His Holiness travelled a great deal and met more and more heads of state. Back in Dharamsala, he liked spending his few moments of spare time studying holy texts, reading books about animals, studying the Second World War, or looking at scientific journals. His curiosity remained insatiable and very eclectic.

Observing him during his long working day, I was struck by the intensity of his Buddhist practice. For him the Tibetan cause took precedence over everything else, but he was always very understanding towards other people. When, for instance, one of my nephews married Danielle Aeschiman, His Holiness asked them to come and join us in India, where my nephew ran the leading Tibetan journal.

Now that my children had grown up, they met the Dalai

Lama less often. Nevertheless, they were never refused an audience, because His Holiness was also considered the head of the family. One day, when my two daughters were suffering from stomachaches and headaches, His Holiness asked them if they ever took Tibetan medicine and who their doctor was. They replied together: 'Amala!' He was unable to hide his surprise. A few days later, he received me in his residence and advised me to stop playing at being a doctor with my children and to take them to see a real one.

The first delegation sent by His Holiness had visited Tibet in 1979. On its return I talked to the members about the situation in my country. I could not help comparing this to the genocide of the Jews. Moreover, I often advised young Tibetans to study the lessons of history and asked them to show a determination comparable to that of the Jewish people. We had a lot to learn from these men and women who, in spite of their sufferings, had never lost confidence.

In September 1979, while the first delegation was still in Tibet, a little girl of eight arrived in Dharamsala. She was called Dawa. Her parents had entrusted her to Tibetans who were returning to India, expressly asking them to lead her to His Holiness. Another group of children arrived the following year. The Chinese Communists seemed to have begun a process of some political openness, even allowing refugees to visit their families in Tibet but with a written undertaking that they were overseas Chinese! When they arrived in Tibet, they were given children to take back to India so that they could be given a Tibetan education with us.

Men and women also escaped into exile, some of whom had spent years in Communist prisons. Among them was Dr Tenzin Choedrak, His Holiness's personal physician, who had been allowed to leave Tibet. The Dalai Lama asked these men and women to go round the settlements and speak about their experiences under the Chinese occupation. These encounters did much to strengthen the refugees' motivation because, it must not be forgotten, we received very little news from Tibet.

The arrival of little Dawa at the TCV in Dharamsala practically caused a riot. Everyone wanted to see her and talk to her. We realized that the situation in Tibet must be very bad if parents were taking so great a risk in sending their children to us to be educated.

We were amazed by the general condition of the children arriving from Tibet. They all had the tanned complexions of people who live out of doors and appeared to be in fine shape. However, when we pulled up their eyelids, we could see that they were anaemic. In fact, they were all suffering from malnutrition. One sign worried us very much: as Tibetans normally have absolutely black hair, the dark brown hair of these children was yet another indication of very poor health.

We first of all looked after the children's sores and stomach problems in hospital, before treating the lice and giving vaccinations. After two weeks, the young refugees were put in the warm atmosphere of the homes. These children only spoke Tibetan, because most of them had not been to school. Only the older ones spoke a little Chinese.

We were very surprised by the amount of food that these children took in at each meal. The foster mothers did their best to calm their fears by explaining to them that here there would always be enough food. The children were very happy to be able to sleep in a bed and to slip under sheets and blankets and to have new clothes and shoes.

1980 marked a turning point for our community. At the New Year I was in Bylakuppe, where there were two Tibetan settlements. The oldest dated from the early 1960s; the other was more recent. The refugees in this region of southern India had asked me to look after their destitute children. It was nevertheless impossible to take them all in at the TCV in Dharamsala, because more and more children were arriving from Tibet, Nepal and the other settlements in the South.

Realizing the assistance needed for the destitute children, we felt it would be of tremendous help to build a Children's Village in the South to care for them. The cooperative society that ran the two settlements allocated some land for us. At the time, there were 30,000 Tibetans living in this Indian State of Karnataka, amongst whom there was a high proportion of destitute children. It only remained to find the funds. I contacted the SOS Children's Village in Holland, whose Secretary General I had met in Vienna in 1978, during a convention of representatives of SOS Children's Villages throughout the world. They energetically took the matter in hand and obtained the necessary money.

Returning to Dharamsala in March 1980 I was immediately called by the Secretary of His Holiness to come to the Palace. His Holiness asked me if I would lead a third delegation to Tibet to study the situation of education in our homeland. I felt a mixture of apprehension and pride, but I replied to him without the slightest hesitation: 'I will go, as you wish me to.' During the following days, I looked at the photographs taken by previous delegation, of beautiful landscapes, clear streams and impressive mountains. I could not, however, forget the horrors endured by our people.

PART III

1980–1995

12

A Tragedy Revealed

In 1980 I went back to Tibet for the first time. The population's poverty and silent suffering persuaded me to keep a diary of my three-month-long journey across the country that I had left in 1949. What follows is an account of my own personal reactions. I feel that it is my duty to publish a report on the atrocities committed by the Chinese Communists on the Tibetan people. The whole world must hear about this. I also believe it is vital that the slow agony resulting from this barbarity be made known to the international community.

One of the most irritating experiences of my journey was having to endure the permanent lies and deceit of the Chinese. Everywhere, we had the greatest difficulty in obtaining anything apart from false figures and statistics. Everything was done to prevent us from coming into direct contact with the population. This censorship considerably slowed down and handicapped our work. We opposed it vigorously, deciding to take up the challenge with complete honesty and objectivity.

It was my heavy responsibility to lead this third delegation to Tibet. It had been given the name of 'educational delegation' and its objective was to study the educational conditions in the country. It was composed of three teachers, three heads of Tibetan schools in India, a photographer and myself.

Before leaving Dharamsala, the Tibetan government in exile

gave us a detailed list of the towns and villages we were to visit. Our mission was also to observe the regions that the first two delegations had not been able to visit. Besides studying the education system, our task was to study the condition of the entire population and, if possible, inform it of the activities of our exiled government.

Our first halt was China, where I was struck by the strange feeling of sadness that seemed to engulf the population. Practically nobody smiled. The inhabitants of Beijing looked like empty, feelingless robots, devoid of emotion. I thought that I could see fear in their faces. It was also shocking to see the uniformity that ruled over this society: from top to bottom of the social scale, the Chinese no longer gave any importance to personal taste in clothing. Only the top government figures wore clothes that were made to measure from the finest materials. Everyone else put up with the usual blue or green uniforms. This was no doubt what the Chinese meant by equality; to me it seemed like a tragic joke. Those at the top of the hierarchy lived like kings, leaving the poor ordinary people without much to live on.

In Beijing, we met the Panchen Lama and Phuntsok Wangyal, who had both spent long years in prison. Phuntsok Wangyal was one of the first Tibetan Communists to collaborate with the Chinese, but he very soon began to oppose them. He was thrown into prison in 1957, with all the members of his family following him there, including his two-year-old daughter. His wife later died in prison. When I met him, it was only a year since he had been freed and he found it extremely difficult to talk, even in Tibetan. He had to spend most of those years in solitary confinement, without the right to speak. Completely cut off from the outside world, he had even been unaware of his brother's detention for 14 years in a neighbouring cell.

We realized that it would be impossible for us to keep to our original itinerary. The Chinese officials reproached us for wanting to visit too many places and for having an itinerary that was too ambitious for such a short amount of time. They told us that the first delegation had taken four months to see half as much. I replied to this by reminding them that it was absolutely essential that we respect the terms of our mission, but we could spend more time in Tibet should they judge it to be necessary. The Chinese then asked us to list the sites that were a priority for us, promising to think the matter over. At the next meeting, an official said that we were too demanding and that certain places were simply inaccessible during this rainy season. We then immediately proposed to travel on horseback, or even on foot.

Our delegation finally lost the argument, the Chinese claiming to be concerned for our safety. They kept on reminding us that we were, after all, their guests. I pointed out to them that if we paid all the expenses, we would be free to go where we wanted to. The reply was quick in coming. All at once, all the cars that had been used by the previous delegation were out of order and, using this as a pretext, an itinerary was arranged for us that conformed to the wishes of the Chinese Communist Party. In the end, we had to bend to their instructions. Even then we were kept waiting, as apparently the final decision had to be taken by the local authorities at the places we wanted to visit.

Sometimes, we were not even allowed to stop at places where hundreds of Tibetans had gathered to meet us. The local authorities announced coldly that they were not entitled to make such decisions and strongly advised us to keep to the itinerary laid down by Beijing.

Our convoy was composed of four large vehicles, with myself often in the leading one. One day, though I cannot remember where we were going, a group of Tibetans formed around us. I unwound the window to hold their hands and speak to them. Unfortunately, they spoke an Amdo dialect that I did not understand very well. The woman official seated next to me urged me to close the window again. I refused fairly bluntly. After two weeks in my own country, I was beginning to feel pretty exasperated by the authoritarian behaviour of the Chinese. A few days earlier, we had been entertained by nomads who served us boiled meat and *momos*. Apparently they had not eaten these traditional dishes for years, as the repressive behaviour of the Chinese extended to all areas of Tibetan life.

So when the window incident occurred, I said to the head of the Chinese delegation: 'Either you let me meet the Tibetans and carry out the mission that His Holiness sent me here for, or I leave with the entire delegation. I have not made the journey here from India to see Chinese in Tibet. I am here to meet Tibetans in their country.'

That evening in the inn, we were as usual locked in our room; I felt that I could no longer bear this deplorable situation. My cries drowned the voices of the interpreter and the zealous official. After a while, the Chinese minders came to ask me to calm down and insisted that it was impossible for us to go back. I repeated to them that if I could not speak to the Tibetans, I might as well return to India. Then I suddenly exploded, pouring out everything that I had on my mind. I had had enough of seeing my countrymen dying of hunger and I was not blind to the masquerades and pretences. The following day, my minder covered herself with excuses and pretended that she had asked me to close the window because of her rheumatism. I advised her to change vehicles. As for myself, I said that I considered that I had the right to behave as I wished. She said that she was the head of the delegation and therefore had to remain next to me. From that day on, whenever we were in the car, I got out the *mala* which I always kept with me and which had been blessed by His Holiness. Throughout the day, I recited the mantra *Om mani padme hum*. I think I must have murmured thousands of prayers like this, irritating my companion even more as she of course did not know their exact meaning.

We also noticed that the Chinese Communists had absolutely no shame and did not hesitate to tell lies. They would say something and then, two minutes later, contradict it. Hardly had something been said, than it was immediately denied and the contradiction attributed to our lack of understanding. Amongst other shameless statements made since the welcoming reception in Hong Kong, the authorities assured us that religious freedom was now respected in Tibet and that the monks were allowed back to their monasteries. They conceded that, during the Cultural Revolution, certain counter-revolutionaries had indeed been tempted to suppress religious practice, but invariably ended by saying that today the Tibetans were free.

One of the first monasteries we visited on arriving in Tibet was Tashi Kyil, in the province of Amdo. I did not really know what to expect from this visit and my feelings were rather confused.

In spite of my mistrust of the Chinese, I could not prevent myself from sustaining the hope that I would find this great holy place intact and still alive with religious activity.

I could almost hear the deep, serious voices of the monks resonating as they read from holy texts and the sound of the pilgrims as they knelt. I imagined the habitual, almost imperceptible, murmur of the faithful saying countless prayers on the path between the temples, carrying with them offerings of khatas, the white silk scarves that are a sign of devotion, so as not to be empty-handed when paying homage to the gods. These scarves signify the auspicious character of the visit and are also used to accumulate merit. I imagined the faithful offering butter lamps to the Bodhisattvas in order to overcome the difficulties of their present life, and the moving sight of children placing pins and needles in the divinities' clothes, a symbolic expression of their desire to sharpen their youthful minds. For several minutes I could practically breathe in the scent of the incense and see the strange shadows of the statues, which seemed animated with life. I felt inside myself the silence and serenity of the room lit by the flickering of a thousand butter lamps.

We were welcomed at Tashi Kyil by seven old monks, the only people there apart from a few workers engaged in renovating the monastery. This restoration work had been decided on after the first delegation's visit and a large part of the buildings had been restored to their original appearance. A few butter lamps even burned in the main temple. However, the entire monastery was filled with an unreal atmosphere; it felt physically and spiritually empty. I realized to what extent we had been manipulated by the Chinese officials. It was a long time since this temple had been a haven of peace.

Instead of experiencing the serenity habitually associated with such a place, my companions and I felt distressed. Had we been deceived because we were foreign visitors? Or had perhaps our contacts been convinced of the truth of their scandalous and shocking propaganda? For us, as Tibetans in our own country, this visit was exasperating and deeply upsetting.

Before the Chinese invasion, any devout person could go to the monasteries, which were also places of learning and an inherent part of our way of life. The Chinese occupying forces had transformed these places into either sterile museums, visited by only a few carefully chosen visitors, or piles of stones. They had organized exhibitions showing the monks leading a life of luxury and plenty in the midst of a traditional, poor Tibetan society. The bearded monks were presented as cruel and pitiless individuals.

Wherever there were some parts of the monasteries still standing, such as at Tashi Kyil, Sera, Drepung or Tashi Lhunpo, the Chinese had the nerve to draw attention to the freedom accorded to the practice of religion in Tibet. At Tashi Kyil, I managed to go into the monastery kitchen, where I found no evidence to suggest that anyone had recently lit a fire there. I even wondered if the seven old monks had not simply been brought there for the duration of our visit, perhaps temporarily dragged out of a forced labour camp to which they would later be sent back by the military authorities. The Tibetans have an unshakable faith in the teachings of Buddha and this is what gives them the strength to withstand the brutality of the Chinese.

We had reached an agreement with the Beijing authorities which allowed us to go to Taktser, the little village where my parents came from, and also where His Holiness was born. I was delighted at the idea of this visit as I had never seen our village. It had only appeared in my childhood dreams when Amala told me about life in this region of Amdo. We hoped to be in Taktser on 6 July, His Holiness's birthday. Arriving from Siling, we stopped on the way in a small village where my brother-in-law Phuntsok Tashi's sister still lives with her family. I met her and we breakfasted together in her little mud-brick house, which was completely empty except for one wooden cupboard and a few stools.

We then reached Taktser, where we celebrated His Holiness's birthday by burning incense and saying some prayers, I was able to go for a short walk in the village. Hardly anything remained of our house, except for two rooms giving on to the inner courtyard and the four outside walls. All the rest of the house had been destroyed. Before we arrived, the Chinese had put up a large gate and my cousin's sister had been given the task of looking after the house. Out of the 30 families who had previously lived in Taktser, only four remained. All the other inhabitants were Chinese.

The small rooms that gave on to the courtyard were being used as classrooms. My cousin's son taught there. Our visit fell during holiday time and there was not a single child to be seen. I was able to say a few prayers in the courtyard. My cousin wore her best clothes and had made us some bread. A little later, I discovered that Chinese officials had preceded us 48 hours earlier and distributed new clothes and food. My cousin, like all other Tibetans, had not eaten meat for a long time.

In spite of the continual pressure on us, I felt at ease here, happy to spend a few moments in this landscape that had been so dear to my parents and brothers and sister. Taktser was the happiest memory of our Tibetan journey. To reach the village, it was first of all necessary to cross a curious hill with red soil. Amala had told me how tiring it had been to fetch water from the well every day. I therefore went to see it, intending to show Amala a photograph on my return. The wells held only a few drops of horrid-looking liquid.

The day went by very fast and it was sad saying goodbye to my cousins and Taktser. At dinner, on our return to Siling, I said a prayer aloud, as it was the Dalai Lama's birthday, asking for His Holiness to live another 1,000 years. The interpreter translated my words to the official who never left us for a second. She immediately became very angry. We had organized a little party and played some modern music. The Chinese appeared to be astonished by our tastes; I explained to them that these were the result of an excellent education in the Indian missionary schools.

The officials asked us many questions about India. They kept on telling us how a sudden change in climate had led to the death of numerous Tibetans. I replied to them that the first refugees had indeed suffered, but that this was nothing compared with the brutality experienced in their own country under Chinese repression. I above all insisted on the fact that we were free in India: free to have emotions, free to express ourselves and to practise our religion. We had monasteries there and schools where our children received an education that was admired by many.

When I consider the sufferings our people endured and remember all that I heard and saw in Tibet, I realize how difficult it is to convey the tragic story of the Tibetan people to the outside world. I must, however, mention the lives that were broken by the aggressors' oppression. It is perhaps not known that if parents did not smile before the 'spectacle' of their son's death, or if they did not applaud, or thank the Chinese for having killed their child before their own eyes, they were then condemned to death as well. Very young children were forced to see their parents being dragged through the streets of the village or town and then beaten, stoned and finally executed, simply because they had committed the crime of serving the previous regime or were heirs to landed property.

Women were punished just as cruelly, when their husbands, suspected of resistance, had been executed or had succeeded in escaping to India. I have lists of the names of many of these rape and torture victims but, to preserve the safety of their families, I must not cite them.

In every region we went through, we heard the same stories of atrocities. The Tibetans told us about their personal experience of the Chinese terror. They considered the entire nation to be in peril, faced by a situation of the utmost horror. Their country's agony seemed to them inexorable.

As I listened to these accounts, looking at the emaciated faces and fleshless bodies, I could not prevent myself from shedding tears. The delegation I led lived in a state of permanent shock. We often cried with the people who had come to meet us. We could see how moved they were at being able to talk to us for the first time in 30 years. Sometimes, after talking amongst ourselves about the day's experiences, exhaustion and discouragement overcame us and we sobbed silently.

It was very moving to observe the spiritual and mental force that our countrymen displayed, in spite of everything they had been through. Risking their lives, they cried: 'Long live the Dalai Lama! May he live for 10,000 years!' The population nevertheless lived in a state of horror. I was aware of the presence of informers and spies working for the occupying authorities. Therefore, we took infinite precautions during our conversations, and this added to the difficulties of our mission.

In 1961, the General Assembly of the United Nations had adopted resolution 1723–XVI, explicitly recognizing the right of the Tibetan people to self-determination. The United

Nations asked the government of the People's Republic of China to put an end to 'practices that deprive the Tibetan people of their fundamental rights and freedoms, including that of self-determination'. In 1965, this resolution (2079–XX) was reaffirmed by the General Assembly.

At the same time the iron fist of Communism tightened its grip on our country. Fewer and fewer refugees managed to cross the Himalayas. The few people who managed to do so brought news that was all the more tragic because most of them still had family members in Tibet. They had no way of knowing what had become of them.

Since then, up to 1965, China divided Tibet into five parts: the major parts of eastern and southern Kham region were incorporated into the neighbouring Chinese provinces of Sichuan and Yunnan respectively; a large part of Amdo was named Qingahi province; a smaller part of Amdo was incorporated into the Chinese province of Kansu.

On 9 September 1965, China formally established the 'Tibet Autonomous Region', regrouping under its rule the whole of the region of U-tsang and a part of Kham. The Chinese deprived many ethnic groups – including the Sherpas, the Monpas, the Lhopas, the Tengpas and the Jangpas – of their Tibetan identity. All these populations, who considered themselves Tibetans, were arbitrarily classified as separate Chinese minorities.

Tibet had never suffered from famine before the Chinese invasion. There had been lean years, but the people had had easy access to the stores of the government or the monastaries, as well as those of the aristocracy or rich farmers. In 1949, the Chinese military and civil authorities fed their personnel from the state stores and forced the Tibetans to sell their cereal reserves for derisory prices. The 'liberation' meant poverty for everyone. Agricultural production was divided, with the smallest part going to the peasants who, from then on, had to exercise careful control over their daily consumption. Until 1949, barley was the basic Tibetan foodstuff. The Chinese replaced it with wheat, with drastic consequences. Badly adapted to the Tibetan climate, the wheat did not ripen and most of the crops froze. (The land, intentionally left fallow, had once only served as pasture.) The Chinese authorities carried out a policy of intensive farming and the enforced settlement of nomads. Entire flocks of livestock perished and the farm land became infertile. Famine then swept over the entire country.

The Chinese invasion of 1949 had a further tragic consequence. Tibet was transformed into a vast prison and the territory was scattered with labour camps. The massacres, tortures, murders, attacks on monasteries, and the extermination of entire villages and nomad populations constituted the basis of documents collected by the International Commission of Jurists in 1960. We learnt that the People's Liberation Army had put down hundreds of revolts in Kanlho and Amdo between 1952 and 1958, killing thousands of Tibetans in the process. I remember the testimony of the Panchen Lama who, in 1963, speaking of the population of Golok in the region of Amdo, which had been reduced from 130,000 to 60,000 inhabitants, said: 'If a film was to be made about all the atrocities perpetrated in the province of Qinghai, the spectators would be horrified. After the massacres around Golok, bodies were thrown from the top of a hill into a large ditch. The soldiers forced the families of the dead to celebrate the rebels' successful extermination. They even forced them to dance on the corpses before they were in their turn murdered by machine-gun fire.'

After the uprising in 1959 at Lhasa, between 10,000 and 15,000 Tibetans were exterminated in the space of three days. I read in a Chinese report that, between March 1959 and October 1960, 87,000 Tibetans lost their lives in central Tibet alone.

The exiles who had managed to escape the wave of arrests recounted the atrocities committed in the camps. On average, about 70 per cent of the inmates died. At Jang Karpo, for example, in the wild plains of northern Tibet, over 10,000 people had been packed into five prisons and forced to work in the borax mines. Each day, between 10 and 30 of them had died from hunger, exhaustion or physical assault. Within a year, more than 8,000 prisoners had died. During the building of the hydroelectric plant at Lhasa Ngachen, supposedly built by the People's Liberation Army, three or four bodies were burnt or thrown into the nearest river every day. In Kham, an ex-prisoner, Adi Taphe from Nyarong, told us that between 1960 and 1962, more than 12,000 Tibetans died in a lead mine in the region of Dartsedo in eastern Tibet.

In Lhasa we saw 30,000 of our countrymen. The visits followed one another in an exhausting rhythm, from five in the morning until two the following morning. It took all our energy not to leave anyone out and to listen to all those who wanted to talk to us. We divided the work. At night some of us remained in our rooms while the others visited the inhabitants. Two small girls served as our messengers, bringing us letters for His Holiness. Both of them knew the mantras very well and recited them with me. Although I, of course, remember them very well, I cannot mention their names because this would place their lives in danger.

The day of our arrival in the capital was very moving. We approached from the direction of Shigatse, then, on turning a corner, we suddenly caught sight of the Potala. The building was as extraordinarily beautiful as ever. The delegation settled into an inn and, as soon as I could, I looked out of the window. The Potala stood majestically on a hill in the moonlight. The sight of a small light flickering made me feel nostalgic. Later, I learnt that, apart from a caretaker in one room, no one now lived in the immense empty palace. Remembering my childhood and my visits to His Holiness, I was unable to hold back my tears.

Lhasa was now very different from the city of my childhood. Arriving in front of our family house, I found the railings padlocked. The residence, with its windows painted in blue, appeared lifeless. The following day I asked what it was used for now and was told: 'It's an inn for Chinese army officers!' Besides the Potala, it was the only place that I recognized in Lhasa. Nearly all the town had been destroyed and Chinese-style constructions replaced the older edifices. When we went to the Jokhang, the sewers were overflowing because there was no proper sanitation system. The street lamps had bulbs, but there was no electric current. The Chinese development was, of course, just a façade. Roads built by Tibetan prisoners were merely to facilitate the movement of huge numbers of troops and Chinese settlers. Electricity was available only in the quarters inhabited by the Chinese. Buildings were in a state of advanced dilapidation, almost ruins. Traditionally the walls were whitewashed every New Year, but this had not been done for 10, 15 or even 20 years.

The population lived in continual fear of reprisals. When we met Tibetans in the street, they often walked with lowered heads. The inhabitants explained to me that during the Cultural Revolution, they had not been allowed to raise their eyes and they had kept this habit ever since. Every evening they had indoctrination sessions, brain-washing that began at sundown and went on until midnight or one in the morning. People were even careful in the presence of their own children, fearing that they might repeat conversations heard in the family home. In Lhasa, all radio programmes were in Chinese. The news was broadcast from Beijing, as was recorded music and even gym lessons. The invader had imposed Beijing time and the Tibetans were therefore forced to live according to a time that was entirely different from the one they were accustomed to.

During these three months, I think I shed enough tears to fill several buckets. We would cry every day with the Tibetans who came to see us. It was torment for us to be unable to do anything for them, but the simple fact of listening to them brought them a little comfort. In front of the door to our room an official photographed everyone who entered. We asked our visitors if they were not frightened of being recognized. They said that it did not matter to them, explaining that they needed to make this visit, even if it lasted only for a short time, and were prepared to sacrifice their lives.

I remember a terrifying story told by a woman who came to see me. She had three children, including a little daughter of six. As they had become weaker and weaker, to the point where her daughter could no longer stand up, she had decided to mix remains of tsampa with her own blood, saying that she had made them a soup. She had given them this mixture three times a day and in this way had saved her daughter from certain death.

The Chinese Embassy in Holland issued an official statement accusing me of having invented this story. Several years later, after an earthquake in the Soviet Union, *Time Magazine* reported that a mother, trapped with her child under the ruins, had cut her finger in order to feed the child with her blood and had like this been able to save its life.

In spite of all the strong emotions and permanent sadness, my mission to Tibet turned out to be interesting and much more gratifying than I had expected. Due to lack of time, and due to pressure from the Chinese authorities, we were unable to go all over the country or to widen our field research. However, the population responded enthusiastically to our visit. The Tibetans showed extraordinary eagerness to meet and talk to us, taking enormous risks and choosing to ignore the warnings that were given out in advance of our arrival. They described to us the deceptions schemed up by the Chinese, the masquerades organized to prevent our meeting them, and the sufferings and atrocities that they had endured for 30 years. Their courageous behaviour made up for all the inconveniences of the journey. Every day we witnessed the unshakable faith of the Tibetans in His Holiness the Dalai Lama, their hatred of the brutal occupying regime, and their thirst for freedom. With every moment they spent with us, we became closer to them, and this often enabled us to foil the machinations of the Chinese Communists.

Our journey lasted 130 days, 105 of which were spent in Tibet, from 1 June to 3 October 1980. We visited 41 towns and numerous villages and nomad settlements, making this exhausting 8,500-mile journey on roads that were almost impassable. Everywhere we went we were welcomed by the mayor and his deputy, who gave long speeches full of figures and statistics to show us the progress that had been accomplished in our country under Deng Xiaoping's leadership since 1959, the date of the Dalai Lama's departure into exile. The errors committed by the Gang of Four were also mentioned, but 'everything was going well in the Tibet that we were fortunate to be visiting'. These boring meetings, devoid of any meaning, took longer and longer. The larger the town, the longer the speech became.

I can confirm that the majority of Tibetans live in Tibet like animals. They have lost their families, identities, religion, houses, and monasteries. But even though they are suffering from total exhaustion, their mental faculties are undamaged. Throughout the journey, I was able to observe the extent to which their determination was stronger than ever. All these men and women said: 'We have a spiritual and temporal leader, the Dalai Lama, who cares for us. Everything else is just a question of time.' At Gormo, where I met some Muslims from Turkestan, one of them said to me: 'You are lucky, you have something that we do not have: the Dalai Lama. Like us, you

Tibetans have lost everything but, thanks to His Holiness, your cause is still alive. We no longer have anyone and our battle seems to be lost.' Historically the Tibetans, the Uighurs of East Turkestan (Xinjiang) and the Mongols have been close neighbours; our common fate of being subjected to Chinese communist rule has brought us closer than ever before.

13

Encounters with an Oppressed People

During our journey, I managed to listen to BBC radio. This is how, for instance, I learnt of the death of Indira Gandhi's son in an airplane crash. My minder asked me a great many questions about the Indian Prime Minister and about the political changes that would follow on the death of her heir. I explained to her how, from 1959, first of all Prime Minister Nehru and then Indira Gandhi had generously helped the Tibetan refugees and why we were very grateful to India, but she did not really like listening to this kind of thing. In fact, she wanted above all to know whether Indira Gandhi's second son was also involved in politics. I replied to her: 'No, but perhaps he will be now!' Like all the Chinese, she no doubt thought that the Gandhis would leave the international stage. I then added: 'Indira Gandhi is a very strong personality. Her son's death has no doubt affected her enormously, but she still has a lot of resources. Besides, India is not China.' I once again noticed this Chinese official's backward mentality. It was inconceivable to her that a woman could be prime minister.

Wherever we happened to be, I was always aware of the extreme laziness of the Chinese accompanying us. Every afternoon they would have a long nap and insisted that we do likewise. Needless to say, this was the last thing we wanted to do and we used these moments of peace to disappear. Equally, when they retired to bed in the evenings, we would take pocket torches and go out to meet the Tibetans. The officials no longer dared lock the doors of the guest house since our rather vehement dispute.

All along our route, the Tibetans discreetly handed us letters for the Dalai Lama and these were distributed amongst the members of my delegation. Each member carried a bag for this purpose, which he never let out of his sight as the letters could have compromised their writers. By the end of the journey, we had collected nearly 7,000 letters, most of them for His Holiness.

As we had expected from the beginning, at each meeting we were subjected to a relentless litany about the unprecedented progress that had been accomplished in the field of education. The Chinese statistics were as follows: 430 primary schools with 17,000 pupils; 55 secondary schools with 10,000 pupils; and 6,000 schools opened by the population itself, where some 200,000 pupils received government grants. The authorities even anticipated taking over the running of these establishments. To this list were added an additional 22 secondary schools with 2,000 pupils and four further educational establishments of about 560 students. Everywhere we went, the officials bombarded us with their figures, no doubt in this way hoping to hide a less impressive reality.

I must stress that we were given no opportunity to verify these figures. We also discovered how difficult it was to arrange a visit to a school. We did not want to visit all the hundreds of establishments that they talked to us about, just one or two in each province that we went through.

We were told, however, that the schools were closed everywhere for the summer holidays. I could not understand the logic of shutting them in the middle of the warm season in a country where the winters are so long and hard. No real school buildings existed, let alone heated ones. As for the children, they did not possess any warm clothes. Transport was limited to military trucks and a few buses. 'The schools are closed for the summer holidays,' was the usual excuse, repeated to us day after day, from our arrival in Tibet on 18 June until our departure on 23 September. To start with, we tried to see at least the buildings, even if the pupils were not in them. But then we realized that the Chinese used this expression as a euphemism for there being no school, or to prevent us from inspecting a school that did exist. Sometimes our interpreter would pretend that the headmaster was absent and that there would therefore be no point in visiting an establishment without the presence of the person in the best position to answer our questions.

Nevertheless, in order to carry out our mission effectively, we had to find a way to overcome all these obstacles. We were, in fact, able to observe 92 establishments. These figures included the training institutes in the different regions of Tibet, the national schools for minorities in Beijing, such as Shenyang, Lanzhou and Chengdu, where there were Tibetans studying, and the primary schools that we glimpsed in Beijing before our departure for Tibet. This figure also took into account the Muslim school in Lhasa and a Mongol school in the district of Daku Zong in Amdo. In fact, we visited 70 establishments in Tibet and this enabled us to make an objective judgment about the state of education there.

In 16 out of these 70 establishments, no Tibetan was taught at all, and in eight others it was taught only after primary school. Most of the village schools and the majority of the primary establishments whose existence had been indicated to us, and in which Tibetan was supposed to be taught, did not even exist. Everywhere else, the academic standard was extremely low. The teachers themselves mostly had no education beyond primary school level.

In Beijing, the authorities had described a Tibetan education system that had greatly improved over the last 20 years and which now had 300 times as many pupils as in the past. According to their estimates, only 13 schools had existed prior to 1950. This calculation, of course, left out the thousands of monasteries and other institutions, subsequently destroyed, which had also served as schools, often excellent ones. Moreover, the old monastic schools had also taught the Tibetan language and culture. The schools created by the Chinese, on the other hand, aimed first of all to indoctrinate our children so that they would learn to detest their civilization and religion, and even their family and their own people. It would appear that the Chinese really appreciated our old education system while at the same time they rejected our culture! This hypocrisy and deceit have irreversibly destroyed the educational system in Tibet.

Leaving aside the few exceptions mentioned above, only 40 per cent of the pupils in the 70 schools we visited were Tibetan. The Chinese occupied 70 per cent of the teaching jobs. The authorities themselves gave us these figures and therefore could not contest them. We indeed had every reason to be very worried by the situation.

In some villages, the Chinese even went so far as to create a school just for the duration of our visit. In one school under a tent that we were shown, everything was brand-new: the tent, children's clothes, tables and blackboard. Even the grass under the carpet was tender and green. A teacher explained the subtleties of Tibetan grammar to children who did not even know the alphabet! The situation was so ridiculous that even the Chinese officials accompanying us seemed embarrassed. The authorities had organized a lunch inside the tent. Once our delegation had been installed, the people outside began to walk round the tent, praying, bowing and generally showing us every sign of deep respect. I gave a speech conveying His Holiness's best wishes to our countrymen. At the end of the speech a couple began a very melancholy traditional song with words describing how much they have suffered under these new rulers and tears began to flow down our cheeks.

At one point, we halted between Toe and Chuni at a place called Gormo. This was a very unusual event as it did not feature on our schedule. There was not a child to be seen in the school here and, although it was not yet ten in the morning, the headmaster explained to us that they were having lunch. When I asked him at what time classes started, he replied, 'at eight', and then, correcting himself, 'at seven'. He hurried to add that the lunch break would last until two in the afternoon. In the meantime, we had been able to have a look at the place: the building served as a storehouse for firewood. I suggested we continue on our way as it was obvious that classes would never be starting.

In the brigade of Kangsto, near Chaktso, in the division of Nagchu, our delegation visited a primary school of 37 pupils run by two teachers. One of them appeared not to want to answer our questions at all. The pupils had no carpet to sit on in the tiny classroom. In Lhasa we visited a primary and infant school where children, barefooted and dressed in rags, carried stones and earth in baskets. It goes without saying that the level of education there was desperately low.

In Jarak Linka, the delegation visited an establishment which served as a showcase for foreigners. More than half of the 1,500 pupils were Chinese. The occupying authorities had insisted that the Tibetans put on their best clothes. We later learnt that this school was reserved for the children of officials who had sworn allegiance to Beijing. At Nyitri Ghey Chik, in the administrative area of Kongpo, 200 of the 441 pupils were boarders. They were asked to provide their own food because, so the headmaster told us, the school received no grant from the Chinese government or the local authorities.

I could cite many more examples of cases where the Chinese Communists tried to take us in and which would prove that even the notion of education is a farce in Tibet. But what would be the point of this? Any sensible person who has read so far will have clearly perceived the gravity of the events that were taking place in my country, and will understand that Tibet was, and remains, pitilessly oppressed under the yoke of the Chinese, whose number exceeds that of the Tibetan population.

Today, Chinese power is expressed by the presence of 7.5 million Chinese settlers, backed by the might of reportedly 300,000 armed soldiers. The Communists have enslaved a deeply pious and peaceful country which did not possess a single modern weapon and where a fifth of the male population lived in the calm and serenity of the monasteries. Our people's tragedy can be summed up in a single sentence: the Chinese People's Republic illegally occupies Tibet. As long as the invader's troops remain on Tibetan soil, this tragedy will persist, whatever else they may pretend. The longer the occupying forces remain, the worse the situation will become. It is not possible to believe that a colonial power can occupy a country, decimate its population and systematically destroy its culture with the intention of serving that country's interests.

During the three months of our journey, I observed our people's tragedy with my own eyes. Hundreds of accounts confirmed the existence of a systematic and total programme of exploitation of Tibet's natural resources. Entire forests had been razed to the ground and the land transformed into vast deserts. China used foreign help, particularly from Japan, to exploit the country's mineral resources. Of course, the Tibetan people derived no benefits from this policy of devastation.

The Chinese affirmed that they had brought progress to Tibet by building roads, bridges and houses. Once again, this was a barefaced lie. They had improved the transport network only to facilitate continuous and massive transfer of the Chinese population and their systematic pillage. As for new houses, these were allotted only to Chinese settlers and the few Tibetans who collaborated with the occupying authorities.

While Tibetans die from hunger, the best land, cultivated by the Chinese, serves to feed the thousands of settlers or to provide foodstuffs for export. We were shown around an abattoir and cold store at Marchu, where 3,000 sheep and 7,300 yak are slaughtered every year. What happens to this meat? It is sent to various Arab nations. The same happens at Dholen Zong, where 40,000 sheep and 40,000 yak are slaughtered annually to provide China with meat, wool, fur and leather. These are two examples among many others.

Before leaving for Tibet, I had expressed a particular wish: to be able to photograph the wildlife and flora. I clearly remembered an abundance of wild animals and different kinds of plants. When I had been younger, I had imagined that there were more animals than men in my country. In fact, I discovered that the stags, wild donkeys and antelopes that had been there during my childhood no longer existed. Even the trung trung, the famous black-necked Tibetan crane, was no longer to be seen.

In spite of Chinese professions to the contrary, the situation seemed to be worsening. All official transactions took place in Chinese and the Tibetan language had no official worth.

The Tibetan nomads and farmers were all listed, put into bogus municipalities, production gangs and other subdivisions. The members of these groups were given a certain number of instructions which, in theory, normally took into account each member's capacities and aptitudes. The population carried out extremely hard tasks such as the construction of waste-water systems, sewers and rudimentary dams. The inhabitants of Shigatse were even forced to build dikes on the river between Gyantse and Shigatse, to reduce its width. After the heavy summer rains, the river swelled and swept over the dikes, flooding the entire region for 30 miles. Many Tibetans lost their lives in these mad enterprises, working to the point of exhaustion. Many also had their backs broken by the weight of the stones they had to carry.

In the towns, a large part of the population that was still fit was employed on building programmes. These included the making of unmetalled roads, airstrips, communications infrastructure and electrical installations. Each worker received between one and a half and two and a half monetary units for his work. Transactions were monitored and restricted by the obligation to use coupons for purchases. The result of this system was that even those Tibetans who had been able to keep back some savings were unable to buy extra food or clothing.

The Tibetans lived in little wooden shacks or mud huts because the prohibitive rents prevented them from occupying separate houses. We closely observed the mixture of Tibetans and Chinese on the streets. The Chinese wore excellent quality clothing and above all seemed to be in perfect health. The Tibetans wore rags and were often ill.

The highly developed road system enabled a large amount of traffic to circulate on the major routes. We particularly noticed heavy vehicles, most of which were military, that served to transport the troops of the People's Liberation Army and military equipment for the barracks. On their return journey, the trucks carried the local agricultural produce towards China, as well as livestock and Tibetan mineral extracts.

The gangs of workers were essentially composed of Tibetan officials from the period prior to 1959. Imprisoned and then subsequently set free, they had been unable to return to their families or their homes, which had been either confiscated by the authorities or, frequently, destroyed after their arrest. These gangs, which were to be found throughout the country, were a form of cheap labour for the invader. None of our attempts to meet our countrymen held in these camps met with any success. In Shigatse and Emagang, we were told that we would not be able to cross the river at Emagang because of the heavy seasonal rains. We had a similar response when we tried to see the brigade at Kongpo Phagmotrang, where Tibetans were employed clearing forests. Although the population had no heating, truck loads of trees were leaving for China.

During the second delegation's visit a serious incident had occurred. While they were visiting the ruins of Ganden monastery, one person had shouted 'Long live His Holiness'. He was immediately arrested and imprisoned and the second delegation was instantly asked to return back to India. For this reason, initially the Chinese official in charge did not allow us to go to Lhasa but we were taken instead directly to Shigatse from

Nagchu. As Thubten Jigme Norbu, my brother, was at the time making a private visit to Tibet and was in Lhasa, I was in spite of everything given permission to telephone him. I even asked the officials for permission to see my brother before he left. To my great surprise, they accorded me a day to go from Shigatse to Lhasa and back. This enabled me to spend several hours in the company of my elder brother and sister-in-law. We talked about what the delegation had seen and expressed our horror at the Chinese barbarity.

However, in the end our delegation was able to spend two weeks in Lhasa. On our arrival in the Tibetan capital we were welcomed by a huge crowd. I gave a speech and talked at length about His Holiness's good health and the efforts of the Tibetans in exile, whose aim was the same as theirs: the liberation of Tibet. That evening at around midnight, the interpreter came to my room and led me to the woman official in charge of our group. She interrogated me rigorously: 'You talked about a common aim for all Tibetans. What did you mean by this?' I explained to her that it was His Holiness's concern to act for the wellbeing of all Tibetans, whether they lived in exile or in Tibet. At the end of the meeting, I was asked never again to use the word 'aim'.

The population was intensely moved by our visit. As the Chinese had forbidden all gatherings on the morning of our departure, a crowd of Tibetans began to form from the previous evening onwards in order to see us for the last time. I spoke to them again, using exactly the same words as before. This time, the officials did not say anything and, anyway, we were leaving the next day.

One Sunday, some monks came to fetch us to take us to the Jokhang. After a lot of difficulty we managed to shake off our escort and set off towards the temple. The monks showed us a statue, explaining that during the Cultural Revolution a bullet had passed right through it. A few minutes later, the Chinese arrived. The officials immediately began to reprimand the monks: 'Today is Sunday, a day off, so why have you opened the gates?' I once again noticed the stupidity of the Chinese way of thinking. According to their strange conception of religious freedom, the temple should remain open during the week when people were working and closed on the day when the Tibetans were able to take us to the Jokhang. I had also heard that every evening, at closing time, a truck retrieved the butter that the Tibetans had offered to the deities. The Chinese took the butter to biscuit manufacturers, further proof of our brave people's systematic exploitation.

I was also very shocked at the sight of the many thousands of Chinese that lived in the Kongpo Valley. The surrounding countryside was still very beautiful and the temperature agreeable, but only a few Tibetans lived there. Their place had been taken by Chinese settlers who had built factories, including one which made blankets. When I left Tibet, I also had to resign myself to another calamity: I had seen children and met a great many women, but throughout the months of our stay I had seen practically no babies or pregnant women.

When I arrived in Chengdu I was exhausted after these two weeks in Lhasa and slept all the time, doubtless for two reasons: I had difficulty in digesting the region's rather heavy cooking and I was also suffering from the after-effects of my sleepless nights in the Tibetan capital. The officials wanted to take us to a silk factory and a jade manufacturer, but I refused. In Beijing, I had also turned down an invitation to see the Great Wall.

Our journey to Tibet made us realize how extraordinarily lucky we were to live in India: we were a free people in a country, albeit a foreign one, which treated us as guests. In Tibet, the Tibetans were slaves, a fact that was made evident to us every day. How could we possibly believe the Chinese and the lies that they had been telling us for so long? Sometimes, I even wonder whether they have reached the point where their inventions now seem to them to be the truth. I do not believe that hope can exist in such a system. The Chinese imagine that they are a superior race while we are not worth anything at all. They consider us to be a backward, barbaric people and enslave us so that they can more easily exploit the riches of our country.

I realized to what extent the number of Tibetans who still had the means to defend our cause or bring about any change in this tragic situation, was diminishing. We are reduced to a situation of waiting. The population shows, on the whole, exceptional courage and remains entirely devoted to His Holiness the Dalai Lama and the government in exile. However, after 30 years of suffering, the life of the vast majority is reduced to a struggle for survival. As for the few Tibetans who are trusted by the Chinese, they are the worst sort of scoundrels and will do anything to satisfy the occupying forces. People like this have been a problem in all countries. The Communists have given them just enough education to obey orders, which they vilely execute. These people no longer have any understanding of traditional Tibetan culture. Placed by the Chinese in high administrative posts, they imagine that they exercise real power, whereas in fact they are manipulated by the Chinese who have turned them into tyrants over their own people.

Forgive me if I repeat here, for the sake of the Tibetans in exile, to what extent our freedom in India, and the other host countries, is precious. It is only here that we can prepare our country's future. We are neither backward nor barbaric, as the Chinese say, and certainly not when compared with what they have done in our country. We must hold our heads up and, above all, sustain our thirst for democracy.

The Chinese should feel guilty and ashamed. Instead, this supposedly great new China is trying at all costs to deceive the rest of the world. Is that its karma? The truth cannot be stifled for ever. The day of reckoning is approaching for China. Today we are witnessing its exploitation of our people. What is the point of brutal economic development when a people's dignity is continually ridiculed!

We still have a long way to go. We must work unceasingly in every area, because this is the only way to meet the challenge imposed by the occupier. We must also appreciate the true value of everything we have in exile, and never forget the wisdom proffered by the Dalai Lama. His Holiness thinks of Tibet and of those who suffer there every day. He makes preparations for our nation's future with the government and with all of us. He has often said: 'I believe that no matter how strong the wind of evil may blow, the flame of truth will never be extinguished.' We must always keep these words in our mind.

After the invasion of 1949, China imposed a huge programme of collective farming. The nomads and farmers saw their flocks confiscated, and they were themselves divided into brigades and communes. Those who were allowed to keep their flocks had no commercial rights over them. The Tibetans had to try and stay alive with an average annual diet of 5 or 6 pounds of butter,

10 pounds of meat and 4 or 5 khels (between 25 and 30 pounds) of tsampa. During the early 1960s the famine worsened inexorably. The occasional refugees who managed to cross the frontier told us how their countrymen now fed themselves on rats, dogs, worms and anything that was remotely edible. Besides, almost every family had been a victim, either physically or mentally, of the systematic repression inflicted by the Communist authorities in charge of Tibet.

From 1966 onwards, the key words became 'total Sinisation' with, as its first consequence, a total ban on the Tibetan language, which was considered a religious language. The monks, nuns and qualified Tibetan lay teachers were ordered to leave their jobs. Even Tibetan grammar books were declared to be 'books of blind faith' and everything was done to make their use impossible. In their place, the little leaflets of Mao Tse-tung's thoughts and the bulletins of Chinese propaganda were integrated into the school curriculum. Children were told that religion was only a superstitious practice, an outdated belief; the Tibetan language, useless and backward, was presented as the heritage of an old-fashioned, barbaric and oppressive society. Those on good terms with the invader were considered to be progressive; others were classified as counter-revolutionaries, reactionaries or enemies of the working classes. An entire generation of Tibetans was brought up completely ignorant of their own civilization and history. Chinese words with Marxist connotations replaced the Tibetan names for houses, roads and squares. Tibetans were even forced to change their family name for a Chinese name. Norbulingka, His Holiness's summer palace, was given the new name of 'the people's public park'.

A few months after the annexation of Tibet, the Beijing government declared: 'The Chinese Communist party considers that its ideology and that of religion are two forces that cannot co-exist. The differences between the two, that is to say between science and religion, can be compared to light and darkness, to truth and lies. There is no possible reconciliation between these two mutually opposed points of view.' Mao himself added: 'To be sure, religion is a poison. It has two big faults: it attacks race and the country's progress is held up. Tibet and Mongolia were both poisoned by religion.'

In the mid-50s the occupying authorities realized to what extent religion constituted the main obstacle to their total control over Tibet. From 1956, the monasteries, temples and centres of culture were systematically ransacked and then totally destroyed. First of all, mineralogists visited the sites to find and carry away all the precious stones. Then, other teams arrived and marked all the metal objects, which were then taken away in trucks by soldiers to an unknown destination. Finally, once the beams and pillars had been taken away, the walls were dynamited and the sculptures destroyed in the hope of finding further precious metals. Only a pile of wood and stones remained, whatever had survived the fires. Hundreds of tons of valuable statues, tankas, works of art in metal and other treasures were taken by road to China and sold on the international art markets of Hong Kong, Singapore or Amsterdam, or, even worse, melted down.

Contrary to Beijing's official statements, the greater part of Tibet's cultural and religious heritage was destroyed between 1956 and 1961, and not during the famous Cultural Revolution of 1966 to 1976. Out of a total of 6,259 monasteries and nunneries, only 13 remained in 1976. Amongst the ruins were the monastery of Samye, the first Tibetan monastery, built in the eighth century; the most important Sakyapa monastery; the one at Tsorpu, one of the most prestigious Kagyupa monasteries; Ganden, the oldest and most venerated of the Gelugpa monastic universities; Mindroling, one of the most famous Nyingmapa spiritual centres; Menri, the oldest and most sacred Bon monastery ... Out of 592,558 monks, nuns and rinpoches, more than 110,000 were tortured and put to death and more than 250,00 forcibly derobed.

We also learnt that huge sterilization and abortion campaigns had been enforced throughout the country.

14

Progress in the Village

After a brief stop-over in Hong Kong and two days in New Delhi, our delegation arrived back in Dharamsala. We were received immediately by His Holiness. We were so moved that we were unable to hold back our tears.

His Holiness welcomed us warmly and asked us to give a detailed account of our journey. We gave him a complete report in an audience lasting a few hours. I handed him the 7,000 letters that we had brought back with us as well as several manuscripts that were saved from destruction. His Holiness wanted us to tell our exiled countrymen what we had seen in Tibet so that they could know about their country's real condition. After the return of the first delegation in 1979, they had avoided talking too much. As two further groups were to visit Tibet, they had had to show a certain prudence so as not to compromise these ventures. But the second delegation, after its unexpected departure from Tibet, had been contacted by various journalists when it returned to India. Public awareness of the situation in Tibet began at this point.

We were stopped by many Tibetans in the street who asked us questions about our stay. It was difficult to reply to them all. His Holiness asked us to brief first the Kashag and then the entire population. I sent a newsletter to all our friends and to the children's sponsors who wanted to know what was happening in Tibet. Several weeks later, I also wrote an article. The first three days were spent reporting to the Kashag. I was very moved and cried whenever I thought of the horrors we had encountered. Indeed, it took me a long time to recover.

Amala bombarded me with questions on my return. She was then 80 years old and knew that she would not return to Tibet. This period was very difficult for her. I was forced to tell her in detail about everything we had seen. Because of her age, I would have preferred to hide certain things from her but, overwhelmed by emotion, I felt obliged to reveal the extent of the tragedy that had overcome our people. I also told her about the family and friends I had seen again in Lhasa and Takster, and our meetings with the people. I pretended that the Chinese authorities had promised that the situation would improve after the visits of the three delegations. But Amala was not to be deceived. To try and distract her, I suggested that she watch television, but she was not interested. Besides, shortly after our return, my mother's younger sister arrived with her husband and three children and, once again, the account of the horrors began.

The shock was really terrible for Amala. She had always been extremely active although she suffered from high blood pressure. But, because of this awful and distressing news, she had a stroke and the entire left side of her body was paralysed. Fortunately, Tibetan medicine has an extraordinary remedy for this type of illness. After a few months, her condition had much improved, although I had to support her when she walked. Amala had understood that she would never again see her country. She had until then always hoped that she would end her days in her village of Taktser. It was disastrous for her to lose this hope.

Life went on at the Tibetan Children's Village. 23 October 1980 was going to be an important date: we would then celebrate the 20 years of our existence. We decided to make the commemoration a very special occasion. His Holiness honoured us with a visit and attended competitions between the schools: football, basketball, debates and recitations. I was able to compare what we had done in India, in a land of exile, with what I had just seen in Tibet. There, the schools were mere fronts, and the children were deprived of real teaching and were most often illiterate. Here, on the other hand, more than 400 student representatives from TCV schools throughout the country had gathered in Dharamsala for this celebration. The games opened with a parade. The entire staff were able to relish the work that had been accomplished. These festivities encouraged us to continue our work.

I found myself divided between joy and sadness: the joy of seeing hundreds of happy children surrounded by their foster parents; sadness because my mother's health was declining day by day. Lobsang Samten had returned from the United States and settled in Dharamsala. My younger brother also lived at home with his wife and two children. I paid very frequent visits to Amala and it was clear that her strength was failing.

The Dutch SOS Children's Village invited me to Amsterdam, but I hesitated at the thought of once again leaving Dharamsala. Amala was confined to bed and I found it very distressing to see my mother, who had been so active, totally dependent on her my sister-in-law and two servants. She herself had difficulty in putting up with their dependence. She urged me to leave: 'You're not a doctor, therefore you cannot help me!' In Amsterdam, ten days later, a telegram arrived announcing her passing away on 12 January 1981. I cancelled all my engagements and returned immediately to Dharamsala. Unfortunately, because of the astrologer's calculations for the funeral, Amala was cremated on 14 January, the day before my arrival.

The entire population of Dharamsala was in a state of shock at the announcement of her death and, on the day of the cremation, all the people gathered to pray. The shops were closed. The day after the funeral, I discovered an immense crowd massed on the side of the hill to pray for Amala. I could not stop crying, because Amala was much more than a mother. For several days I went to the place where she had been cremated and prayed at length as this was the only thing that I could do for Amala. At the time, His Holiness was in Bodh Gaya, the principal place of pilgrimage for Tibetans, where the Shakyamuni Buddha had attained Enlightenment.

Amala was truly the pillar of our family and the link between myself and my brothers. Her death did not change our relationships, but our occupations and families took up a lot of of our time and we saw one another less. My brothers, who used to spend all their holidays with Amala, no longer had any reason to come to Dharamsala, except to visit His Holiness on important occasions. I realized to what extent she had been the soul of our family.

In the 1980s, my family was to be found in many different parts of the world. Thubten Jigme Norbu still lived in the United States with his wife, Kunchok Yangkyi, and his three children, Lhundup Namgyal, Kunga Gyaltsen and Jigme Kunden. Gyalo Thondup was in Hong Kong. His two sons, Tenzin Khedroop and Ngawang Tempa, lived in Darjeeling. Their mother, Diki Dolkar had been greatly affected by the death of her first child, Yangzom Dolma, in 1982. Lobsang Samten's children, Tenzin Chukie and Tenzin Namdhak, were at university and his wife, Namgyal Lhamo, still worked for the government in exile. My youngest brother, Tenzin Choegal, lived in Dharamsala with his wife, Rinchen Khando. Their two children, Tenzin Chonzom and Tenzin Lodoe, attended school at the TCV.

We continued our work tirelessly. For the first time all the heads of the TCV schools met together in a group called the 'Management and Finance Committee'. In meetings opinions were exchanged and the difficulties of each establishment, especially those involving education, hygiene and health, discussed. The organization worked in an entirely democratic manner, serving the various villages and schools. With the children and staff, we were in fact one large family.

Since we were dispersed over a wide geographical area, these meetings were extremely necessary. We were all part of an organization formed to serve our children, and they were our country's future. At the time we were having problems with the school in Ladakh. No one wanted to go there as the winters were very hard, like those in Tibet; most of our teachers had lived in the south of India and found it difficult to withstand the severe cold. We therefore organized the teachers into teams on a rota system: teachers from the south went to Ladakh, while those who were in Ladakh came to Bylakuppe and Dharamsala.

In May 1982, Doctor Hermann Gmeiner, president of SOS Kinderdorf, inaugurated our village in Ladakh, and decided to build seven homes for the Ladakhi children. I made it a point of honour that the foster mothers should be from the region. The other priority was the teaching of Ladakhi, a language derived from Tibetan. In 1975, when we first started our work in Ladakh, the village was situated in the midst of a vast expanse of sand and rocks. Little by little, the children and village staff began to transform their establishment into a small oasis, in the extreme north-west of a region that borders on Tibet. In 1981/82, they planted trees and made small gardens. Today the village is an example of what can be done through continuous work and strong willpower.

Wherever I went, it was also my duty to talk, and I always used the opportunity to mention the situation in our country. Evidently, the Beijing government did not appreciate our comments. On several occasions relations were almost at breaking point, because they did not want the world to know the truth. In the meantime, among the numerous Tibetans who continued to cross the border, there was an increasing number of children. Between 1980 and 1982, more than 1,000 managed to reach Dharamsala. Several hundred were admitted to the TCV and to Mussoorie. The others, who wished to become monks, were sent to the different Tibetan monasteries in India. Every year the number of young people between the age of 6 and 20 rose, and so did the number of monks. After the return of our delegation, an average of 4–5,000 refugees arrived each year from Tibet, including children, adults and monks. Some of them settled permanently in India, others simply came on pilgrimage and then went back to Tibet – they had to leave the name of a member of their family in order to guarantee their return and 'good behaviour'. They were also forced to indicate the length of time they would be away. These pressures were terrible: if they did not return, the lives of their family back in Tibet were at risk.

Children were often entrusted to the travellers to India if the parents themselves were unable to go. But, between 1987 and 1988, the Chinese authorities tried to further tighten the borders. However, quite a few, including children, managed to cross the border illegally, after several weeks' walk through the mountains. Some died on the way. Quite a few lost a finger or a toe, or their legs had to be amputated on their arrival. On arriving in a deplorable condition in Kathmandu, their only aim was to study and seek His Holiness's blessing. Travellers brought us groups of between 10 and 20 such children.

The TCV staff at the village looked after them. It was terrible for these children to have people endlessly asking them the same questions about the awful events they had lived through in Tibet. I therefore decided to ask the staff not to question them any more, except in certain very specific cases. Only the people who were directly responsible for this duty were allowed to listen to their tales. It was above all necessary to help them to exorcize all these horrors from their past. In the junior classes this took the form of drawing; the same subjects were always repeated: Tibetans in chains and monks shot by Chinese soldiers. The children hardly ever used colour.

At the TCV in Dharamsala, the number of children went up from 1,000 to 1,200, then to 1,500 and finally to 1,700. Today, 2,200 children live amongst us. The homes, which were originally intended to house 25 children each, now house double that number. In one house, a record 55 was reached, which of course was far too many. These children had undergone serious psychological trauma and required very special attention. The foster mothers were particularly overwhelmed. Therefore, we placed some children in TCV, Lower Dharamsala, and at the TCVs in Bylakuppe and Pathli Kuhl. In this way, our numbers dropped a little, although we still have over 2,000 pupils.

However, there was absolutely no question of us turning away children from Tibet because of overcrowding in the homes. They had come to India to be educated near His Holiness; they represented not just our only hope but also the only hope for their parents. Luckily, the sponsorship system went very well during the 1980s. The entire world began to be aware of the real situation in Tibet: 6,000 monasteries destroyed, 1,200,000 dead, no education system, widespread illiteracy, fundamental human rights violation and cultural genocide. Above all, the sponsors had become aware of the importance of their role. Even though the number of children increased every day, so too did the amount of aid.

The smallest children were looked after from the moment of their arrival, and the foster mothers gave them a lot of love and attention. Thanks to this care, little by little their wounds were healed. Only those who had witnessed torture and murder, especially that of their parents, had difficulty in recovering. The mothers of the homes were then asked to give these children special attention.

The condition of the young people between 13 and 20 was even more delicate. We decided to open a school for them in Bir. The establishment specialized in training young people with serious psychological problems who had sublimated their experiences and emotions. They arrived longing for their new-found freedom, but they were extremely aggressive and always on the defensive. Most of these young people had been born during the Cultural Revolution and we had difficulty in winning their confidence because they had grown up in an atmosphere of continual mistrust. Following our advice, the establishment head, Gen Tenzin La, gave priority to sports such as basketball, volleyball and football. He told us that they needed to replace the balls every day because the children transferred all their hate of the Chinese and their past repression onto them. Gen Tenzin La had been one of my sister's first colleagues.

We also taught them manual skills. Because the students were unable to maintain attention for several hours of lessons in mathematics, English or Tibetan, the part played by sport and manual work was stressed. Each pupil was in this way able to work at his own speed. Gen Tenzin La took them in small groups, sometimes individually, and spent time talking to them. He listened to news of their families and tried to find out their origins and the route they had taken to reach India. He told them that they were here thanks to His Holiness, who was giving them a chance to be educated that they must not miss. In my ardent desire to see these adolescents emerge from hell, I frequently went to Bir.

Many of the young smoked and refused to learn but, not knowing what else to do, remained in the homes. The dormitories were overcrowded and we had a great deal of trouble in dealing with the problem. Rootless and permanently scarred by their life in Tibet in an oppressed society, they had difficulty in adapting to their new freedom. However, with patience and a great deal of attention, the situation improved. We devoted time to explaining to them that we were there to help them and to be of use to them, and that their future was very important to us. The adolescents who had been at Bir for two or three years helped us and also spent a lot of time talking to the new arrivals. This helped enormously.

In 1991, rather serious problem arose; violent clashes occurred between the students, sometimes with stone throwing. We were to a certain extent responsible. We had accepted young people of 20 and over, with the oldest being 30. There were then over 700 pupils living in Bir, most of them between 13 and 16. Gangs formed around various leaders and the tension became unbearable. The Indian police even had to intervene to break up and calm the disputes. First of all, we decided to expel the leaders and to speak to all the others in groups of 20. They all reacted in the same way: it was not possible for them to live with men over 20. An age limit for attending Bir was therefore fixed.

But what were we to do with the others? The most conscientious were allowed to continue their studies and an occupation was found for the rest. Since this day, Bir has not had any problems. After being trained, those who wanted to do so were encouraged to return to their families in Tibet.

Every moment spent with these adolescents was proof that the Chinese had constantly violated human rights. China may continue to claim that it has given Tibetans an education, but what are a few educated people worth when compared with the permanent and massive violation of fundamental rights? It was not enough to train an individual to be a minister, or to turn nomads into people's representatives. These rare appointments only existed to hide an enormous tragedy.

15

The Struggle of Tibetan Women

As a woman and mother I have always deeply resented the unspeakable destruction of my country by the Chinese. By 1980, the Tibetans were no more than a minority in their own country. I had met many children of between seven and ten. When I asked their mothers why they had not had any other children, they invariably replied that they did not know why. In fact, they had been sterilized when giving birth. Such behaviour is cruel and unspeakable! This is where my fight as a Tibetan woman comes into play.

For 33 years, I have devoted my life to children. I do not know anything about politics and I am certainly not a politician. I do not work for honours or for a monument to be erected in my memory. I want to remain honest to myself and to my religion, Buddhism. I sincerely want to serve the children and this is my contribution to the Tibetan cause.

I have never been trained in any particular educational skill and have had to learn everything as I went along. When I was confronted with a problem, I had to solve it quickly; I therefore learnt fast. When, in 1964, His Holiness told me to continue my sister's work, I simply rolled up my sleeves and got on with it. Of course, I have often been asked to talk on the subject of Tibetan women and their situation in Tibet, but my priority, my concern, remains the children.

On the other hand, there is an association of Tibetan women

very motivated and active. They do an extraordinary job and play an important role in the society of exiled Tibetans. They are not only actively involved in the Tibetan struggle for justice and freedom, but one of their priorities is to take up the issues that deeply effect Tibetan women, including denouncing the sterilization and abortion programmes that the Chinese have enforced. It is unthinkable for a mother not to be able to choose the number of children she wishes to bring into the world. In an age of contraception and family planning, there is nothing more horrible than sterilization or the death of a child in its mother's womb. I try to associate with the work of these women as much as possible but, as I have said, the work at the Children's Village takes priority and there is also a lot else to be done.

I regret that so little has been written on the role of women in our society. In fact, one can infer from this that the activities and aspirations of half the Tibetan population have not been accorded the importance they merit. Our ancestors have left us what is probably the richest collection of religious literature in the world. On the other hand, writings on the role of women in the evolution of Tibet over the last 2,000 years are very few.

I am, however, very happy to observe that, over the last few years, Tibetan women have taken the initiative to participate in a more active manner in the social life of their country. Unlike in the past, when they concerned themselves almost exclusively with domestic tasks, today more and more women take part in areas as diverse as business, finance, industry, the arts, literature, politics, government and sport. What is more, they are trying to define a new identity so as to rid themselves of the stereotyped image of the housewife.

These attempts have been encouraged and facilitated by exile. The Tibetan community living abroad, whether in India, Europe or the United States, has been confronted with new ways of thinking. It has seen the world differently. I am not a historian and I do not consider myself to be a specialist on the Tibetan question. Nevertheless, I would like to talk about the status of women in Tibet with regard to their more important role since the 1959 uprising in Lhasa. The reader will then be able to realize the exceptional degree of independence which women had enjoyed in traditional Tibet.

As a general rule, Tibetan women have always held a high

social position. It was perhaps less high than that demanded by feminist movements in Western countries, but better than that in many Asian countries. Thus, even though the traditional structure of Tibetan society was patriarchal, women's feet were never bandaged as they were in China. In the same way, cases of female infanticide, such as those in India, were unknown. The position of the Tibetan women 'is on par with their exceptionally independent character – they are free economically, and have their own property which makes divorce easy. They often manage their husbands' finances. Their economic position is as strong among herdsmen as among cultivators' (R A Stein, *Tibetan Civilization*).

Tibetan historians writing about the second century AD have made reference to a kingdom of women in the south-east of Tibet. These women held political power; the men were either warriors or servants. Greek legends also mention a similar kingdom in the west of Tibet that even Alexander the Great was unable to subdue. But these kingdoms had practically disappeared when Tibet entered the era of written history, around the seventh century AD.

Under the rule of the Yarlung dynasty (seventh to ninth century AD), the mothers of Tibetan emperors played an important political role. Tibetan empresses and princesses played a very active part in government affairs. They were amongst the first Tibetans to be attracted to Buddhism. In 1926, in *We Tibetans*, Rinchen Lhamo wrote: 'With us neither the one sex nor the other is considered the inferior or the superior. Men and Women treat each other as equals . . . Husband and Wife are companions and partners.' And in 1949, Lowell Thomas's *Out of this World* noted: 'In Tibet, unlike most Asiatic countries, women have had equal rights with men since the early days of Buddhism.'

Religion is perhaps the only area where women are not considered equal to men. The Tibetan word for woman, *kyemen*, means 'of inferior birth'. In Rita M Gross's book on Yeshe Tsogyal there is a poignant account of the frustrations encountered by Tibetan women desiring to teach Buddhism: 'Inadequate women like me with little energy and an inferior birth incur the world's hostility. When we go begging, the dogs are hostile. If we possess food or wealth then thieves molest us. If we are attractive then we are bothered by people. Even if we do nothing the tongues of malicious gossips turn against us. If our attitude is improper than the whole world is hostile. Whatever we do, the lot of a women on the path is a miserable one. To maintain our practice is virtually impossible, and even to stay alive is difficult.' In reply, Padmasambhava taught Yeshe Tsogyal the Buddhist view of the equality of the sexes: 'The human body is the basis for the attainment of wisdom. The body of a woman and the body of a man are equally suited to this task.' Yeshe Tsogyal surmounted all the obstacles posed by her sex and reached 'the state of Buddha'. Besides Yeshe Tsogyal, other remarkable women are to be found in Tibetan history.

The role of women in Tibetan religious life is still minimal compared with that of men. Out of the thousands of reincarnations recognized by Buddhist tradition, only three women are to be found: Machik Labdon from Lhoka in the south of Tibet; Shugseb Jetsun from Lhasa; and the most famous, Samding Dorje Phagmo, who was the mother superior of the monastery of Samding, near the banks of Lake Yamdro Tso in southern Tibet. In *Tibetan Women: Then and Now*, Indra Majupuria relates how, after the Chinese invasion, Samding Dorje Phagmo, then 18, renounced her vows and became a member of the Chinese People's Consultative Committee, an organization made up of important Tibetans, but without real power.

The invasion with all its atrocities was the catalyst for Tibetan women to group together and form a cohesive political and social force. In the east of Tibet, the growing number of demands and atrocities by the Chinese provoked a revolt against the People's Liberation Army. This protest spread across the entire country and culminated in the 1959 uprising. That year, the women of Lhasa created the Tibetan Women's Association.

Two days after the National Uprising of 10 March, they descended into the streets of Lhasa. In *Daughter of Tibet*, Rinchen Dolma Taring recounts that the demonstrators 'were bravely led by Serong Kunsang (also known as Kundeling Kunsang) who was like a Tibetan Joan of Arc. Usually she was shy and respected us and would not speak freely to us, but now she instructed me to go to the Indian Consul General to ask India to help Tibet – which I did. She was a real heroine. Poor woman, we heard that when she was arrested and interrogated; after the uprising, she said that her actions were all her own responsibility and that no one else should be blamed. She was beaten and lost an eye and was later shot dead.

The Lhasa women had made many anti-Chinese posters and when I joined them they were lined up around the Barkor shouting slogans – 'From today Tibet is independent!' and 'China must quit Tibet!' Our women were more fierce than our men.

Like Kundeling Kunsang, other women paid with their lives for their resistance against the Chinese oppressor: Ganning Sha Choela, Tawutsang Dolkar, Demo Chimi, Tsongkhang Mimi, Ani Trinley Chodon, Gugarshar Kelsang and Risur Yangchen ... I mention these names as representatives of all those who were killed, aborted, sterilized, tortured or raped.

Even though the Chinese had repressed the Tibetan people's uprising, there was renewed longing for a free and independent Tibet. From 1966 to 1976, China, and therefore Tibet, was involved in the torment of the Cultural Revolution. In China, this was above all a campaign launched by Mao to remove all possibility of opposition. In Tibet, on the other hand, their aim during this troubled period was to eradicate the culture and traditions of the country. In order to combat this vast human and cultural genocide, a nun from Nyemo, a few miles from Lhasa, provoked an uprising. Unfortunately, this movement organized by Ani Trinley Chodon met the tragic fate reserved for all Tibetan uprisings. Its leader was captured and executed in front of thousands of inhabitants of Lhasa.

In 1979, when His Holiness the Dalai Lama sent the first fact-finding delegation to report on the situation in Tibet, Tsering Lhamo, more commonly known as Rangtsen Ama, fell foul of the Chinese authorities. A huge crowd had gathered around Norbulingka, His Holiness's summer palace, and Tsering Lhamo had shown her support for the Dalai Lama by shouting that the Chinese should leave Tibet. After the delegation left, she was arrested, and was only released from prison in 1982, after the intervention of Amnesty International. Her son, Lobsang Chodak, who was also imprisoned, is said to be still detained. Tsering Lhamo eventually succeeded in escaping from Tibet and today lives in Dharamsala.

I will here add a few words concerning Tibetan nuns. In the last few years they have led a non-violent movement to restore freedom in Tibet. As spearheads of most of the recent demonstrations, many were imprisoned and tortured, and large numbers died in labour camps or prisons after horrible sufferings.

One demonstration particularly moved me. It had been organized, in May 1988, by nine nuns from the convent of Shungseb, near Lhasa. They were immediately arrested for shouting slogans against the Chinese, interrogated and tortured. One of them, Ani Kelsang Pelmo, later related in the *Tibetan Bulletin*: 'All of us were separately interrogated. I was asked who our ringleader was, whether we had outside support and what the purpose of our demonstration was. To save my fellow nuns, I said I was the ringleader and that we had no outside support. 'We are simple nuns, pursuing our religious studies but you have arrested our lamas, our monks and nuns. It is to tell you to release them that we have staged the demonstration.'

Driven to fury by Ani Kelsang Pelmo's determination, the Chinese officials set an Alsatian dog on her. The dog leapt at her throat and knocked her over: 'I imagined that I was going to be killed; but I managed to pick up a stone and hit the beast on the head. Later, the officials accused me of having killed it.' The interrogation went on for a long time. Ani Kelsang Pelmo persisted: 'I have already told you that I was the leader and that we had no outside help. Even if you kill me, I have nothing else to say. One of the officials replied: "OK, what does it matter if we kill you. Maybe we will finish you all off and give your bodies to the dogs to eat."'

The nine nuns were released three months later. They were able to flee to India and today also live in Dharamsala.

Even if the experience of exile is painful, it must be admitted that it has enabled the women of Tibet to evolve. Liberated from the taboos which had previously confined them to specific occupations, they have with time acquired a modern education and, because of this, can now contribute to improving the condition of the Tibetan community in exile. For example, in the medical corps, women now outnumber the men.

I will also take advantage of this book to pay special homage to those women who, in exile, fulfil the role of foster mothers to thousands of Tibetan orphans, children whose parents, during their flight in 1959, died on the roads or were killed in fights. Besides education, these young have a desperate need for love and attention. It was to assure them of both a decent education and a harmonious emotional environment, that the TCV was

My first marriage to
Lhundup Gyalpo

Tempa Tsering, my second
husband, with two of my
children

(Right)
Lhundup Gyalpo
with our three
children: Tenzin
Choedon (1966),
Kelsang Yangzom
(1968) and Tenzin
Choedhak (1972)

Discovering the horror

Fear can be seen in the eyes of the children under Chinese occupation.

Canton, 1980. The second Tibetan delegation on its way to Beijing. To the left, the Chinese translator.

As soon as we arrived in Tibet, we realized that oppression had not diminished the faith of the Tibetan people.

My brother Gyalo Thondup, the Panchen Lama and Phuntsok Wangyal (from left to right).

Life at the Tibetan Children's Village

(photographs by Tenzin Dorjee)

Life at the Tibetan Children's Village

His Holiness inaugurates the Tibetan SOS Youth Hostel in Delhi
with Mr Helmut Kutin, President of SOS-Kinderdorf International
and Mr J N Kaul, President, SOS Children's Villages of India.

Dharamsala, 1994. With Village Directors and School
Principles of TCV branches

1993. Here in Ladakh,
the elderly are also
looked after by TCV

Dharamsala, 1978
The first TCV graduates

Bir, 1995. The new homes at the TCV SOS School in Bir

Taking oath in front of His Holiness. The first woman elected as a Kalon (minister) in the first election of the Kashang (Cabinet) members.

My favourite photograph: His Holiness the Dalai Lama with children in traditional Tibetan dress.

Dharamsala, 1995. Myself with TCV children

Kalimpong, 1976. Amala

created. At the beginning, when the children were still traumatized and had to adapt to a new culture without the help of their parents, the foster mothers gave them their love. With the benefit of a modern education, these children have become balanced people, while still remaining aware of their cultural roots. Today they contribute greatly to the development of the Tibetan community.

But the energy of the Tibetan women in exile is above all devoted to the struggle to re-establish freedom in Tibet. It is towards this end, with His Holiness's encouragement, that the Tibetan Women's Association works. It also aims to preserve and promote our religion and culture and to improve the social conditions of the community in exile.

The TCV takes up nearly all of my time. Self-taught, I was absolutely unprepared for such a job. I therefore had to work very hard and to read a great deal, often to the detriment of my own family life. When a children's village was built in Ladakh or Bylakuppe, or a school created in the valley of Kulu, my sole concern was to watch over the successful running of these establishments.

After I returned from Tibet, I continued to travel frequently. I spent less than six months a year in Dharamsala, even though my home and children were there. My role had changed somewhat. Above all I lent my help to those who worked in the children's villages. We had also been very lucky. Often, the children from the TCVs went on to gain further qualifications before returning to work with us in positions of responsibility in the schools and children's villages around India. Today, 75 per cent of the staff come from the TCVs. These people, about 40 years old, now have their own families and their children are receiving a Tibetan schooling in our midst. Tashi La for instance, a Tibetan who works in our office, had been part of the first group of children who arrived at the village. She finished her schooling, then married and had three children. One of her daughters teaches at the TCV school in Bir.

Today, there are over 11,000 children in the TCVs. I cannot therefore take on other activities. I must also prepare those who will take over, because it is essential for a country to have the greatest possible number of potential leaders. At the TCV, when I am absent, the management makes decisions and is responsible for them. The young must also take the initiative. After 33 years of service the villages are working very well. I am like a mother to them: I first of all listen to the people, advise them – and sometimes shake them up too.

The Tibetan cause must take precedence over everything else and remain at the centre of our preoccupations. I often talk about this with the children at the TCVs. As both individuals and Tibetans, they must recognize their responsibility to Tibet, and to the 1,200,000 Tibetans who died and all those who still suffer there.

His Holiness's response to the Chinese has been through non-violence. This is certainly the best solution for the Tibetan cause. It is the same for any people, anywhere in the world. Today we live in a nuclear age. During the 1970s and 1980s the Soviet Union and the United States engaged in an unbridled arms race for military superiority. Now the Soviet Union has broken apart and the Berlin Wall has fallen; everyone is now recommending arms reductions and the destruction of the nuclear arsenal.

In this astonishing world, His Holiness has always spoken up for peace and universal responsibility. With universal responsibility, it becomes possible to support peace and non-violence. Where does peace begin if not in men's hearts? If everyone was at peace within themselves, it would be easier to talk about peace at a world level. The world is more than ever in need of peace. It is the responsibility of us all. We must not think just about ourselves, but about our children, grandchildren and great-grandchildren. It is indeed essential to instil peace in the minds of the young. At the TCV we constantly reflect on the best way to do this.

His Holiness proposes to transform Tibet into a vast Zone of Peace where Tibetans can live in harmony with nature. I find this idea absolutely magnificent and noble. But how can it happen? It is first of all necessary to understand that peace is not a geographical or physical concept: it must first of all exist in people's hearts and minds. It must therefore be taught to children so that they may learn to live in peace.

I am convinced that education is the means by which we can attain this objective. I try to put this into practice in the TCV. For example, each time I see two children arguing, I immediately

intervene. In fact, fights are rare in the village. But w
happen, we talk to the children and teach them to excha
different points of view. They must realize that it is so
stupid to fight. Then the children can go off once more to
play together.

We also live in an age of communication. But, overwhelmed
by our various activities, we do not make sufficient time to talk
or communicate. Many human values are not developed. When
people sit down at the same table and listen to one another,
things usually sort themselves out. For me, peace is positive and
quarrels, above all war, are negative. I always say to children
that they should lean towards positive things, and act in the
same way.

We are at the dawn of the twenty-first century, but what a
world we live in! We may have made prodigious scientific
discoveries and technology has undoubtedly developed to an
extraordinary extent, but, with all this knowledge, we are
incapable of living in peace and respecting each other. What is
the real meaning of all this progress and the evolution of our
society? Our objective should be to make things better
for everyone.

In exile, few young Tibetans are impatient. They sometimes
feel frustrated at not being able to combat the Chinese with
violence. They would like to be able to use terrorist tactics, like
the Palestinians. But what would that change? Tibet would be on
the front page of all the world's newspapers for a day or two. In
fact, our people would lose all the credit and respect that today
its non-violent position attracts.

Every Tibetan is driven forward by the hope of returning to
Tibet. I am convinced that our efforts will not be in vain.
However long it takes, the day will come when we will return
with dignity to a country that will once again be free. Perhaps
tomorrow, perhaps in 10 years, perhaps only in 50. But whatever
the date, we are determined to take our destiny in our own
hands. Why do we have this hope, this inner force? I suppose
that suffering creates hope. Hope generates energy. We must use
it to give the best of ourselves. What is happening to Tibet is
terrible. We have lost our country and witnessed unspeakable
atrocities. But these events have also strengthened our
determination to survive, to become independent once again
and to safeguard our cultural identity.

The Chinese first of all invaded Tibet; then they destroyed our unique cultural heitage and colonized the country. We are determined to resist them and to take up the challenge, because they must not succeed. Our struggle is made possible through education. As long as there are children having a Tibetan education, our culture will survive. In this troubled period of our country's history, I say to myself that I am lucky to have been born the Dalai Lama's sister, to be able to make myself useful to the Tibetan cause and to serve my people. Each year, hundreds of children, like Kalsang Gyaltsen, whose escape story is told in the next chapter, and many others like him, cross the Himalayas and risk their lives to receive a Tibetan education next to His Holiness the Dalai Lama.

16

A Child's Story

The period of relative liberalization that followed the return of the delegations again gave many Tibetans the opportunity to flee their country. More and more children also took the road to exile to have a Tibetan education. Their parents knew that in keeping their children with them they were condemning them to indoctrination by the Chinese. As soon as the children arrived in the village they were were given all possible care and attention. When we had gained their trust they eventually told us about the sufferings and trials they had been through. Because of these testimonies, we lived the horrors of the Tibetan tragedy day by day. It is not possible to recount here all the broken lives; instead, I will take one story as an example. It is the tale of Kalsang Gyaltsen, the second of a family of three children, who was 12 years old at the time of these events.

Born in the north of Tibet, in the Chang Thang plains, Kalsang Gyaltsen lived in a nomad settlement on the edge of a mountain. The neighbouring forest contained leopards, wild cats and brown bears. The mountain peaks were white, but the opposite slope of the mountain looked black. On one side the nomads raised sheep, on the other, the Tibetans mostly bred yaks. A river flowed close to the encampment, on the opposite bank of which there were pastures. The landscape was magnificent. In the winter, the nomads lived inside one-roomed houses, built close to the forest to make the gathering of wood easy. In the summer, they pitched their black tents made from yak wool on the vast expanses of land where their animals grazed peacefully.

Kalsang Gyaltsen's mother, a nomad, came from a neighbouring region. The family included several monks and, in particular, an important and rich lama. When the Chinese arrived, they were immediately branded as reactionaries. His grandparents underwent thamzing sessions, where they were jeered at, insulted and beaten. His grandfather died as a result of these repeated beatings, but his grandmother survived. His great-uncle was also tortured with heavy logs that the Chinese rolled on his arms and legs.

Kalsang Gyaltsen's father came from a fairly poor peasant family from central Tibet. After his marriage, he in turn became a nomad. Kalsang Gyaltsen was unable to give us any further details about his family. In Tibet, older people's names referred to the names of places and regions. The Chinese had changed these names and it now sometimes became very difficult to know where people came from. At the time, his mother was 38 and his father 42. Born in 1978, Kalsang Gyaltsen was 12 years old when he decided to flee. His parents had told him how the Chinese had destroyed all the monasteries in the region and had assembled all the nomads of the camp and taken all their possessions: jewellery, carpets and sacred objects. Afterwards, the Chinese had forcibly settled them, placing them first of all in camps before transferring them to various municipalities.

The Tibetans were put in groups of 30 and heavily taxed by the authorities. Each family regularly paid an average of 25 gyamas (500 grams) of butter per dri, whether or not it gave milk, and two gyamas of milk per sheep. If their production exceeded this quota, the family could keep the surplus. On the other hand, if the animals fell ill or were eaten by wolves or by brown bears, they had to pay the difference in cash. The sheep were frequently victims of wild animals and sudden avalanches, and this system therefore increased the population's anxiety. In bad years, Kalsang Gyaltsen's parents even had to buy butter and wool.

Sometimes they managed to thwart the authorities' plans. As the region was pretty inaccessible, the Chinese only went there infrequently. The inhabitants, warned of their approach, had time to hide the sheep in the mountains. Kalsang Gyaltsen's parents owned three horses, 35 dri, 20 yaks and 100 sheep. The milk dri and the young animals were kept in a pen and the yaks usually remained in the pastures. The animals were marked and each family could easily recognize which were theirs. The herds were gathered once a week so that a check could be kept on their numbers.

During the winter, which was extremely harsh in these regions, the river froze. In order to have water, the boy's family melted blocks of ice inside the house. The leopards and wild cats, famished and paralysed with cold, came down from the mountains and regularly attacked the herds. The yaks were not in much danger, except when the wild cats managed to isolate one. They would then leap onto its back, bite its throat and let it bleed to death. A wolf was easily identifiable, but the cats could slide into the midst of a herd of sheep and decimate it, in spite of the helpful presence of dogs.

To improve the household's income, Kalsang Gyaltsen's father sometimes went to Lhasa. He then needed a pass, which cost 15 yuans a day. A long-term permit could cost as much as 10,000 yuans. In order to cross the border into Nepal, Tibetans had to know Chinese or Tibetan officials in Lhasa. A passport cost 4–5,000 yuans. Monks were not able to procure one, even if they had a 1,000 yuans. On the road between Kham and Lhasa, Kalsang Gyaltsen's father bought a little merchandise from the Khampas which he then resold in his municipality. He took great care because he was not allowed to trade.

One day, Kalsang Gyaltsen saw two strangers arrive in the area. They were tall and fair, with large noses and funny hair. He regretted not being able to speak to them. They came and went with complete freedom and Kalsang Gyaltsen envied them enormously. He was still able to move freely in the village, but adults needed a pass at all times. This document had to be stamped by three or four administrations and it was usually almost impossible to obtain all the stamps. Any person discovered without a pass was made to pay a fine and sometimes imprisoned for several days. Although the villagers met few Chinese soldiers, informers were hidden everywhere, and this made the atmosphere even more strained.

No school existed in the region. When Kalsang Gyaltsen asked his father why, he cited the promise that the Chinese had made when the people's municipalities had been created: to bring progress to Tibet and build schools. More than 30 years later, famine had spread across the entire country, and the schools remained non-existent.

There was also a monastery in his village, called Balong, where 130 monks lived. His mother had explained to him how, as soon as they arrived, the Chinese military had murdered the lamas, pillaged and ransacked the sacred works of art and destroyed some of the buildings. They had installed lavatories in what remained. The *mani* stones were used to pave roads. In the 1980s, the region's inhabitants put the stones back in the monastery, which was then reopened, although only 17 monks were allowed to live there. Two or three Chinese came every month to count the monks, among whom there were no *tulkus* or reincarnated lamas.

Refusing to spend the remainder of his days looking after sheep and yaks in these conditions, Kalsang Gyaltsen told us that he took the decision to leave his family. He wanted to study and hoped to meet Gyalwa Rinpoche, the name by which Tibetans refer to His Holiness. Like some of the young Tibetans sent to Lhasa to study, he hoped to know a happier destiny. He naturally spoke to his parents about this, and they took him to the Chinese school of Nagchu Kha to enrol him there. The director of the establishment asked for 500 yuans a month for books, board and teaching. His parents were unable to pay such a sum. Kalsang Gyaltsen tried to hide his disappointment, understanding that the official was in fact trying to dissuade his parents by asking for such as astronomical sum. He then declared that he would like to become a monk at the monastery of Balong, where he would also be able to study. However, their quota of monks had already been reached. He would then secretly try his luck with the monasteries of Drepung, Sera and Ganden. In the event of failure, he was prepared to go as far as India.

Kalsang Gyaltsen began to prepare his plan a year before his departure, fixed for the 15th day of the first Tibetan month of the year of the Horse of Iron (March 1990). He worked out very precisely which road he would take to reach Lhasa. So as not to arouse suspicion, he carefully asked questions about the region, speaking mainly to experienced travellers, who thought that he was just a very curious child. Kalsang Gyaltsen felt that he was being deceitful.

Before Losar, his mother always got out his best clothes from the trunk where they were kept in mothballs. He wore them for a few days and then hid them, persuading his mother that he had carefully put them back himself. He then hid the pointed stick that his brother used to guard the flock of sheep. Because it was Losar and they were not visiting the pastures, his brother did not notice. He also hid a torch and set aside sheepskin clothes, to which he added a pair of Chinese tennis shoes which he hoped would be less slippery on the mountain rocks.

The day before his departure he decided to remain close to the house and tried to hide his nervousness and anxiety. After nightfall and the evening prayers, the young boy suddenly felt heavy of heart. He wondered about the future. That evening, he waited until all the family were asleep. His father had said a few mantras before blowing out the petrol lamp, and time seemed to crawl by. Finally, he silently slipped out of his bed, took his clothes rolled into a ball, opened the door with great care and then shut it gently behind him.

It was cold in the clear night. He quickly put on his clothes. Kalsang Gyaltsen saw from the moon that it was only 11 o'clock. He had chosen the 15th day for several reasons: the full moon would enable him to see where he was going until daybreak and no one would be surprised to see him outside at this hour because the 15th day of the first Tibetan month is considered a favourable day for saying mantras. Some people prayed all night.

It was almost impossible to get through the very deep snow without the help of yaks. Four enormous beasts preceded Kalsang Gyaltsen and cleared a path up to the summit of the mountain. When he had crossed over the first pass, he was again able to see the dark shadows of the yaks on the snow. He advanced very slowly, from pass to pass. By daybreak, he had crossed three passes and had reached a completely deserted spot. He opened his bundle and immediately went to sleep.

The boy walked like this for three nights. During the day, he hid in the mountains. Remembering the children's stories about devils and ghosts who haunted deserted places, he recited prayers to dispel his fear of the unknown. The road to Lhasa was straight, but Kalsang Gyaltsen preferred to avoid it. He was also very frightened of the enormous hounds that were big enough to scare wolves and sufficiently ferocious to kill and devour a child.

On the first day, when he was not sleeping, he played on the rocks. The place was quiet, with only a few birds and yaks, and rabbits who stood on their hind paws and observed him from a distance. The next day, Kalsang Gyaltsen got blisters which, because of the cold, burst and then bled. He suffered a lot. Then his skin began to peel, exposing a second skin which was almost raw. He now hardly felt the hunger that had been nagging him; since his departure he had eaten nothing but snow.

On the third evening, just after sundown, Kalsang Gyaltsen heard a wolf howl. The animal could not have been very far off. Suddenly he felt very lonely and began to tremble with fear. This predator seemed to be closer than the devils and ghosts. He tried to think what to do and in the end relied on good luck to escape. He lay down in the shelter of a rock and prayed, thinking very hard of Gyalwa Rinpoche. Little by little, he fell into a light sleep, imaging that Gyalwa Rinpoche was standing close to him, stroking his neck and telling him to resist and not to be frightened. His fear gradually disappeared, the wolf calmed down, and he slept deeply.

Early in the morning, his body was terribly swollen and numbed by the cold and he could not move. Luckily, his shoes had laces and he was able to take them off to rub his feet and warm them in the sun. Until now he had slept during the day, when the cold was still bearable. At night the temperature fell considerably. It took him an entire morning to get up and set off again. It now became vital to find a bit of food and shelter.

Kalsang Gyaltsen came down from the mountain to rejoin the main road to Lhasa. He continued walking for a whole day, reciting mantras in a low voice, the prayers that he generally said in the evening with his father. The Tibetans that he passed behaved kindly. Most of them thought he was lost or an orphan and put him up and fed him. Other asked him far too many questions for his liking and he decided not to say anything. He wanted to avoid being handed over to the Chinese authorities or meeting his father's trading partners, who would inevitably warn his parents. He spent three days with a family, bandaging his wounds and helping them with their various tasks. These worthy people suggested that he stay with them, but Kalsang Gyaltsen refused and continued on his way.

On the twentieth day of the second month, after 35 days, he

arrived outside Lhasa. Kalsang Gyaltsen decided to get rid of his baggage so as not to attract attention. That night, he found refuge in a house belonging to merchants. In the kitchen, the mother, eldest daughter and son asked him a lot of questions. While he ate, Kalsang Gyaltsen told them a story about a pilgrimage that made them laugh a lot, but did not satisfy their curiosity. So he added a few dramatic details about his family history in order to explain why he was alone. Then he pretended to be tired and the family at last left him alone. He silently sought the blessing of *Jowo* in the Jokhang.

The following morning, the elder son of the house offered to take Kalsang Gyaltsen to the Jokhang on his motorcycle. He had never ridden on such a beast, nor seen so many people. In the Jokhang he prayed to Jowo Rinpoche at length, asking for his help to reach India and to grant long life to Gyalwa Rinpoche and all his family. His companion wanted to help him, but he thanked him politely as he intended to hide in the Jokhang, where he was found by a monk going about his tasks. The monk led him to his small room, full of holy works and with a large number of thanka hanging on the wall. The boy explained that he wanted to get as far as Sera, where friends were waiting for him. Suddenly, two policemen, a Chinese and a Tibetan, burst into the room. The monk later explained that this kind of intrusion had become routine for the monks who were under constant suspicion. When the Tibetan asked him where he came from, Kalsang Gyaltsen said that he was a cousin of the monk's and that he was called Dawa and came from Nagchu Kha. The monk did not contradict him and the two men left the room.

Before reaching Sera, Kalsang Gyaltsen had to pass several guard posts where Chinese policemen stopped and questioned all those approaching the monastery. Meeting a monk, Kalsang Gyaltsen explained his intention to study sacred texts and become a monk. The monk told him that it had now become very difficult to do these things. A future monk needed to be well-connected, because his parents and family had to be questioned to check their political reliability by the Chinese authorities. Only then did the authorities give him authorization to live in a monastery. The candidate then had to find a master and place himself under his protection. Before being able to take part in the monastery's activities he had to do manual work for two years, remaining as discreet as possible.

Kalsang Gyaltsen asked to stay several days in Sera. A policeman watched his comings and goings inside the monastery, but it was easy to avoid him. The boy had to face the truth of his situation: at that time it was practically impossible to become a monk in Tibet. He decided to escape to India. By then many of them had already been expelled or arrested for taking part in demonstrations. The security forces regularly photographed demonstrators. Once the monks had been identified, Chinese policemen and soldiers encircled the monastery and led them away. For a first political offence they were mostly taken to prison, beaten and then sent home. The monks were forbidden to return to their monastery. The second time, the demonstrators were not only beaten but locked up for over a year; the third time they were either given life sentences or executed.

The police allowed only groups of two or three monks who had parents in Lhasa to leave town. Each monk always had to carry his pass with him, even when he was taking part in religious rituals.

Kalsang Gyaltsen set off again towards Lhasa. When night began to fall he was unable to find shelter and had to settle under a porch in the company of several beggars and a group of pilgrims from Amdo. Their dialect was difficult to understand, but he managed to exchange a few words with them and they shared a meal. At dawn, he continued on towards Ganden. There he encountered far fewer monks than he had in Sera, and they all seemed very young. The place looked desolate and sad. He had been told that after completely destroying the monastery the Chinese had begun its reconstruction. He was therefore surprised not to see any building in progress. In fact, the oldest monks had been taken away after the last demonstration and no outside person was authorized to take part in the building works. The living conditions at Ganden were far worse than those at Sera. The few monks were stuck in minute cells. Kalsang Gyaltsen stayed with them for a few days, but gave up for good the idea of studying in Tibet.

The boy remained in Lhasa for two weeks, living mainly in the monasteries. In the town he avoided lodging with the citizens, preferring to sleep outside under porches with beggars or pilgrims. It was necessary to be very careful, because he had been warned of the presence of numerous informers; he had to distrust everybody. All the same, people were generous to him and gave him food. In Ganden, Kalsang Gyaltsen had explained to a monk that he did not even have a bowl. The monk had then given him one in white enamel.

Kalsang Gyaltsen wanted to visit the Potala, but the Dalai Lama's palace was closed for renovation! No Tibetan was allowed into Norbulingka. However, he did manage to get in, even entering by the main entrance. He noticed a group of foreigners surrounding a Chinese guide. Drawn by curiosity, Kalsang Gyaltsen slipped among these people whom, he thought, had a strange appearance; he began to imagine a Marxist propaganda exercise like the kind of meetings his father had talked to him about. The sight astonished him. Some of the men were taking notes, others had cameras on their shoulders. The women, like the men, were tall. Their hair was of an extraordinary variety of colours: orange, yellow, brown and black. The young boy had never seen hairstyles like these. Their clothes also seemed to him extraordinary: trousers that were baggy or tight, long or short skirts like decorative vases, large jackets of every colour of the rainbow. He said to himself that they must all come from different countries and each be wearing their respective traditional costume.

When the Chinese stopped speaking, they all went towards Mingyur Potrang, Gyalwa Rinpoche's residence. They walked in a disorderly manner and he followed them. Apparently the foreigners appreciated his presence. One of them slipped a kind of envelope into his hand. The group went into the palace and the Chinese began to speak again, obviously commenting on the surroundings. The boy in this way saw the place where Gyalwa Rinpoche had lived. In one of the rooms there was a very simple bed. The group stopped for a long time in front of a fresco with the faces of several men painted in such a realistic way that they could have been about to talk. Gyalwa Rinpoche was certainly amongst them. Suddenly the guide, who had just noticed Kalsang Gyaltsen's presence, pointed at him. Everyone turned round to look at him. He gave a big smile to a lady who wore a kind of long mane; she returned the smile. The guide looked at him for a long time and then apparently decided to ignore him. The visit continued.

That night, Kalsang Gyaltsen slept in the park of Norbulingka. He found a very agreeable spot under some weeping willows. Just before daybreak, the birds began to sing above him in the clear sky. He felt the approach of spring; the branches were already carrying tiny buds. He opened the paper that the foreigner had given him and tasted the soft, brown mixture. Not liking it very much, he placed it back in its wrapping.

On leaving the park, he set off towards the monastery of Drepung, where he spent the day getting lost in the mazes. Then he met a monk whom he asked to write a letter to his parents: 'Dear parents, I am in Lhasa. When this letter reaches you, I will certainly be very far from here. I intend to go to school. Don't worry, everything will be all right.' Kalsang Gyaltsen deliberately omitted to say that he was going to India. A few days later, in the Barkhor, he met a merchant from a region near his own. This man promised to give the letter to his father. Now, he could leave Lhasa.

Kalsang Gyaltsen took the road towards Shigatse, the second largest town in Tibet, walking all day and stopping at night in farms. At one point, he thought of going directly as the crow flies, but then he resigned himself to going by the main road, which prolonged his journey. The inhabitants of Tsang seemed to him to be very poor compared with the regions where the nomads lived. The clothes seemed less warm and meat and butter were scarce. In the north of the country, he was sometimes given meat and butter when he begged. Here he was given only tsampa. Kalsang Gyaltsen stopped for five days at Sakya, then at Shigatse. He visited the monastery of Tashi Lhunpo and admired the mausoleum of the Panchen Lama.

His family had not particularly liked Panchen Lama and his father had told him one day that he did not like the way in which he had negotiated with the Chinese. He had instead placed his hope in Gyalwa Rinpoche. In spite of this, when he saw the Panchen Lama's intact body preserved in the mausoleum, the boy was unable to suppress his admiration and was filled by an indescribable feeling of grace. An ordinary person's body would have decomposed, but something impressive emanated from Panchen Lama.

Kalsang Gyaltsen left Shigatse and reached a crossroads. The road to the left was the one usually taken to cross the border to Nepal; that to the right led to Mount Kailash, from where one could also reach Nepal. Kalsang Gyaltsen's adventure did not end on Mount Kailash. At this point he met a learned monk called Geshe Senge, who carried out a divination and advised him to take the longest road to the border. After a long and treacherous journey through the mountains, he managed to arrive in Nepal.

In Dharamsala, Kalsang Gyaltsen often thought about his parents, and the moment when they first noticed his disappearance. His feeling of guilt was nevertheless fairly rapidly erased by the prospect of the future: studies, his contribution to the liberation of his country, the help that he would be able to bring to his parents when they were old.

At the TCV, thousands of similar stories have been told to us, all equally distressing. Some of them ended very badly, but this tale will serve to encourage tomorrow's Tibetan children.

The Chinese know that the essence of Tibetan Buddhism resides in a mental and spiritual development acquired through long study, under the direction of qualified lamas. They discourage these teachings through fallacious campaigns against the faith, reducing it to superstitious practices or blind faith, to the detriment of an honest presentation of its real nature. The policy that has been implemented by the Beijing government aims to slowly eliminate Tibetan culture and transform the country into an uneducated nation, good enough only to be exploited and manipulated by its occupier.

The present reconstruction of monuments and monasteries fits in with the strategic objectives of Communist China, both political and economic. The monuments serve as museums for tourists and are no longer temples of learning. In independent Tibet, the large monastic universities were centres of learning for a great many intellectuals and students from all over Central Asia. These institutions each welcomed between 3,000 and 10,000 students.

Before the Chinese invasion, Sera counted 7,997 monks; there are now about 300 there. There were over 10,000 monks at Drepung, whereas today there are no more than 400. Ganden had 5,600 monks; today it has 150.

Between 1980 and 1985, my life remained centred around the children's village. My journey to Tibet had influenced me considerably and reinforced my conviction to follow the path of justice. My work often took precedence over my family life. In

1970, my husband, Lhundup Gyalpo, left the Department of Finance, considering that the government in exile had sufficient staff. He wanted to devote more time to our three children's education. In 1973, he opened a restaurant in Bangalore, which also made it possible to help my mother a little. We therefore spent the winter holidays in the south of India, with Tenzin Choedon, Kelsang Yangzom and Tenzin Choedak. I often entrusted them to my husband and returned to Dharamsala to look after the children at the TCV.

The village site at Bylakuppe was consecrated on 17 July 1980 by His Holiness and officially inaugurated by him on 16 February 1984 in the presence of Mr Raghupathy, the Minister of Information, Broadcasting and Tourism of Karnataka State Government; Mr Helmut Kutin of SOS Kinderdorf International; and other foreign representatives, particularly the Dutch Ambassador in New Delhi. The village was, in fact, built thanks to the help of SOS Kinderdorf Holland, whose president was Yvonne Praxmeyer. The government in exile was now functioning well, the settlements were well established and His Holiness often visited the various regions of India. He was also frequently invited abroad, I saw him very rarely.

I had spent the winter of 1984 in Bylakuppe and, once the inaugural ceremonies for the new village were completed and operating smoothly, I returned to Dharamsala. It was March, just before the end of the school holidays and my three children were with me.

One night in May, at about two in the morning, I was abruptly woken by knocking at the window. I could also hear shouting. It was Diki Dolkar who wanted to speak to me urgently. She had her son with her. I let her in and she told me that my husband had been killed in a car crash. I immediately thought of our three children and burst into tears. Diki Dolkar tried to console me. I must be courageous for their sake, she said. Shocked, I did not know how to tell them the news. Diki Dolkar and my nephew remained with me until morning, discussing all the problems that we would now have to deal with. At six, I woke Tenzin Choedon, Kelsang Yangzom and Tenzin Choedak.

His Holiness was in Japan at the time. I decided to go to Bangalore immediately with all three children. We set off as soon as I had got my things ready and put them into Gyalo Thondup's car. All the village staff were very sympathetic and everyone wanted to help.

On my arrival I went to the police station to claim the deceased's body. I was told that the car had burnt and that not much remained of my husband's body. My children came everywhere with me; I considered that they were old enough to understand what was happening, especially my two girls. Tenzin Choedon was already 17, Kelsang Yangzom 15; Tenzin Choedak was a boy of 11. We obtained the death certificate at the police station and made arrangements for the cremation.

The employees of the family restaurant came to my help, as well as Tsering Wangyal, the head of onw of the Tibetan settlements in the area. Lawyer friend, John de Souza and his family, were a great help. Mr D'Souza was a very warm-hearted gentleman. Although he is no more, I have necome very close friends with his family. A lot of rumours were going around about Lhundup Gyalpo's death. Murder was even talked about. Indeed, no one knew what had happened. He had set off in the car that night and had never been seen alive again. The following morning, my husband's assistant, Tenzin Choglang, recognized the number plate of the crashed car from the newspaper, and immediately had informed Diki Dolkar in Byla Kuppe.

It took six days to get everything done. The children's village sent two people to help me organize the funeral. After three days I asked them to leave as they also had a lot of work to do at the village. The astrologer made his calculations and we arranged the prayers. A large number of Tibetans came to the cremation. A new period of mourning began for me.

We were still at Bangalore when His Holiness returned to Dharamsala. His Holiness rang immediately. It was a tremendous comfort for me to hear his voice. He understood my grief, but asked me to be strong as I was not alone in the world. Accidents of this kind are part of life, he added, and the world's newspapers report them all the time. I remember that on the day His Holiness rang me, there were headlines in the paper about a fire in Japan that had caused hundreds of deaths. I thought about the people there; they too were experiencing unhappiness. This gave me some strength.

Tenzin Choglang knew all about the running of the restaurant and suggested to me that he look after it. Just before his death, Lhundup Gyalpo had been preparing to open a second restaurant. Under the given circumstances, I could not possibly take on the additional responsibility. I therefore re-negotiated the deal and returned the new restaurant to my husband's uncle.

Diki Dolkar, Gyalo Thondup's wife, had always acted as a mother to me. She invited us to spend several days in New Delhi, and then we returned to Dharamsala. His Holiness had left for Kulu, where he likes to go to rest and meditate. I joined him there with my three children. During the ten days I spent there I was able to have several long conversations with him. We had lunch together and often took the car up into the mountains. I also benefited from the teachings given by His Holiness to the inhabitants of Lahul and Spiti.

In Kulu, I mentioned the rumours of murder that were circulating after my husband's death. I had also talked about them with Gyalo Thondup and Diki Dolkar, who had suggested that I engage a detective. His Holiness advised me not to do this. He explained to me that it was not positive to have a vengeful mind. My children thought the same. Some people accused me of not investigating thoroughly the real reasons for the accident; the majority, however, understood my determination to protect my children and to avoid any unpleasant publicity for our family.

Tenzin Choedon, my eldest daughter, was at this time considering becoming a doctor. She had begun science studies at the university of Chandigarh. After her father's death, she decided to remain with me. She took great care of the house and visitors and followed a correspondence course. After a year, she left to study at Simla. I remember the day when we had taken her to the university for the first time, when she was 15. Thanks to an education which had begun when she was very young and her hard work, she was two or three years ahead of the other students.

However, Tenzin Choedon had serious health problems. She was running a high temperature and trembled. At first we thought she had a bad cold, but during one of these attacks, the village doctors prescribed blood tests and discovered that she had malaria. I therefore spent a lot of time looking after her during the year she spent in Dharamsala.

In the meantime, my second daughter, Kelsang Yangzom, had finished her secondary education and I enrolled her at the University of Bangalore. Her sister, who had just passed her exams, decided to go there as well, to help Tenzin in the running of the restaurant.

My life continued to run its course in the Tibetan Children's Village. My son had been 11 when his father died. At this age, a boy needs a man's presence. However, thanks to my brothers and the male staff of the village, Tenzin Choedak did not suffer too much from the absence of a father.

I then discovered how marvellous my children were. When they were smaller, I cuddled and played with them. When they grew up, I talked to them a lot. As my husband spent only six months of the year with us, from early I encouraged them to develop a sense of responsibility. For instance, they helped me to prepare a menu when we had visitors. We openly discussed our problems. After Amala's death, they were sometimes alone in the house. I had therefore taught them to manage a small amount of money and, apparently, they coped very well.

17

The Seeds of the Future

After my husband's death I was very depressed. His Holiness the Dalai Lama gave me continual care and support and I was able to see him whenever I wanted to. I would wait for his audiences to end and then spend a quarter of an hour with him. He always appeared the same towards me, as indeed he did towards everybody: a good and open man, someone who personified compassion.

At about the same time, His Holiness had to go to Switzerland to confer the Kalachakra and he asked me to accompany him. As the Alexandra David-Néel Foundation was becoming more and more active, I first of all went to Digne-les-Bains in France to meet the sponsors living in the area, and then met up with His Holiness at Rikon in German-speaking Switzerland. The Kalachakra lasted for five days. Many of the Tibetan refugees who are settled there took part, as did an impressive number of Westerners. I had met a lot of them in Dharamsala, but I had never seen them attend one of His Holiness's teachings. Many of them were preparing to become Buddhist and a few of them as monks too; in fact, during the previous years several hundred Buddhist centres had sprung up in Europe and the United States.

All the audience now understood that the Tibetans, with their ancestral culture, philosophy and religion, carried a message of peace and compassion for the Western world. For those trying to find their way amongst the teachings of Buddhism, His Holiness was without doubt the best qualified guide. I think the reason for this is simple. He always repeats: 'I am only a simple monk', and yet he personifies love, compassion, peace, non-violence and tolerance. At the same time, he would, I think, have been very happy to spend his life quietly studying sacred texts, meditating and praying.

In this atmosphere of happiness and contemplation, the future appeared to be more promising. With many Westerners turning towards Tibetan culture, this could but serve our cause. Societies dominated by technology and materialism were beginning to open up to our values, those of a civilization that the Chinese Communists wanted to wipe from the surface of the earth. Perhaps, one day, the same Chinese will realize the extent of their error and then hope will be rekindled in the Tibetan people.

At the end of the Kalachakra, feeling much better, I decided to return to Dharamsala to resume my activities. Many letters awaited my arrival and replying to them took a long time.

In 1985, a new tragedy struck my family. His Holiness was returning from Switzerland. Lobsang Samten was then to accompany His Holiness from Delhi to Dharamsala. In the afternoon of the day of their departure, he said he had too much work at the Tibetan Medical Institute and cancelled his journey. A few days later, after returning to Dharamsala myself, I received a telephone message: Lobsang Samten was unwell. I immediately contacted my sister-in-law, Namgyal Lhamo, and advised her to go to New Delhi as fast as possible. Three weeks later I arrived in the Indian capital. Lobsang Samten was in hospital with jaundice and was declining rapidly. He was suffering a lot and we decided to transfer him to the Holy Family hospital, where he fell into a coma. He was later admitted to the All India Medical Institute. His two children, Tenzin Chuki and Tenzin Namdhak, both at university, joined their mother. Unfortunately, Lobsang Samten never came out of his coma and died after 12 days. He was only 53.

It was the end of September and the heat in New Delhi was stifling. However, we were determined to cremate the body in Dharamsala. We took it there by night, after having it embalmed. His Holiness was terribly moved by his brother's death, because they had grown up together and Lobsang Samten had sworn to serve the Dalai Lama all his life.

Once again struck by misfortune, the family could not hide its grief. His Holiness continued unceasingly to give us the courage and energy to continue on our path. His Holiness's personality helped us to overcome our immediate preoccupations. His teaching stresses the ephemeral character of life on earth and advises us to accept death, which, for a Buddhist, is not an end because it will be followed by a rebirth according to the cycle of the Wheel of Life which leads us towards Enlightenment. I cannot remember ever having seen His Holiness cry at the time of someone's death. However, when confronted with man's violence, cruelty and repression, he sometimes sheds a few tears – for instance, in front of the Berlin Wall or, of course, at the mention of the Tibetan tragedy.

Work continued at the Children's Village. The Educational Development and Resource Centre (EDRC) was created in 1985. This organization enabled us to reflect on our education system and at the same time publish our own Tibetan books and education manuals. We had quite a number of children at the TCV who spoke English and Hindi, but it was essential that they attained a comparable level of proficiency in the use of their own language, Tibetan. The centre's first mission was not just to translate works but also to bring about qualitative changes in the way we educated our children. It took us a year to complete this task for the primary schools. At last, all our lessons could take place in Tibetan and this system was extended to all the Tibetan primary schools in India and Nepal.

Around this time, I became aware of a document, the contents of which did not really surprise me. On 20 February 1986, an English teacher at the University of Tibet in Lhasa approached the Chinese authorities with the following observations: most of the funds reserved by the Beijing government for the Tibetan students are used for young Chinese; 70 per cent of Tibetans are illiterate; the most qualified teachers look after the Chinese, the others are given to the Tibetans; many rural schools were closed after the decollectivization of the land and pastures, either because there were not enough pupils or not enough teachers.

We had at that time started another project in the south of India. The Tibetan colony had given us some land near Bylakuppe. I thought that it would give the TCV children a chance to work on the land and that they would become a model for the population for different methods of farming. Our children, with their education and training, started the cultivation of fruit, inter-cropping, crop rotation and vegetable growing. This set a good example for the settlers and I was very pleased.

Also, with the help of funds from Japan, we built a temple, on the summit of a hill overlooking Dharamsala. An old monk lived there and he devoted a lot of time to the children. The adults of the village also go there frequently. After a while, the area around the temple was considered a 'peace zone', where everyone meditates and prays. Again, this set a good example to many others.

On 20 April 1986 we received some very sad news. Dr Hermann Gmeiner, the president of SOS Kinderdorf International, had died. I was extremely upset. The staff and children of the TCV greatly felt this loss and we prayed for him. His generosity and sympathy will be remembered and cherished for as long as there are destitute children.

One Saturday in 1986 around one o'clock in the afternoon, I was just about to go up to the temple, when there was a terrible noise in the mountains which then echoed around the valley; it seemed like a premonition or bad omen. The site of Dharamsala had in the past experienced large earth tremors, the most serious having occurred in 1905, when the British still lived in the village. Several of the victims were buried in an Anglican chapel about half a mile from McLeod Ganj.

That day, my cousin was with me, and we stopped in her house near the main temple. The ground then began to tremble, making a deafening racket. I huddled next to the door thinking of the village children. My cousin prayed. We could hear people shouting outside. The quake lasted for a few seconds. Then calm returned and I went out, relieved to see that the temple and other buildings were all intact. I ran as far as His Holiness's residence where, apart from a few cracked walls, there seemed to be no other damage. Luckily the telephone line had not been cut either. I telephoned the Village and found out that four houses had caved in, covering the children's beds with stones. Luckily, at that time of the day, they were all having lunch outside and none of them was hurt.

His Holiness was reading in his residence when the quake occurred. The Dalai Lama lived in an old building which had been renovated, but the wall between the roof and the ceiling had not been solidly constructed or cemented. Some stones had been dislodged and one of them had fallen, just missing his head.

One thing was obvious to us: His Holiness could not live in such an exposed place, on the edge of the mountain. This last quake had reached 7.8 on the Richter scale. There was an English architect living in Dharamsala who had considerable experience of earthquake-resistant buildings. He designed a residence for His Holiness which could withstand such a phenomenon.

The news spread around the world very quickly and we received a great many letters. Money also arrived so that we could begin the reconstruction immediately of the four collapsed houses. The population performed many pujas. Since then, Dharamsala has not had another serious earthquake.

About this time there had been a change in my personal life. Tempa Tsering, who since 1973 had worked in different departments including the office of His Holiness. Since late 1985, we had seen one another quite frequently .One day, he asked me to marry him. Before taking my decision, I wanted to tell my three children. They replied: 'It's your life, it's therefore your decision!' I also spoke to Gyalo Thondup and he reacted in exactly the same way as the children.

We celebrated our marriage with a simple civil ceremony in New Delhi. Shortly afterwards, Tempa Tsering heard that he was going to be transferred to Bangalore. I was to be separated from him for many months, but we had decided to give priority to our work and to continue to serve the Tibetan cause. My husband moved in with my two daughters, Tenzin Choedon and Kelsang Yangzom, in the rented family house in Bangalore. Tenzin Choedak stayed with me to finish his secondary schooling in Dharamsala. We both went to bangalore during the school holidays.

Tempa Tsering had worked actively for the Tibetan cause. In Bangalore, he became responsible for five settlements which had a total population of nearly 32,000 Tibetans. Today he is the Secretary for the Department of Information and International Relations.

As I was the Dalai Lama's sister, many Tibetans expected me to become a nun after Lundup Gyalpo's death. I am not particularly affected by other people's opinions. Honesty is the most important thing, to be true to oneself. During a long conversation with Diki Dolkar, we had talked about this point and I had said to her: 'I'm not going to pretend to be someone else. I don't do anything on the sly. This is not my nature and I want to be faithful to myself Furthermore, I want the people to know me and recognize me as I am.'

In 1986–7, more and more children arrived in Tibet. At least 1,500 were living in the village; others had left us to study elsewhere. We had to find jobs for some of them. Our education system was now working very well, and we were thinking about improving and developing the programmes.

With some relaxation of the restrictions, it became possible to travel from the West to Tibet, especially in light of the Chinese desire for foreign exchange. More and more tourists went to Lhasa and the other regions. The Tibetans in exile began to realize the extent of the Chinese domination over their country and the tragedy that had begun almost 40 years ago.

In 1987, I went to Paris, where I took part in a demonstration that drew together the Tibetan community in France and friends who were sympathetic to our cause. Nearly 300 of us marched down the Champs Elysées to the Embassy of the Chinese People's Republic on the avenue Georges V. We first of all chanted slogans in front of the building, then recited the prayer, 'The Word of Truth', written by His Holiness. I saw a Chinese official at a window filming us and others taking photographs.

In Lhasa, the Chinese had violently put down the demonstrations of 27 September and 1 October 1987 and that of 5 March the following year. They had even opened fire on the demonstrators, mainly monks and nuns. Nearly 2,500 people were arrested. However, this did not put an end to the protests. There were more than 150 demonstrations of this sort in Tibet between 27 September 1987 and the end of 1992. Before 1987, although many demonstrations had taken place in Tibet, the international community had not been informed.

On 12 December 1986, the People's Republic of China had ratified the United Nations' convention against torture, but nothing changed in our country. When former political prisoners arrived in Dharamsala, they were looked after by our Security Department and they recounted to them everything they had endured: kicks, clubbings, beatings, electric shock treatments … The cruellest and most perverse methods were used to drag out confessions: dogs were unleashed on prisoners, nuns were raped, electric shocks ... In all, 33 different methods of torture were commonly practised.

The many offers of support from the free world in support of our cause warmed my heart, but I could not stop myself thinking about all those who suffered in Tibet. The Communist authorities attempted to stifle any spontaneous act of protest: perhaps by a dozen nuns, or by a few monks carrying a Tibetan flag and shouting their anger against the invader. Arrested and tortured, some of them did not survive. Those who are still alive today carry the signs of their suffering. When they managed to flee, sometimes after years in prison or labour camps, they were immediately looked after by the Kashag Secretariat and doctors. The latter were sometimes powerless in the face of the terrible psychological and physical damage caused by torture.

The Chinese occupiers cared little for human life, especially when it came to subduing our countrymen. Tibetans over the age of 20 who were arrested were frequently condemned to life imprisonment or forced labour. The policy implemented by the People's Republic of China in Tibet was always one of double standards: the administrative authorities talked about religious freedom but the forces of repression prevented the study of religious texts and practices. 'Don't trust the Chinese Communists. They don't think what they say and they don't say what they think. As long as the Chinese are in Tibet, His Holiness must not come back here ...' These terrible words, heard hundreds of times, have remained engraved on my memory since my journey to Tibet in 1980.

In 1987, the children in our villages were involved in a three-month campaign to help the less privileged, organized by SOS Kinderdorf International with the United Nations. The eldest children were sent into the neighbouring villages to help homeless families. We gave them the money necessary to buy building materials and build houses, helped by professionals. The family lived temporarily in a tent, then, when the construction was completed, moved into their new home. I was much in favour of this initiative, even though it cost between 20,000 and 25,000 rupees per village. It was a way of thanking the Indian government for all they had done for us and of strengthening the links between the Indian and Tibetan peoples.

We also had excellent relations with a British teacher training college. In 1987, those in charge began to send their managers to Dharamsala to set up workshops and exchange know-how with our staff. They also went to Ladakh and the south of India. This programme still continues today, its principal objective being the improvement of the general level of education in our children's villages. The British teachers generally stayed with us for about a year. That same year, we decided to set the TCV common exams at Classes V and VIII for all the TCV schools.

The purpose of the Common Exams is to test the language and mathematical skills of the children. So, papers were set for Tibetan, English and Mathematics. The entire exam is centrally conducted from Dharamsala. This enables us to evaluate our pupils' abilities. I think that this exam is very useful for children who have reached the end of their primary education.

Cultural and intellectual activities common to all the schools were also developed: Tibetan music and singing, and traditional dancing. This permitted us to organize competitions between the different establishments. These events took place in Dharamsala one year, in Ladakh the following year, and then in Bylakuppe. They extended the horizons of the young people who often spent years in the same place with very little opportunity to travel.

Tempa Tsering and I continued our respective efforts. My two daughters, Tenzin Choedon and Kelsang Yangzom, and my son, Tenzin Choedak are all living in Bangalore and are looking after the restaurant business.

I frequently visited the different children's villages and spent much of my time with them. I also went abroad to meet children's sponsors in Switzerland, France, Holland, Britain or the United States. Because of my country's situation, I wanted to make as much effort as I could. Public speaking is a calling for me. It is impossible to take this role of spokeswoman from me at a time when the Chinese want to reduce the Tibetans to silence, or to prevent me using my voice to speak for all the unfortunates who are imprisoned or tortured. I also speak about the role of women in Tibet as I am often asked about this.

Even though the Chinese authorities do everything they can to prevent children escaping, hardly a week goes by when they do not arrive in the village, usually in a pitiful state. They cross the Himalayas during the night, even in the middle of winter. I am grieved every time I listen to their stories. It is necessary to act, emotion is not enough. I love the children, and I want to use this love and compassion. The best thing I can do, I think, is to make life a little easier in our children's villages and allow the children to have the education for which they have fled their country.

The foster mothers, who gave their help first of all to Tsering Dolma and then to me, became far too old to work so hard in the homes. They deserved a rest. We therefore started a retirement home. Now we look after both children and old people. In Pathli Kuhl, in the children's village, we built a home for the men and women who toiled on building and road construction sites in the valley of Kulu, sleeping all the time in tents. Most of these people had fled with His Holiness and ended up completely destitute. It is our duty to take care of them.

I was 49 in 1989 and, logically, more than half my life was behind me. The time had come to reflect, to sum up and ask myself: 'What have I done with my life?' I was really happy to have served the Tibetan children, even if I feel terribly sad each time I see them arriving in Dharamsala, in complete physical and mental distress.

I have always tried not to become hardened by these tragic events and, indeed, I think that it is important to consider their positive side. Groups of children regularly arrive from Tibet and others are sent to us from the refugee settlements. What they tell us is terrible. I always try to put myself in their place, rather than listening with an adult's less attentive ear; this gives an entirely different perspective. In fact, working only from a sense of duty is fatal and it leads to routine and ages the heart. By listening in an understanding way to a child, we can feel how much he needs us. I then say to myself: 'It doesn't matter how many children there are, what matters is their life. We have to look after them, because if we don't, what will happen to them?' I also think about the difficulties of the foster mothers. A home shelters on average 30 children; if, one morning, we entrust them with 10 more, their task is not easy, but we do not really have a choice.

I believe that either you have fixed ideas, or that you are capable of adapting – at any age. There must always be room for things that are new. For my part, I have never believed in predetermined solutions; I want to resolve difficulties according to the circumstances in which they occur. The situation in Ladakh is not the same as that in south of India. However, certain principles remain unchangeable. I attach major importance to universal notions of truth, justice, compassion and goodness; I am therefore extremely wary of my ego, which I do not impose on anyone.

18

The Voice of Peace

The fourteenth Dalai Lama has always pursued the path of negotiation to resolve the Tibetan issue. On 21 September 1987, addressing the Human Rights Committee of the American Congress, he proposed a Five-Point Peace Plan:

1 Transformation of the whole of Tibet into a zone of peace;
2 Abandonment of China's population transfer policy which threatens the very existence of the Tibetans as a people;
3 Respect for the Tibetan people's fundamental human rights and democratic freedoms;
4 Restoration and protection of Tibet's natural environment and the abandonment of China's use of Tibet for the production of nuclear weapons and dumping of nuclear waste;
5 Commencement of earnest negotiations on the future status of Tibet and of relations between the Tibetan and Chinese peoples.

Personally I regret the total rejection by the Chinese authorities of His Holiness's propositions and numerous appeals to reach an amicable solution to the Tibetan problem. The atrocities committed against our people must cease. To my greatest sorrow, the efforts consistently made by His Holiness have so far remained without result.

A very important event occurred in 1989: His Holiness, was awarded the Nobel Peace Prize. I heard this happy news on the radio while I was in our Children's Village at Bylakuppe, South

India. The award citation read:

> The Norwegian Nobel Committee has decided to award the 1989 Nobel Peace Prize to the fourteenth Dalai Lama, Tenzin Gyatso, the religious and political leader of the Tibetan people.
> The Committee wants to emphasize the fact that the Dalai Lama, in his struggle for the liberation of Tibet, has consistently opposed the use of violence. He has instead advocated peaceful solutions based upon tolerance and mutual respect in order to preserve the historical and cultural heritage of his people.
> The Dalai Lama has developed his philosophy of peace from a great reverence for all things living, upon the concept of universal responsibility embracing all mankind as well as nature. In the opinion of the Committee, the Dalai Lama has come forward with constructive and forward-looking proposals for the solution of international conflicts, human rights issues and global environmental problems.

I could not withold my happiness and immediately sent a card to His Holiness, with my congratulations. Tibetans everywhere were overwhelmed with joy and happiness, as at last the Norwegian Nobel Peace Committee had recognized His Holiness's dedication to peace, harmony, tolerance and Universal Responsibility. For us Tibetans, this news was without doubt the best that we had received for many years. His Holiness was then in the United States. The community prepared a great celebration for his return and thousands of people from all over India, Nepal and Bhutan flooded into the streets of Dharamsala. He was met by a huge crowd at Delhi airport.

The anniversary of the TCV fell on 23 October, so we celebrated both events together, with great joy and emotion.

His Holiness then went to Norway. My brother Thubten Jigme Norbu and his wife were fortunate to be present there. I was not able to go to Oslo as I was in hospital with hepatitis. I personally feel that the speech that His Holiness gave on this occasion was certainly one of the most important that he has ever made. His Holiness emphasized the necessity of finding a harmonious balance between material development and man's spiritual progress, and presented the practical solutions which would guarantee the freedom of his people and assure stability and peace in Asia.

Only a return to Tibet could have brought the Tibetan people more intense joy. The awarding of the Nobel Peace Prize to the

Dalai Lama reinforced our determination and motivation. At the TCV anniversary, we all (management, foster mothers, cooks and drivers) swore to work even harder. Thanks to His Holiness's efforts, the Tibetan situation was gaining gradual recognition and concern from many countries in the world. The work of the government in exile, our representatives abroad and the heads of the departments had at last been recognized. The courage of the refugees, and of those Tibetans who continued to suffer in their country for the cause of freedom, had also been indicated. Everyone realized that the path of negotiation and non-violence followed by His Holiness represented the only method that could, one day, break the oppression of the Chinese Communists.

1990 was marked by the elections for the Assembly of Tibetan People's Deputies (Tibetan Parliament) and the creation of a Tibetan Constitution Redrafting Committee, a commission charged with the responsibility for drafting the charter for the government in exile and a constitution for tomorrow's Tibet.

In May 1990, in an effort to further democratize the Tibetan government in exile, His Holiness dissolved both the Kashag and the Assembly of Tibetan People's Deputies and convened a special congress of the Tibetan people in exile. He informed this congress that all appointments by the Dalai Lama were void and that the people should take greater responsibility in the affairs of the government. He, therefore, asked the congress to elect an Interim Kashag, which would take on the responsibility of government for one year, draft a charter for the exiled Tibetan community and hold a general election for the Assembly of Tibetan People's Deputies.

In the charter, the term of the Assembly had been increased from three to five years and the number of Deputies was increased from 12 to 46. All Tibetans above the age of 18 were eligible to vote and any Tibetan above the age of 25 was eligible to stand as candidate for the Assembly. The Assembly was delegated the responsibility of electing the kalons (ministers).

As a functioning democratic system of government, the responsibilities of executive, legislature, and judiciary were clearly defined. The rule by man has been changed to rule by law.

In May 1990, when I was in Bangalore, I received a telephone call from Dharamsala to inform me that the Special Congress had elected me as one of the three kalons and that I should report immediately. On my arrival in Dharamsala, I immediately went to His Holiness's office to explain that I did not want to become a kalon as I was not capable of taking on such a role. 'For the first time in Tibetan history, a woman has been elected a kalon,' the secretary retorted. It was an important moment, and I must not shed this responsibility. After the meeting I rang Tempa Tsering. My husband encouraged me: he said to me that I had no choice, and if it later turned out that I could not fulfil my functions, it would always be possible to resign.

On 12 May, I was sworn in, in front of His Holiness, accompanied by just two other ministers, Kalsang Yeshi and Tenzin Namgyal Tethong. To tell the truth, I did not feel at ease, or happy. When I took the oath I had to read the text in Tibetan … a terrifying moment. As my knowledge of the language was poor, I made a great many mistakes. Afterwards we were invited to a traditional ceremony with tea and rice. His Holiness gave us a khata and we then went to the temple to pray.

On the return route, a large crowd was waiting to congratulate me. I was covered with khatas. A delegation from Amdo wanted to talk to me but, in all honesty, I felt more like crying and telling them that people had made a bad choice at a time when Tibet had so many problems. In my opinion, the community already had a sufficient number of talented people. I had no idea about politics; my only talent lay in the field of education.

Suddenly I found myself saying to the people I met: 'I thank you for having elected me, but I'm not happy about it.' Everyone mentioned my success with the TCV and explained that it was important to work for education within the government. They asked me to implement my practical field experience within the Kashag. I also received hundreds of letters from old students who had been at the TCV in the 1960s and 1970s and who now lived in different parts of India, Japan, Nepal, Bhutan or Europe. They congratulated me on my election. I suffered inwardly for not being able to share this happiness with them.

The next day, I went to the Kashag for the first time. Not being accustomed to written Tibetan, I thought that I would be out of place there. All the texts were written in Tibetan and I had to ask for help to read documents. Their content was explained to me and I spent a lot of time thinking. His Holiness had expressly asked me to keep my job at the TCV, which was then still expanding. My colleagues were working there on other projects and new programmes; I therefore intended to leave the cabinet at the first opportunity.

In fact, I offered my resignation four times. The first time, in 1991, His Holiness replied: 'We need you.' In 1992, I was still part of the government. The next year, in July, I remember taking my courage in both hands and writing a letter to His Holiness, in English, because it is the language I know best. His Holiness at last accepted my resignation and, as directed by him, I was able to devote myself entirely to my work at the children's village.

During my tenure as Minister for Education, one of the things that I was able to accomplish was the introduction of the Tibetanization programme in all the Tibetan schools, including those managed by the Indian Ministry of Education. I met the Indian Education Minister along with all the concerned officials, and was able to convince them of the importance of teaching the young children through their mother tongue. Since 1986, education at the TCV up to primary level has been in Tibetan. The Tibetan language constituted an essential support for our religion and culture; it was the basis of our cultural identity. After the long years of exile, contact with Tibet became rarer, and it was imperative that we preserve and maintain our language. Today, I must express my gratitude to the Indian government for the understanding of our concerns and objectives. Since the end of 1993, our young people have been able to receive their education in the Indian-managed schools in Tibetan, using TCV books and manuals. This represents great progress and I am very happy about this.

We have continued to develop the structures and services of the TCV. In Delhi, a youth hostel, financed by SOS Kinderdorf International, was inaugurated in 1991 by His Holiness in the presence of the Speaker of the Indian Parliament, Mr Rabi Ray, and the President of SOS Kinderdorf, who had been one of the children at the first children's village in Austria. The hostel enabled us to receive an ever larger number of students, who had previously been dispersed across major Indian cities, often in deplorable conditions. Today the hostel has capacity for 220 students and it is completely full. Next to the Tibetan SOS hostel there is a large park where Indians come to meditate and practise yoga. During the monsoons, the park is frequently flooded; we have therefore made the hall of the hostel open to everyone.

We have also considered training our young people in the new technologies and the study of alternative energy. In Tibet, we have little wood, gas or fossil fuels, but we do have a lot of water and a sky that is often sunny. In the SOS Technical Training Centre in Nepal, the young have learnt to make the solar water heaters that we have installed in all the TCVs. In Bir, the adult education cycle takes four years. In Dharamsala we have started a much needed Teacher's Training Centre along with the Educational Development and Resource Centre (EDRC), offering a library and a documentation centre. Since obtaining his Master's degree in the United States, Ngawang Dorjee, our Education Director has looked after the work of this centre as well as overseeing all the educational programmes which we have for the children.

As there is an urgent need for more vocational training for our young people, in 1996 we were able to acquire some suitable land in the Indian State of Uttar Pradesh to establish a separate Vocational Training Centre. Once again the SOS Kinderdorf came to our assistance and they are funding this project. It is being handled by Phuntsok Tashi who has much experience in this kind of work. He was one of the children who was sent to be educated in the early 1960s in the Pestalozzi Children's Village, England. This project is in good hands and we are hopeful that the first trainees can be accepted by 1998.

Time has gone by. My own children have grown up and left the family nest. I spend most of my time travelling and looking after the Tibetan Children's Village. My husband, Tempa Tsering, is also very occupied in serving our government as Secretary for the Department of Information and International Relations. He is in permanent contact with support groups abroad and His Holiness's representatives in the different capitals of the world. My eldest daughter has been elected to the National Assembly of Tibetan People's Deputies.

At 56 I have the feeling that I know myself well, as if I am looking at myself in a mirror. When you believe in reincarnation, if such an understanding of your own personality has not been achieved, then the next existence is not very promising. I think that today I live in peace with myself. Free of my fetters, I am able to act. My work in the children's village represents a sequel to the work started by my elder sister in 1960. I have not done this out of self-interest; I devoted myself to this task as a sister of the Dalai Lama.

The work of the Tibetan Children's Villages is most important as our children are the seeds for the future who will flower tomorrow. As long as there are Tibetans in exile, there will be children who will need our service. I consider good education as the essential prerequisite for national development and progress. Therefore, this work must go on without having to rely on any one individual.

The time to step down is close at hand and I am happy that due to the decentralized approach that I have always emphasized, we have in all our branches a host of dedicated and energetic trained people doing different work at all levels. They are able to shoulder this great responsibility of taking care and educating the children, citizens of a future democratic Tibet.

Today, I am alive, but who knows what may happen tomorrow. I have seen several members of my family die, but when I compare these losses to the 1.2 million dead, victims of the occupation of our country, my personal loss is insignificant. Throughout my adult life, death has been present. I am conscious that life is not eternal and that one must think about one's impermanence.

I do not pretend at 56 to have a profound Buddhist experience. I have followed a few teachings, but the essential thing for me is to be able to feel that I can carry out my own introspection honestly. I have always asked myself, doing for myself or for the benefit of the children that we care for?'

Today, I know that I have no fears of the future.

Epilogue

Today, after 37 years of existence, the Tibetan Children's Villages carries on its mission for the service of Tibetan children in exile. Here, each child finds the love, care and environment essential for a good all-round education, and is brought up as a Tibetan. This crucial task also lays the foundations for the future of our nation.

We are given support and encouragement from India, as well as numerous other countries. Thanks to their support, we are able to preserve our freedom to act for the Tibetan cause and to maintain our cultural heritage. We have a unique, ancient culture and heritage which is useful in the lives of our people and has the potential to make a contribution to other peoples of the world. We, therefore, consider that it is our duty and our top priority to ensure the preservation of this culture. In our own country, under the Chinese occupation, our culture or anything that identifies Tibet as a separate entity suffers systematic destruction and is on the verge of annihilation. Our culture is alive only in exile.

We continue to receive very painful news from Tibet, which has now been made a colony of China. Tibetans have not only become an insignificant minority in their own country because of the massive influx of Chinese people but are treated as second-class citizens. Political repression has intensified, and teaching of Tibetan language, culture and history is increasingly curtailed, with the danger of it being completely eliminated in all the schools. Under various campaigns, people are deprived of their religious freedom – many monasteries are being closed down and many monks and nuns are being expelled. Even keeping a photograph of His Holiness the Dalai Lama is considered a crime. The latest in this cycle of Tibetan resistance and Chinese repression is the episode of Chadrel Rinpoche, whom the Chinese authorities in Shigatse sentenced to six years of imprisonment on 21 April 1997, for his role in the search for the Panchen Lama. This sentence was condemned around the world.

The fate of Chadrel Rinpoche is inextricably tied to the fate of the eight-year-old, Gedhun Choekyi Nyima, the boy recognized by His Holiness the Dalai Lama on 14 May 1995 as the true reincarnation of the Panchen Lama, who died in 1989 in his traditional religious seat of Tashi Lhunpo Monastery in Shigatse.

China put Chadrel Rinpoche in detention on 17 May 1995 in Chengdu and accused him of 'leaking state secrets' to the Dalai Lama, which the Chinese authorities claim enabled His Holiness to recognize Gedhun Choekyi Nyima as the Panchen Lama.

Chadrel Rinpoche's real 'crime' was his well-known view that the discovery of the new Panchen Lama was a religious issue and needed to be given religious sanctity which only His Holiness could provide, and only then would it become acceptable to the majority of the Tibetan people.

The imprisonment of Chadrel Rinpoche has implications far beyond the fate of one individual Tibetan. It touches on the fate of Tibet itself and on the question of who will lead Tibet in the future. By the recent imprisonment of Chadrel Rinpoche and the continued detention of the Panchen Lama, China is giving notice to the world that only Beijing has the authority to select the Panchen Lama and by implication the next Dalai Lama. Sticking to such a policy would be a tragedy for Tibet and for those areas which come under the Tibetan spiritual and cultural influence. Above all, it would be a tragedy for China because Tibetans would not tolerate such humiliating interference in their core spiritual beliefs.

I want to salute Tibetan women who, with extraordinary courage, at the fourth United Nations conference on women, reminded the whole world of the real situation of our fellow countrymen in Tibet.

We remain confident for the future. His Holiness the Dalai Lama and the government in exile relentlessly devote their time and energy to the continuation of this sacred struggle. They have the support of Tibetan communities throughout the world, as well as all those who are sensitive to what is at stake in our cause.

This support gives us hope and confidence that we will one day return to our country. As envisaged by His Holiness the Dalai Lama, we want to live in harmony with nature in Tibet in the hope that it will become a land of peace and contentment, and a model example for men and women who cherish human values.

I decided to write this book so that the tragedy of the Tibetan people and the difficulties they face may be better known. May all those who, like us, value freedom and justice be aware of the developments of our recent tragic history and give us their support before Tibet is lost and Tibetan culture becomes a museum piece.

APPENDICES

Glossary

Achala: honorary term for sister.

Amala: honorary term for mother.

Ambag: breast pocket of chuba.

Amdo: region in the north-east of Tibet.

Apso: a Tibetan terrier, usually referred to as a Lhasa Apso.

Aya: Hindi word for a nanny.

Barkhor: precincts of the temple of the Jokhang. Pilgrims walk round clockwise, reciting prayers.

Bodhisattva: a being who has reached Enlightenment and is ready to become a Buddha, but who renounces this final liberation so as to deliver all living creatures. The Bodhisattva remains in this world of suffering, where he acts out of pure compassion, without any form of attachment.

Bon: the original Tibetan religion.

Buddhist Schools: Tibetan Buddhism is rooted in Mahayana Buddhism (Greater Vehicle), teachings of the Buddha which were developed from the first century AD onwards. Introduced in Tibet in the eighth century, Tantric Buddhism (Greater Vehicle) gave birth to lineages or schools:

The Nyingmapa School – School of the Ancients – was established in the eighth century and groups together the earliest teachings, introduced in Tibet by Padmasambhava, also known as Guru Rinpoche.

The Kagyupa School – school of oral transmission – appeared in the eleventh century. Marpa, nicknamed 'the translator', returned from India with the teachings of India masters which he passed on to his famous disciple, Milarepa.

The Sakyapa lineage – named after the monastery in western Tibet it originated from, was founded by Khion Konchog Gyalpo in the eleventh century.

The Gelugpa, 'the Virtuous', resulted from the reform initiated by Tsongkhapa in the fifteenth century. The Dalai Lama essentially belongs to the Gelugpa lineage, but also studies the teachings of the three other schools. All schools recognize him as the temporal and spiritual leader of all Tibetans.

Cham: a sacred Tibetan Buddhist dance.

Chang: barley beer.

Changtse-Shar: the residence of the Dalai Lama's family before the Chinese invasion, located between the centre of Lhasa and the Potala.

Chemar is a mixture of tampa (roasted barley flour) and butter and is placed in a container as offerings to deities during festive occasions, especially at the celebration of the Tibetan New Year (Losar).

Chogyal of Sikkim: title of the former sovereign of Sikkim.

Chola: honorary term for the eldest brother.

Chuba: Tibetan dress.

Dalai Lama: Dalai is a Mongol word meaning ocean. Lama is a Tibetan equivalent of the Indian word 'guru', meaning spiritual master. Put together these words are often loosely translated as 'Ocean of Wisdom'. But Dalai Lama is first of all the title of the spiritual leader and most eminent religious character in the Buddhist world, who is also the temporal leader of Tibet and its head of government. The Dalai Lama is the incarnation of Chenrezi, the Bodhisattva of Compassion.

Dhama: drum of Ladakh.

Dharma: Buddhist teaching. The order of things, the cosmic system and absolute Truth. In plural form, written without a capital letter, dharmas are the phenomena ordered by this law.

Dresil: sweetened rice.

Dri: female yak.

Dro-ma: potentilla.

Dzomo: the offspring of a cow and a yak.

Gelugpa: *see* Buddhist Schools.

Geshe: doctor in Buddhist philosophy.

Goeku: banner.

Gorshe: Tibetan dance, similar to a quadrille.

Guthul: thick soup into which small objects are dropped as good omens.

Gyalyap: honorary term for the Dalai Lama's father.

Gyalyum: honorary term for the Dalai Lama's mother.

Hors: Tibetan tribe living in the region of Kham.

Jokhang: the most important temple in Lhasa, the Tibetan capital. It is the temple most venerated by Tibetan Buddhists.

Jowo: the most sacred and revered statue of the Shakyamuni Buddha in Tibet.

Kagyupa: *see* Buddhist Schools.

Kalachakra: divinity of Tibetan Tantric Buddhism, and his related teachings.

Kalon: minister.

Karma: the deeds performed by each individual during successive incarnations, which, according to their positive or negative value, lead one towards or away from final release and bliss.

Kashag: council of ministers.

Khabse: New Year biscuits.

Kham: province in eastern Tibet.

Khampa: inhabitant of Kham.

Khata: white silk scarf used as an offering by Tibetans, instead of flowers.

Lama: Tibetan Buddhist master.

Lharampa: highest Buddhist doctorate awarded to monks at the end of their studies.

Lokhor: year.

Lonchen: minister.

Lo-phud: Tibetan New Year offerings of seedlings.

Losar: first day of Tibetan New Year.

Mahayana: in Buddhism there are basically two schools of thought – Mahayana and Hinayana. Mahayana means the 'Greater Vehicle'.

Mala: rosary used to count mantras and to keep continually attentive.

Mani stones: engraved stones; the name refers to the syllables of the mantra *Om mani padme hum*, which is often inscribed on the stones. Mani stones may be coloured, and vary in size – some are as big as rocks. Small mani stones are piled up to form walls called Mendong. Mani stones are found in every kind of sacred place, especially near monasteries and villages.

Mantra: 1) ritual and initiatory formula used in both Hinduism and Buddhism as a form of meditation and prayer. 2) a syllable which, when uttered repetitively or thought of, helps one to gain access to the innermost mind and to influence it. The most famous mantra is *Om mani padme hum*, the mantra of Chenrezi, the Bodhisattva of Compassion. Repeating these words and imagining oneself in the form of this Bodhisattva, helps to gradually release the innate universal compassion.

Mola: grandmother.

Monlam: prayer festival to commemorate the Buddha's victory over heretics at Sravasti.

Momos: traditional festive dish; looks like steamed ravioli.

Namgyal: private monastery of the Dalai Lama.

Nechung Oracle: state oracle of the Tibetan government.

Norbulingka: summer palace of the Dalai Lama.

Nyingmapa: *see* Buddhist Schools.

Padmasambhava: born in Uddiyana, in the north of India, he introduced Buddhism to Tibet by subduing local rebels. He also helped to build Samye, the first Buddhist monastery in Tibet.

Pala: honorary term for father.

Potala: palace of the Dalai Lama.

Puja: practical worship.

Ramoche Tsuklakhang: one of the most revered temples in Tibetan Buddhism, in Lhasa.

Reincarnation: *see* Tulku.

Regent: rules over the country in the absence of, or during the childhood of, the Dalai Lama.

Rinpoche: honorary term for a qualified and enlightened spiritual master. Tibetans call the Dalai Lama, Gyalwa Rinpoche – the Precious Protector.

Rugyen: bone ornaments worn by Tantrists during ceremonies.

Sakyapa: *see* Buddhist Schools.

Sang: Tibetan currency. Tibet issued its own banknotes and stamps as early as 1912. They were hand-painted with wooden blocks (xylographers). Banknotes were made individually, whereas stamps were printed in series of twelve, on local paper. Consequently, colours and the quality of print varied.

Shap-pe: title for a high-ranking Tibetan civil servant.

Shotoen: yoghurt festival.

Sipakhorlo: the Wheel of life; in Buddhism, an image for the cycle of existence.

Suna: flute.

Sungchorawa: place used for instruction in the Barkhor.

Tashi delek: Tibetan greeting.

Thamzing: public punishment carried out by the Chinese Communists. The accused is made to stand for several hours in front of the populace gathered for the occasion. Family, children and friends are obliged to take part. The accused must criticize himself, and those who are close to him must insult him, beat him and even spit on him. Humiliated and held up to ridicule, the accused often asks for a quick death.

Thanka: a Tibetan painted icon on silk or fabric, which can be rolled. It is based on the Indian religious art of the Pala dynasty. Deeply interested in Indian religious teachings, Tibetans scrupulously followed the teachings of Indian, and later Nepalese, artists. Thanka painting was developed in Tibet, in the seventh century, during the reign of Song-Tsen-Gam-po. Around the same time, silkworms, stone mills, paper and ink were introduced into Tibet, and Tibetan writing and grammar became codified.

Torgya: ceremony performed at the end of the year symbolizing the rejection of evil.

Torma: made of tsampa, either round and white or triangular and red. Used in rituals.

Tsampa: roasted barley flour.

Tse School: School at the Summit (the Potala).

Tsi-pon: minister of finance.

Tsokrampa: second-class geshe (doctor). Examination results are announced during the Tsokchoe festival.

Tsongkhapa: founder of the Gelug Buddhist School.

Tsuklakhang: Tsuklakhang is also known as Jokhang and is the Temple in Lhasa. This temple was built to house the gifts of images of Sakyamuni Buddha brought by the Nepalese princess Brikuti who was one of the queens of King Songtsen Gampo who ruled Tibet between 630 to 649 AD.

Tulku: the idea of reincarnation is part of the Buddhist philosophical framework. It is not part of the Buddha's teachings, but is considered by all Asians, whatever their denomination, to be a natural phenomenon. The Buddha taught that the 'ego' or 'soul' does not transmigrate. A life becomes the result of a previous one through a kind of kinetic energy. Any individual who has reached a high level of spiritual development is supposed to be able to direct this energy in a special way at the time of his death, so that it gives birth to a tulku – a reincarnated lama. The tulku is not the same person as the previous lama, but represents the active continuation of his positive qualities, wisdom and blessings. This phenomenon always existed in Buddhism, but no particular attention was given to it. It was not until the eleventh century that a Tibetan lama, Karmapa, talked about his tulku. The tulku was given the same name as his predecessor, thus initiating the first lineage of reincarnation. As the system proved to be useful at both spiritual and material levels, it developed over the course of the centuries, giving birth, in the fifteenth century, to the lineage of the Dalai Lama, and to that of the Panchen Lama in the seventeenth century.

Bibliography

Ani Kelsang Pelmo, 'A Nun Tells Her Story', *Tibetan Bulletin*, August/September, Dharamsala, 1990

Bell, Charles, *Tibet, Past and Present*, Oxford, 1968

— *Portrait of the Dalai Lama*, Collins, London, 1946

Cornu, Philipe, *L'Astrologie tibétaine*, Les Djinns, 1990

Department of Information and International Relations

Department of Religion and Culture, *Chö-Yang*, nos 1, 2, 3, 4 and 5, Dharamsala

Gross, Rita M, *Enlightened Consort, Great Teacher, Female Role: Yeshe Tsogyal*, Snow-Lions Publications, New York, 1989

His Holiness the fourteenth Dalai Lama, *My Land and my People*, McGraw Hill Book Company, New York, 1962

— *Kindness, Clarity and Insight*, Snow-Lions Publications, New York, 1984

— *Enseignements essentiels*, Albin Michel, Paris, 1989

— *Freedom in Exile*, Hodder and Stoughton, London, 1990

— *L'enseignement du Dalaï Lama*, coll. 'Spiritualités vivantes' *Livre de poche*, Editions Jean-Claude Lattes, Paris, 1995

Majupuria, Indra, *Tibetan Women: Then and Now*, M Devi, Gwalior, India, 1990

Petech, Luciano, *Aristocracy and Government in Tibet* (1728–1959), ISMEO, Rome, 1973

Planning Council, *First Integrated Plan*, Dharamsala

— *Integrated Plan, 1995–2000*, Dharamsala

Rinchen Dolma Taring, *Daughter of Tibet*, John Murray, London, 1970, Wisdom Publications, London, 1986

Rinchen Lhamo, *We Tibetans*, Potala Publications, New York, 1995

Snellgrove, D L and Richardson H, *A Cultural History of Tibet*, Weidenfeld and Nicolson, London, 1968

Thomas, Lowell, *Out of this World: Across the Himalayas to Forbidden Tibet*, Greystone Press, New York, 1950

Thubten Jigme Norbu, *Tibet is My Country*, E P Dutton & Co, New York, 1961

Tibetan Young Buddhist Association, *Tibet, the Facts*, Dharamsala, 1980

Tsepon Shakabpa, W D, *Tibet, a Political History*, Potala Publications, New York, 1984

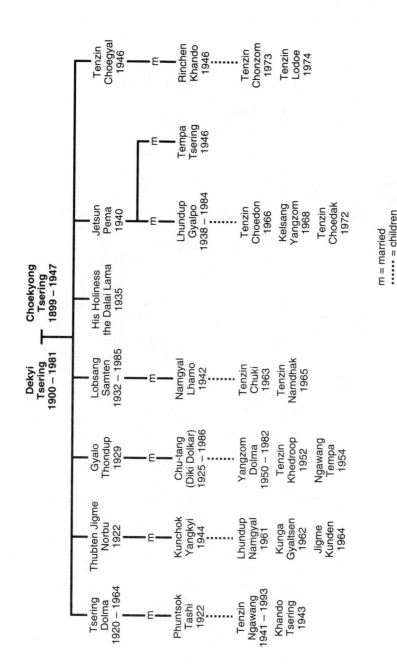

Family Tree

The Institution of the Dalai Lamas

First Dalai Lama	Gendün Drub	(1391–1475)
Second Dalai Lama	Gendün Gyatso	(1475–1542/3)
Third Dalai Lama	Sonam Gyatso	(1543–1588)
Fourth Dalai Lama	Yönten Gyatso	(1589–1617)
Fifth Dalai Lama	Ngawang Lobsang Gyatso	(1617–1682)
Sixth Dalai Lama	Rigdzin Tsangyang Gyatso	(1683–1706)
Seventh Dalai Lama	Kelsang Gyatso	(1708–1757)
Eighth Dalai Lama	Jampel Gyatso	(1758–1804)
Ninth Dalai Lama	Lungtok Gyatso	(1806–1815)
Tenth Dalai Lama	Tsultrim Gyatso	(1816–1837)
Eleventh Dalai Lama	Khedrup Gyatso	(1838–1856)
Twelfth Dalai Lama	Trinle Gyatso	(1856–1875)
Thirteenth Dalai Lama	Thubten Gyatso	(1875–1933)
Fourteenth Dalai Lama	Tenzin Gyatso	(6 July 1935–)

Boundaries of Tibet, India and China

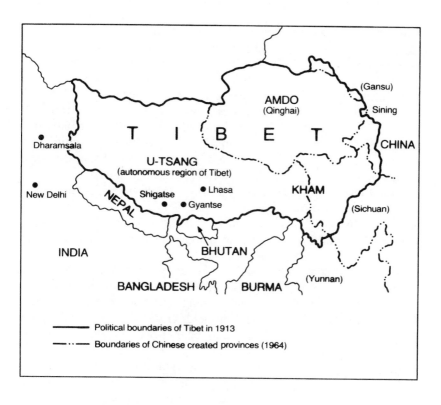

Political boundaries of Tibet in 1913

Boundaries of Chinese created provinces (1964)

Tibet at a Glance

Area	1.5 million square miles.
Capital	Lhasa.
Population	6 million Tibetans, 7.5 million Chinese immigrants (estimate).
Religion	90 per cent of the Tibetan population is Buddhist; Bon (an indigenous religion), Islam and Catholicism are also practised.
Language	Tibetan (a Tibeto-Burman language). Chinese is imposed as the official language.
Basic Food	Tsampa (roasted barley meal).
National Drink	Salted tea mixed with butter; chang (barley beer).
Average Altitude	14,300 feet.
Highest Mountain	Chomo Langma (Mount Everest) at 29,028 feet.
Common Animals	Yak, dri (female yak), bharal (blue sheep), musk-deer, Tibetan antelope, Tibetan gazelle, kyang (wild donkey), ica, panda.
Common Birds	Black-necked crane, lammergeyer, great crested grebe, bar-headed goose, iridescent duck, ibis.
Ecology	Massive deforestation in eastern Tibet, big game poaching, over-exploitation of mineral and other natural resources.
Average Rainfall	Variable. In the west: negligible in January, 1 inch in July. In the east: between 1 and 2 inches in January and 32 inches in July.
Mineral Resources	Bauxite, uranium, iron, copper, chromium, coal, salt, mica, lithium, pewter, gold, oil.
Main Rivers	Zachu (Mekong), Drichu (Yangtse), Machu (Huangho), Gyalmo Ngulchu (Salweem), Tsangpo (Brahmaputra), Senge Khabab

(Indus), Langchen Khabab (Sutlej).

Economy   Tibetans work mostly in agriculture and cattle-breeding. Chinese mainly work for the government, in trade and service industries.

Provinces   U-Tsang (central), Amdo (north-east), Kham (south-east).

Neighbouring Countries   India, Nepal, Bhutan, Burma, East Turkestan, Mongolia, China.

Flag   A mountain, snow lions, and a sun with red and blue beams. It is illegal in Tibet.

Head of State   His Holiness the fourteenth Dalai Lama. In exile in Dharamsala, India.

Spiritual Leader   His Holiness the fourteenth Dalai Lama (full title: Jetsun Ngawang Lobsang Yeshi Tenzin Gyatso Sisum Wangyur Tsunpa Mepai Dhe Palsangpo).

Government in Exile   Democratic (parliamentary system).

Government in Tibet   Communist.

Relations with China   Colonial.

Legal Status   Occupied.

Colonies of Tibetan refugees in India and Nepal

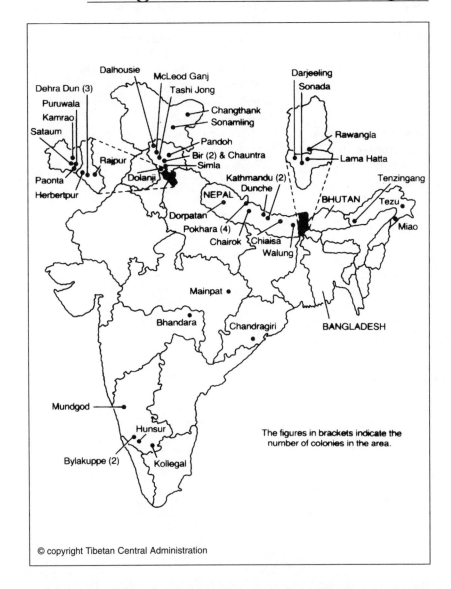

The figures in brackets indicate the number of colonies in the area.

© copyright Tibetan Central Administration

Tibet in Exile

Population	About 130,000 (India 100,000, Nepal 20,000, Bhutan 2,000, Switzerland 2,000, United States 1,500, Canada 500).
Government	Democratic, based on system of popular votes and electoral colleges.
Head of State	His Holiness the fourteenth Dalai Lama.
Ministries	Education, Finance, Health, Home, Information and International Relations, Religion and Culture, Security.
Seat of Government	Dharamsala (Himachal Pradesh).
Seat of Parliament	Dharamsala: National Assembly of Tibetan People's Deputies (46 seats).
International Offices	Tokyo, Canberra, Kathmandu, New Delhi, Budapest, Moscow, Paris, London, New York, Washington, Geneva.
Government Staff	Over 2,000 people.
Government Publications	*Sheja, Tibetan Freedom* (Tibetan), *Tibetan Bulletin* (English, Hindi, French and Chinese), *Tibet Tsushin* (Japanese), *News Tibet* (English).
Independent Publications	*Tibet Times, Rangzen, 60 countries* (Tibetan), *Actualités tibétaines* (French), *Tibetan Affairs* (Tibetan), *Tibetan Review, Tibet Journal, Rangzen, Lungta* (English), *Junges Tibet, Tibet Forum* (German), *Xizang Luntan* (Chinese). Newsletters are also published by various support groups in over 30 countries.

Literacy	75 per cent (92 per cent of Tibetan children attend school).
Army and Police	None.
Government Income	Annual voluntary contribution, trade income and donations.
Official Holidays	10 March: day of the National Uprising 6 July: birthday of His Holiness the Dalai Lama 2 September: Democracy Day 2 October: anniversary of Mahatma Gandhi's birth 10 December: International Human Rights Day Losar – Tibetan New Year (changeable date).
Institutions	Tibetan Institute for Performing Arts, Library of Tibetan Works and Archives, Tibetan Medical and Astro Institute, Central Institute for Tibetan Higher Studies, Amnye Machen Institute.
Tibetan NGOs	Tibetan Youth Congress, Tibetan Women's Association, Tibetan Movement for Freedom, and National Democratic Part of Tibet.
Languages	Tibetan and the language of the host country.
Most Common Diseases	Tuberculosis, malaria, gastro-intestinal disorders.
Economy	Agriculture, farm-produce industries, crafts, small shops, carpet-weaving.
Legal Status	Stateless persons. A few Tibetans have a foreign passport; most Tibetans have an Indian registration certificate.

All information was given freely to the author by the Office of Tibet, 84, bd Adolphe-Pinard, 75014 Paris, tel: (0033) 1 46 56 54 53, fax: (0033) 1 46 56 08 18.

Important Dates

1935	Birth of the Dalai Lama.
1939	Beginning of World War II.
1940	Enthronement of the fourteenth Dalai Lama.
	Birth of Jetsun Pema.
1947	Indian Independence.
	Death of Jetsun Pema's father.
1948	Creation of the State of Israel.
1949	Proclamation of the People's Republic of China.
	The People's Liberation Army invades Tibet.
	Jetsun Pema leaves Tibet for India.
1950	The Dalai Lama retreats to the valley of Chumbi.
	The United Nations debate the Tibetan question.
1951	23 May: Seventeen Point Agreement.
1953	Death of Stalin.
1954	Beginning of war in Algeria.
	The Dalai Lama visits Beijing and returns to Lhasa after a year in China.
1956	The Dalai Lama visits India.
1957	Treaty of Rome.
	Creation of the EEC.
1959	The Dalai Lama leaves Lhasa and begins exile in India.
	10 March: National Uprising of the Tibetan people.
1960	The Dalai Lama arrives in Dharamsala.
	Creation of the Central Tibetan Administration (TAC).
	Foundation of the Nursery for Tibetan Refugee Children.
1961	Jetsun Pema goes to Switzerland to study.
1962	Algerian Independence.
1963	Assassination of J F Kennedy.
1964	Death of Nehru.
	Death of Tsering Dolma, elder sister of the Dalai Lama.
	Jetsun Pema takes charge of the Nursery for Tibetan Refugee Children (now TCV).

1965   War between India and Pakistan.
       The United Nations reconsider the Tibetan question.
1966   Start of Cultural Revolution in China.
1968   May: student upheavals in France and other countries.
1972   The People's Republic of China is admitted to the United Nations.
       Creation of the Tibetan Children's Village (TCV).
1976   Death of Mao Tse-tung.
1977   Deng Xiaoping returns to power.
1978   Peace treaty with Japan.
1979   USSR invades Afghanistan.
       First delegation of the Dalai Lama's representatives visits Tibet.
1980   Jetsun Pema leads the third delegation to Tibet.
1981   Death of the Dalai Lama's and Jetsun Pema's mother.
1982   First exploratory delegation to China.
1985   The Dalai Lama proposes a five-point Peace Plan in Washington.
1987   Upheavals in Lhasa.
1988   Uprisings in Lhasa.
1989   Fall of the Berlin Wall.
       Tiananman Square.
       Dalai Lama receives the Nobel Peace Prize.
       Death of the Panchen Lama.
       Martial law declared in Tibet.
1990   Jetsun Pema becomes the first woman minister in the government in exile.
1995   Beijing questions the Dalai Lama's choice for the reincarnation of the Panchen Lama and designates someone else. Jetsun Pema is given the title of 'Mother of Tibet' by the Assembly of Tibetan People's Deputies in exile.
       May: recognition of the Panchen Lama by the Dalai Lama.

Particulars	Borders	Day Scholars	Staff	Old People	Total
I Villages					
1. TCV Dharamsala	2173	228	278+31	37	2747
2. SOS TCV Ladakh	585	1031	162	42	1820
3. SOS TCV Bylakuppe	795	42	131	2	970
4. SOS TCV Bir/Suja	606		54		660
Total	**4159**	**1301**	**656**	**81**	**6197**
II. Residential Schools					
1. TCV School Pathlikuhi	490	49	66	10	615
2. TCV School, Lower Dharamsala	667	77	78	2	824
3. TCV, School, Hanley Ladakh	156	55	12		223
4. TCV School, Sumdho Janthang	65		7		72
5. TCV School, Bir	606		76	2	684
Total	**1984**	**181**	**239**	**14**	**2418**
III. TCV Day Schools					
1. TCV Day School, Mcleod Ganj		180	9		189
2. TCV Day School, Kulu		55	6		61
3. TCV Day School, Pandoh		12	2		14
4. TCV Day School, Menlha Ladakh		135	8		143
5. TCV Day School, Choglam Ladakh		54	6		60
6. TCV Day School, Agling Ladakh		295	24		319
7. TCV Day School, Nyuma Ladakh	18	29	5		52
8. TCV Day School, Petub Ladakh		15	3		18
Total	**18**	**775**	**63**		**856**
IV. Day Care Centres					
1. TDL, 1st Nursery, Bylakuppe		106	8		114
2. TDL 2nd Nursery, Bylakuppe		107	8		115
3. Kailaspura Bylakuppe		110	8		118
4. ArliKumari, Bylakuppe		60	6		66
5. Gulledhalla, Bylakuppe		121	9		130
6. Purang Camp, Bylakuppe		11	2		13
7. Lakshimpural, Bylkakuppe		7	1		8
8. Chawkur-Bylakuppe		48	5		53
9. Hunsur Creche 'A'		108	10		118
10. Hunsur Creche 'B'		77	7		84
Total		**755**	**64**		**819**
V. Vocational Training					
1. TCV Handicraft Training Centre, D/Sala	59		11		70
2. TCV Handicraft Training Centre, Ladakh	19	16	5		40
3. TCV Vocational Centre, Ladakh	5	2	6		13
4. TCV Farm Project, Bylakuppe			7	5	12
5. TCV Handicraft Centre, D/Sala			12+36		48
6. TCV Thanka Painting, Bir	15		1		16
Total	**98**	**18**	**78**	**5**	**199**
VI. Further Studies					
1. TCV SOS Youth Hostel, Delhi	187		12		199
2. Tibetan Youth Hostel, Bangalore	50		3		53
3. Various College Hostels		270			270
4. Teacher's Training Centre, D/Sala	49		8		57
Total	**286**	**270**	**23**		**579**
VII. Aid Outside TCV					
1. TCV Dharamsala Cantt		1032			1032
2. TCV Ladakh		154			154
3. TCV Bylakuppe		199			199
Total		**1385**			**1385**
Grand Total	**6545**	**4685**	**1123**	**100**	**12453**

Tibetan Children's villages, India (30 April 1997)

List of Principal Donors

1960 to date	Private Office of His Holiness the Dalai Lama
1960 to date	Government of India
1960 to date	Save the Children Fund
1960 to 1964	CARE, USA
1961 to 1992	Mr Eric Muhlmann, Hawaii
1961 to 1984	Miss Nelly Kunzi, Switzerland
1962 to 1991	Swiss Aid to Tibetans, Switzerland
1962 to 1976	Swiss Red Cross, Switzerland
1962 to 1965	American Emergency Committee for Tibetans
1962 to 1982	Tibetan Society of UK
1963 to date	Tibetan Refugee Aid Society, Canada
1968 to date	Dutch Aid to Tibetans, Holland (SHAT)
1968 to date	Tibetan Children's Relief Society, New Zealand
1968 to 1974	Heart Open to the World, Belgium
1968 to 1973	Action 7600, Norway
1968 to 1976	Tibetan Refugee Children's Sponsorship Committee, Australia
1969 to date	Swedish Tibet Committee, Sweden
1969 to 1971	Office of Tibet, Switzerland
1970 to date	Deutsche Welthungerhilfe, Germany (WHH)
1970 to date	United Church Board for World Ministries, USA
1970 to 1984	Tibetan Foundation Inc, USA
1970 to 1982	Norwegian Refugee Aid Council, Norway
1971 to date	SOS Kinderdorf International, Vienna
1971 to 1977	Ms Nadia Proisy and friends, France
1971 to date	Catholic Relief Services, India
1973 to 1974	Radio Mordern, Rotterdam, Holland
1973 to 1974	National Union of Sorohmist Clubs, Holland
1973	Aktie Geef Aktie, Holland
1974 to date	Dr Arthur Furer, Switzerland
1976 to 1980	New Zealand High Commission
1977 to date	Hermann Gmeiner Fonds Deutschland e V, Germany

1977 to 1991	Miriam Dean Trust Fund, UK
1978 to date	SOS France (Village d'enfants SOS dans le monde)
1978 to 1988	SOS-Barnbyarnas Vanner Sverige, Sweden
1978 to date	SOS-Kinderdorpen, Holland
1978 to 1988	Thomas Dooley – Intermed, USA
1978	Save the Children Fund, Canada
1978 to 1982	Norwegian Tibet Aid, Norway
1978	Rotary Club of Switzerland
1978	Kindertehuis de Gensenholf, Holland (Mrs van Gulik)
1979 to date	Dr R Bastiani, France
1979 to date	Ms Morna White, UK
1980 to date	Pastor Diestelkamp and Rev Stimpel, Germany
1980 to date	Aide à l'enfance tibétaine, France
1980 to date	Tibetisches Zentrum, Germany (Waltraud Langner)
1980 to date	American Himalayan Foundation, USA
1980 to 1986	World Federation of Japan Buddhist Association, Japan
1980	18 Temple of Shingon, Japan
1980 to date	Council for Tibetan Education, India
1980 to 1987	Stichting Steinfonds, Holland (Mr Posthumus)
1980 to 1991	Tibet Relief Fund, UK
1981 to date	Mrs Samra Losinger, Switzerland
1981 to 1987	Friends of SOS, USA
1981 to 1982	Narita Temple, Japan
1981	Mrs P Kelder, Holland
1982 to date	German Aid to Tibetans (Mrs Wager)
1982	SOS Norway
1982 to date	SOS Switzerland and Friends of SOS
1982 to 1986	Count Joseph Seilern, Monaco
1982 to date	Mrs Marlies Kornfeld, Switzerland
1982 to date	Mr Donad M Hess, Switzerland
1982 to date	Temple for Spiritual Research and Learning, USA
1983 to date	Tibetan Friendship Group, Australia
1983	CEBEMO, France
1984 to 1994	Kilner Foundation, USA
1984 to 1985	SOIR IM, Sweden
1984	Sanson Limited, Japan
1985 to date	Gemeinschaft zur Forderung, Germany
1985 to 1990	Mr John Borasi, Italy
1986 to 1989	Daeniker Stiftung, Switzerland
1986 to date	SOS UK
1986 to date	Les Amis du Tibet, Switzerland
1986 to date	Foundation Alexandra David-Néel, France
1986 to date	Tibet Fund, USA

1986	Enfants du monde, Switzerland
1986	CCFD, France
1986	TCV Alumini Association
1986 to date	Mrs Lotti Jacobi, Switzerland
1986	Mrs M W van der Haven, Holland
1987 to date	AERT, France (Ngawang Dakpa)
1987 to 1988	SKIP Aid on the Spot, Switzerland
1987 to date	Austerlitz Foundation, Holland (Mrs Kunst Terlaak)
1987 to 1990	Ms Jo Bergmann-Vanderberg, Holland
1987	Mrs Eva Parrot, France
1987 to date	Mrs Dominique Savoy, Switzerland
1987 to date	Mrs Yvette Weber, Switzerland
1987 to 1992	Dr Lobeck, Switzerland
1988 to 1994	ApTT, UK
1988 to date	Tibetan Snowlion Friendship Society, Japan
1988 to 1989	STADT Braunfels, Germany
1988	Mr Hirashi Yoshid, Japan
1988 to date	Tibetan Society Europe, Belgium (Mr Moury)
1989 to 1992	World Association for Orphans and Abandoned Children (Mr Jacques Fischer), Switzerland
1989 to date	Tibet Libre, France
1989	Joan Zulkoski Fund
1989 to date	Centre Bouddhiste Tibétain, France
1989 to date	Friends of Tibet, Switzerland
1989	Mr C Paul, UK
1990 to 1992	Foundation Hergé, Belgium
1990	Nihonji Temple, Japan
1990	Chief of General Affairs Section, Japan
1990 to date	Tibet Foundation, UK (Phunstok Wangyal)
1990	Ms Barbara Hines, USA
1990 to date	Zielonskowski family, Germany
1990 to 1994	Umbrella Project, USA
1990 to date	Verein zur Forderung von Kinderdörfern, Germany (Mr Helmut Schwerdtle)
1991 to date	Danish Tibetan Cultural Society
1991 to date	Coup de main, Switzerland
1991	SIDA, Sweden
1991 to date	STADT Zug, Switzerland
1991 to date	Pestalozzi Children's Village, UK
1991 to date	US Aid through CTRC
1991 to date	ASIA, Italy
1991 to date	Friends of Tibet, Norway
1991	Femmes d'Europe, Belgium
1991 to date	Rigpe Dorjee Foundation, USA

1991	Mrs Naga Machi, Japan
1991 to date	Mr and Mrs Axel Ball, Spain
1991	Arthur Yuen, Canada
1991	Ms Renzo Burkel, France
1991	Mrs Mitsuko Saimomur, Japan
1991 to 1992	Shogo Hamada, Japan
1991 to date	Ms Agathe Drenth, Austria
1991 to 1994	Mr Yoriko Ikada, Japan
1991	Tibetan Community, Switzerland
1991 to date	Sir Robert Folkes, UK
1991 to 1994	Ms Barbara Wagner, Germany
1991 to date	Ms Victoria Sujata, USA
1991 to 1992	Mr and Mrs Harrison Ford, USA
1992 to date	Brighton Tibet Link, UK
1992	Barry J Hershey Foundation, USA
1992 to date	Orientalia, Belgium
1992 to date	Ockenden Venture, UK
1992 to 1994	International Bornehjaelp, Denmark
1992 to date	Tengyeling Buddhist Centre, Canada
1992 to date	Goodricke Group Ltd, India
1992 to date	Institut de recherche physique et conscience, France (Mr and Mrs Drouot)
1992	Mr Klaus Hebben, UK
1992 to date	Mrs Anne Rose Muller, Switzerland
1992	Ms Astrid Popper, Germany
1992	Ms Sonja Bertelle, Switzerland
1992	Mrs Micheline Le Guay, France
1992 to date	Dr Thomas Gysin, Switzerland
1992 to date	Mrs Helena Schmidt, Belgium
1992 to date	Mrs E R De Breuk, Holland
1993 to date	World Council of Churches, Switzerland
1993	United Nations Women's Guild of Vienna, Austria
1993 to date	Institut Tarab Ladrang, France
1993 to date	Mrs Julia Oggay-Zosso, Switzerland
1993 to date	Mr Andrie Vanbenbeyvanghe, Belgium
1994	President Havel of Czechoslovakia
1994	Mrs Yoko Gotoh, Japan
1994 to date	Mrs Fusako Okawa, Japan
1994 to date	Maine Friends of Tibet, USA
1994	Rugby School, UK
1995	Bernhard van Leer Foundation, Holland
1995	European Commission through SCF
1995	Planète Enfants, France
1995	Temple of Hiroshima, Japan

1995	Mr and Mrs Schwyn, Switzerland
1995	Drolma Choeling Centre (Enfants du Monde), France
1995	Mr Bernhard Zoidl, Austria
1995	Dr J H Moon, Korea
1995	Stichting M Huysmann, Netherlands
1995	Ven Kyuse Enshinjoh, Japan
1995	Kurozumi Kyo Shinto, Japan
1995	Mrs M McLaren, USA
1995	Philanthropic Collaboration, Inc, USA
1995	Intern Women's Contact A'Dam, Netherlands
1995	Sanctuary of the Beloved, USA
1995	STADT Baar, Switzerland
1995	Village SOS Sondrio, Italy
1995	Stichting Otten-Philipsfond, Netherlands
1996	Les amis du Tibet, Luxembourg
1996	Pestalozzi Overseas Children's Trust, UK
1996	Mr Jacques Keysers, France
1996	Mr J W Broekhuysen, Netherlands
1996	Fondation Mercier, Switzerland
1996	Dr and Mrs Zimmermann, Austria
1996	Dr and Mrs Bach, Germany
1996	Gaya Network, Japan
1996	Koninklijk Concertge Bouworkest, Netherlands
1996	Tibetan Monastic Institute Rikon, Switzerland
1996	TCV Alumni Association, Nepal
1996	ECH Eversdijk Smulders Stichting, Netherlands
1996	Christian Bachschuster Stiftung Jona, Switzerland
1996	Mrs Martha H Zelgar, Switzerland
1997	Mr B Peytrignet, Switzerland
1997	Mrs L Martin, Switzerland
1997	Dr Hans Rudi Denzler, Switzerland
1997	Dr Schmidt, Germany

You can help the Tibetan Children's Village

– *by sponsoring a child*
You are requested to pay a minimum amount of 30 US$ or £19 per month, either by cheque or by bank transfer.
– *by helping to finance different TCV projects*
You may choose the amount you want to pay by cheque or by bank transfer.
– *by giving donations in kind*
You can give warm clothes (for children and adults), valid medicines – particularly vaccines against tuberculosis – and toys. They will be sent to the various TCV homes.

For further information, write to:
Head Office
Tibetan Children's Villages
Dharamsala Cantt–176216
Distt. Kangra, H.P.
India.

If you choose to send a cheque, please make it out to TCV and send it to the above address.

If you choose to make a bank transfer (the best method), please transfer the funds to account no C–310 300 792 (American Express Bank) in New Delhi.

Index